From Worldly Princess to the Foot of the Cross

The Life and Writings of Saint Camilla Battista Varano, OSC

Translations and Introduction by
Bret Thoman, OFS

From Worldly Princess
to the Foot of the Cross
The Life and Writings of
Saint Camilla Battista Varano, OSC

Translations and Introduction by
Bret Thoman, OFS

Cover design: Tau Publishing design department
Interior page design: Tau Publishing design department

Cover photo and inside photos courtesy of the Poor Clare sisters of Camerino.

For permission contact:
Tau Publishing, LLC
Permissions Dept.
4727 North 12th Street
Phoenix, AZ 85014

ISBN: 978-1-61956-012-3

9 8 7 6 5 4 3 2 1

Published by Tau Publishing, LLC
www.Tau-Publishing.com
Printed in the United States of America.

Tau-Publishing.com
Words of Inspiration

Contents

This book is dedicated
To the Poor Clare sisters of Camerino.
In gratitude for your friendship,
support, and encouragement.

Introduction to the Life of Saint Camilla Battista Da Varano (1458-1524)

By Bret Thoman, OFS

Camilla was the baptismal name that Duke Giulio Cesare da Varano gave to the girl born to him on April 9, 1458. Giulio was a powerful seigniorial Renaissance overlord of Camerino, a small but flourishing city in the Marches of Ancona. He was married to Giovanna Malatesta, with whom he fathered three children. Camilla, however, was one of the duke's six illegitimate children; her mother was a noblewoman, Cecchina di maestro Giacomo. Giulio loved Camilla deeply, and he and the duchess raised her at court together with their three legitimate children. Such family situations were not uncommon in Renaissance noble families then, when marriages were often politically arranged, rather than entered into.

The duke was a competent ruler who strove to keep the nobility in his favor without neglecting the lower classes, including peasants whose support he needed in case of war. Further, he cared for the sick and pilgrims to whom he gave alms in front of his palace and in hospitals he restored. He was generous also to the religious Orders and local churches.

Growing up in the Renaissance court, young Camilla was surrounded not just by political intrigue (Machiavelli was a contemporary of hers), but also by high culture, pomp and splendor. Rivaling the Medici family palace of Florence and the papal residences in Rome, her father's castle boasted some 69 rooms (many ornately frescoed), 4 loggias, 3 cellars, a library, and a stable capable of keeping up to 40 horses. Illustrious poets, historians, philosophers, and painters often passed through as guests of the court. Camilla learned Latin and read the classics; she learned to paint, play musical instruments and dance.

What we know of Camilla comes mostly from her Autobiography, the "Spiritual Life." She grew up vivacious, playful, and passionate for the courtly life. She was sincere, dedicated, and independent to the point of being stubborn. She loved beautiful and pleasurable things. According to her father's plans and desires, Camilla should have been destined to an arranged marriage like her sisters, in order to strengthen the family's power. However, she chose a different path.

Her conversion began during Lent of 1466 when she heard a sermon by an Observant Franciscan friar in which the priest exhorted his listeners to shed a little tear – just one (*una lacrimuccia sola sola*) – each Friday in memory of Christ's Passion. Camilla was only eight years old, but something within moved her to make a promise to do what that friar told her – she actually took a vow. Even though she was just a girl, she was precociously aware that the pleasures of the court would never truly satisfy her soul. She began to see that there was something much more powerful and significant in the cross of Jesus than the intrigues and superficial pleasures around her. And in that penitential devotion of shedding a little tear, her conversion began.

Her new devotion was not without a struggle, though, and she found it difficult to be both faithful to her vow and be present at the court with its worldly pleasures. She said that she would often go into the chapel and squeeze out a tear, then "quickly get up and run away." She also recounts that during this period she was averse to devotional writings, as well as priests, nuns, and friars. Her spiritual life progressed after she discovered a booklet containing a meditation, divided into fifteen parts, on the Passion of Christ. She said it was as if it were designed for "a person who did not know how to meditate." Every Friday, she performed this new devotion on her knees. Then the tears flowed abundantly and her conversion deepened. She began fasting on bread and water on Fridays, reciting the rosary, and scourging her body. Nevertheless, she recounted that she still felt "imprisoned."

It was not until hearing a series of sermons that she was freed. During Lent of 1479, she heard a sermon by a friar from Urbino named Francesco whom she called the "Trumpet of the Holy Spirit." She said his words were like "thunder and lightning that struck her soul" and caused her to fear God. At that point she began to fear Hell and she said she felt freed from her imprisonment of the soul. During this time she made a lifelong vow of virginity and felt the calling to enter a cloistered convent. At this point, she received from God the three lilies described in her autobiography: a hatred of the world, humility, and a desire to suffer badly (*malpatire*).[1]

Her next struggle was with her powerful father, whom she described as her Pharaoh. He clearly had other plans for Camilla. However, she persisted in pursuing her vocation and after a continual deepening of her spiritual life through prayer, confession, and spiritual dialogues with various Franciscan friars, she decided to enter a convent. In 1481, she entered the Poor Clare monastery in Urbino (roughly 50 miles north of Camerino) in the same region.[2] The Poor Clare monastery in Urbino was associated with the Strict Observance within the Franciscan Order; i.e. a reform movement among the Franciscans seeking to 'observe' the original austere Franciscan way of life without privileges or exemptions that had been granted over the centuries. Camilla compared her own story to that of the Jews who were enslaved by the Pharaoh in Egypt. She recounts that God freed her from "the worldly slavery of Egypt" (the secular world) and from the "hands of powerful Pharaoh" (her father). Then she "crossed the Red Sea" (left the world and entered the monastery) where she took the name Battista (Baptist).

She stayed in Urbino for two and a half years where she made her lifelong religious profession. Apparently there was much controversy about which she did not elaborate. It may have had to do with the fact that her father did not want her to be so far from him; or that he, a worldly lord, did not want her to be part of such an austere and penitential movement. Thus, the duke purchased a monastery from the Benedictine Olivetans near his castle in Camerino and, with the approval of the pope, founded a community of Poor Clare nuns. With the encouragement of the Franciscan provincial minister, on January 4, 1484, Camilla returned to Camerino with eight other sisters to reside once again in her native city.

Camilla spent most of the remaining forty years of her life in Camerino with just a few exceptions. Pope Alexander VI, from the Borgia family (in Italy this family name is virtually synonymous with the corruption of Renaissance-era papacy), had divided the lands of the Papal States into fiefdoms, which he subsequently distributed to his (natural-born) sons and nephews. On March 1, 1501, the pope excommunicated Camilla's father for allegedly guarding enemies of the pope and for assassinating the pope's cousin. This caused Duke Giulio to forfeit his feudal rights over the city. In an effort to expand the Papal States, the pope's son, Cesare Borgia, promptly sought to annex Camerino in the spring of 1502. Camilla was forced to flee and seek refuge in the Abruzzo region which was in the territory of the kingdom of Naples. Then Cesare Borgia marched on Camerino with his army, imprisoned Camilla's father, and ordered him strangled to death. The duke's sons met the same fate, with the exception of one. Camilla remained in exile until the Borgia pope's death in August, 1503. With the new papacy of Julius II, Camilla's family was restored to power in Camerino and she was free to return home. Her only surviving brother, Giovanni Maria, was named duke by the pope.

After returning, Battista's role as spiritual mother came into play. She served repeatedly as Abbess in 1500, 1507, 1513, 1515 and once as vicar in 1488. In 1505, Pope Julius II sent Camilla to found a monastery in Fermo where she stayed for two years. Later, in 1521 and 1522 she traveled to San Severino Marches to spiritually reform a community of nuns that had just adopted the Rule of St. Clare. She died in her monastery in Camerino during a plague on March 31, 1524 at the age of 64. Her relics remain there today.

Camilla's spirituality was focused on offering and uniting her sufferings to Christ with him "at the foot of the cross." However, she did not skip over loving service towards her neighbors beginning with her sisters in the monastery. In her writings and other sources, Camilla emphasized living the virtuous life, faithfulness towards her vows, and service towards others as essential to a healthy spirituality. However, she placed a great emphasis on the constant meditation of Christ and his sufferings. In "Spiritual Life," she said that she had engaged in severe penances before becoming a nun, but after entering the monastery, she no longer practiced them; she chose instead to meditate on Christ and his wounds. In "Instructions," she claimed that one reaches God better and faster by thinking constantly of him as opposed to ascetic actions. Also, in "Mental Sorrows," she claimed that many people meditated on Christ's physical sufferings, but by contemplating Christ's mental sufferings (particularly distressing in the Garden of Gethsemane), one could reap more spiritual benefits.

The Canonization

On April 7, 1843, Pope Gregory XVI signed the decree declaring Camilla Battista blessed. On May 11, 1857, Pope Pius IX visited the church of Santa Chiara in Camerino and venerated her remains; he granted a plenary indulgence to those who would make the same pilgrimage to visit her relics. On December 7, 1878, the process of canonization was introduced to Pope Leo XIII and on January 9, 1879, the same pope began the process after approval by the Sacred Apostolic Congregation of Rites. On April 4, 1893, Cardinal Prefect Gaetano Masella issued a decree approving the writings of Blessed Camilla. In 1897, the *Informatio super virtutibus* (Information on her virtues) was presented, but later that year the Order of Friars Minor (OFM) General Postulator, Father Candido Mariotti, could not continue her cause of canonization, resulting in a lengthy delay.

In 1998, the process was once again resumed by Father Silvano Bracci, OFM, who presented the *Positio Super Virtutibus* (Position on heroic virtues), to the Holy See. On December 14, 2004, the consultation of historians and theologians gave a positive opinion about the Heroic Virtues of Blessed Camilla. After the regular session of cardinals and bishops, on December 19, 2005, the *Decreto Super Virtutibus* (Decree on her heroic virtues) was published, which served to advance her cause to the next stage, which was the approval of the miracle. From 2004 to 2007, the curia of the diocese of Camerino pushed for the approval of an alleged miracle attributed to the intercession of Blessed Camilla. On July 12, 2007, the documentation was sent to the Congregation for the Causes of Saints. With the closure on June 18, 2009 of the diocesan process for the approval of the presumed miracle, the Vatican concluded that medical consultation had proved the miracle "inexplicable" from a scientific perspective. On September 22, 2009, the Consultation of Theologians unanimously expressed its positive opinion about the attribution of the miracle. On November 16, 2009, the Commission of Cardinals and Bishops of the Congregation for the Causes of Saints met in Rome and also gave a favorable opinion to the recognition of the miracle. On December 19, 2009, Pope Benedict XVI, authorized the Promulgation of the Decree on the miracle. On February 19, 2010, during the Public Consistory, Pope Benedict XVI signed the decree declaring Blessed Camilla Battista Varano in the Register of Saints and fixing the date of canonization. Finally, on October 17, 2010, Pope Benedict XVI canonized Camilla Battista da Varano and five other saints in Saint Peter's square in Rome.

The approved miracle through the intercession of Saint Camilla Battista for her canonization process involved a little girl healed from a bone deformity caused by rickets. Clelia Ottaviani, daughter of Vincenzo and Elena Ottaviani, was born on September 17, 1871, in the town of San Giovanni di Bieda, near Rome in the Diocese of Viterbo. According to testimony of Clelia's mother, they moved to Camerino in April of 1872, where Clelia lived until her death. Afflicted with rickets, Clelia's bones were deformed to the point that she could not walk since she could not set her feet flat on the ground. In 1877, when Clelia was almost six years old, a relative of hers, Tommasa Dulciotti, brought her to the crypt of

Blessed Camilla where she prayed for her intercession during the three days preceding her feast day of June 2. On the third day, Clelia's bones immediately and without explanation straightened, and the little girl put her feet flat on the ground and began to walk. She ran more than two kilometers home unassisted and without the use of crutches. Later, in 1897, Clelia married a man named Alessandro Carpiceci and they remained in Camerino. She died of bronchitis/pneumonia in the city hospital in Camerino when she was 61.

Her Writings

Saint Camilla was endowed with remarkable intellectual abilities due to her private tutors in the ducal court in which she grew up. She wrote extensively, mostly in the 16th century vernacular Italian of the Marches of Ancona region where she was from, interspersed with Scripture citations in Latin. This was no small feat for a 16th century woman. Her first main work was *Lauda della Visione di Cristo* (Praise of the Vision of Christ), an hendecasyllable work (11 syllable lines) written between 1479-1483. The youthful work describes a relationship with Christ that is familiar and confident, almost casual. She also wrote at the same time, perhaps earlier, a work in Latin on the Passion of Christ. Both these works demonstrate St. Camilla's remarkable command of language in both Latin and Italian, and her capacity as a poet.

In 1483, she wrote *Ricordi di Gesù* (Memories of Jesus), which she rewrote in 1491. Writing of her spiritual life in the form of a letter dictated by Christ himself, she reveals the mystical experiences that occurred after entering the monastery in Urbino. Her best-known work was written in 1488 and represents the apex of her meditations on the Passion of Christ. *I Dolori Mentali di Gesù nella Sua Passione* (The Mental Sorrows of Christ in His Passion) focuses not so much on the corporal sufferings or the physical wounds of Christ, as much on the sufferings of his heart. Published anonymously in Naples in 1490, it was soon translated into many languages.

Between 1488 and 1491 Camilla underwent a painful period in which she felt God's absence. Nevertheless, she wrote various prayers to God, to Jesus Crucified, to the Eucharist, and to the Virgin, all reflecting her profound interior and spiritual life. Also during this time, she wrote her long Autobiography in the form of a letter addressed to Friar Domenico Leonessa. Known as the *Vita Spirituale* (Spiritual Life) she reveals events of her life before entering the monastery, details of her conversion, and other mystical experiences throughout her life as a nun up until that point.

In 1501, she wrote *Istruzioni al Discepolo* (Instructions to the Disciple.) Composed of ten chapters, the work was probably written to a friar named John of Fano, who was provincial minister of the Franciscan Observants in that period. There has in the past, however, been some discussion as to whether or not it was written by St. Camilla Battista; although today scholars have reached a nearly unanimous consensus on its authenticity. Between 1512-1513 she wrote various letters and descriptions of her visions. In 1521 she wrote her most mature work, *Purità del cuore* (Purity of heart) to an anonymous friar, also thought to have been John of Fano. In this final work, she constructs a methodical approach for living the contemplative and spiritual life.

The Spiritual Experience and Background of Saint Camilla

By Father Ferdinando, O.F.M. - Provincial Minister of the Marches, Italy
And the Poor Clare sisters of Camerino

In this reflection, we would like to situate St. Camilla Battista within her historical context, as she inherited a particular spirituality, a culture, a movement of reform to which she dedicated her time and life. History is not born to us today. To think otherwise, in the ways of our contemporary "culture," is a great temptation that has ensnared, we believe, even us in Religious life. Then, to present the spirituality of the newly declared Saint Camilla Battista is an initiative that allows us to look at the pages of Franciscan history – pages that are rich in spirituality. And hers is a richness in large part still to be discovered, but we have been among the first, as we have had the honor of having Camilla Battista da Varano from our own soil. Very few have realized the greatness of this woman. We think, however, that the time is now ripe for a wider recognition, since she has been elevated to the altars of sainthood. Just recently, a large volume was published by the Vatican: "Encyclopedia of Prayer." In the pages dedicated to the most significant schools of spirituality in the Church, five women from the Order of Poor Clares were listed: St. Clare of Assisi, St. Catherine of Bologna, St. Camilla Battista, Bl. Mary Magdalene Martinengo, and St. Veronica Giuliani. Finally, we have become aware of her importance.

St. Camilla Battista hails from a great Franciscan tradition. In the 13th and 14th centuries, there were great personalities within the Franciscan school who taught much, and it is that school which educated also St. Camilla. Within the Franciscan family, St. Camilla was part of a movement of mystics, begun by Francis and Clare, who were not only the founders of Orders, but were people who had the gift of mystical experience. The idea of the mystic may be erroneously understood as monks or nuns living isolated in a hermitage, praying all day long, separated from the reality of the world. Not so. The mystic is one who has encountered God through a concrete and strong spiritual experience, which means first of all that it occurred in life, but then continues through preaching and other events. It is a gift that the Lord gives to some people, to live a combination of deep intimacy with him and with his mystery. Francis and Clare, in this sense, were fully mystics.

In the 13th century, the Franciscan Order had great theologians who were also great mystics, especially St. Bonaventure and St. Anthony of Padua. In the same century, there were numerous women: a Third Order nun, the great Bl. Angela of Foligno, was very similar to Camilla Battista. Another very significant Franciscan woman from the 13th century was St. Margaret of Cortona, who lived a very difficult life and experienced a profound and very intense conversion through grace.

After the death of St. Francis, the Order began to separate into distinct groups. Let us recall the "Spirituals," who distinguished themselves from the Conventuals. They were called "Spirituals" because they wanted to live in hermitages and they paid particular attention to prayer. They were controversial, however, and sought to defend their identity and Franciscan way of life. This involved them in particular episodes of the Church, and they were often misunderstood. Some were condemned by various popes for their rigid stances on the issue of poverty and radical faithfulness to the Rule of Francis, as they did not want to accept the concessions that the popes had issued in the 13th century, which mitigated the Rule as it had been written.

Ubertino da Casale, originally from northern Italy, lived in the Marches, Umbria and Tuscany. He left us a great work in *Arbor vitae Crucifixe Jesu*, (The Tree of Life of the Crucified Jesus.) It was an important work studied by Franciscans and others throughout the centuries, who did not know the author, because Ubertino was condemned by the Church. Angelo Clareno, a Spiritual, was also persecuted by the Church and the pope. In our region, particularly rich in the history of saints, we have in the environs of the hermitage of San Liberato (near Sarnano), the *grotta dei frati* (the cave of the friars), which was the spiritual headquarters of the Spirituals in the Marches. Let us not forget that the *Fioretti*, the "Little Flowers of St. Francis," was written in our region. It was Marchigian-Franciscan written in the hermitage of Roccabruna (also near Sarnano) first, and in San Liberato later.

The fourteenth century was definitely a century that enriched the Order. In particular, to understand the context of Saint Camilla Battista, we must refer to some events that touched this territory of ours. A Franciscan friar of our region, Giovanni della Valle (John of the Valley), began to live the intensive prayerful and penitential life of a hermit. After his death in 1351, his way of life was picked up by another friar, Gentile da Spoleto; but after just three years, he was suspended by the Minister General of the Franciscan Order. Then, in the hermitage of Brogliano near Colfiorito, halfway between Foligno and Camerino, the seeds were planted which would blossom into a very important reform of the Order – that of the Observance.

In 1368, Paoluccio Trinci (a lay friar), the son of the noble Trinci family (a very important family) of Foligno (near Assisi) picked up again this way of life of prayer and penance and founded a harsh and austere hermitage called Brogliano. However, this time this way of life received important support from his family (the Trincis), the Varano family of Camerino, the Pope, and the Franciscan Minister General. In Brogliano, the community focused on faithfully observing the poverty of the original Rule of St. Francis.

In 1405, St. Bernardine of Siena began following this penitential and prayerful life movement. Later, in 1420, St. James of the Marches and St. John of Capistrano followed him. With these great saints, known as the pillars of the movement, we arrived at the height of the Observant Reform. The Franciscans of the Marches region joined enthusiastically the Observants, and there were great personalities who touched this land. This helps us understand the spirituality of Saint Camilla who was born within this historical, ecclesial and spiritual context, which was well-defined in the tradition of the Observant movement and found fertile soil in this land of ours in central Italy. Those who most deeply influenced Saint Camilla as her spiritual fathers were: Pietro da Mogliano, who had been a disciple of St. James of the Marches; Domenico da Leonessa, who was a native of San Severino Marche; and Francesco da Urbino.

From the perspective of St. Camilla Battista within the women's monasteries, there are four fundamental aspects that characterize the feminine branch of the Observant Reform. *The first* is the bond and the relationship of the women's monasteries with the friars of the Observance. The Poor Clare monastery of Santa Lucia in Foligno became the original hub of women's Observant monasteries. Therefore, the women's Observant movement began in central Italy in the same city where Paoluccio Trinci came from. These women's communities were formed in the teachings and through the preaching of the Observant Friars who regularly visited the Poor Clare nuns and served as their spiritual directors and confessors.

The second is the choice of the Rule of Clare. Formed and nurtured in this Observant tradition, these Poor Clares chose the radicalism of Francis and Clare in their way of following the Gospel in poverty. Thus, they embraced the original Rule of St. Clare, although there were other Rules throughout the Poor Clare monasteries. Clare's Rule had been approved by Pope Innocent IV on August 9, 1253, two days before her death. But in 1263, Pope Urban IV wrote a new Rule for the Poor Clares that mitigated poverty and slowly began to replace Clare's Rule in the monasteries. However, with the enthusiasm generated by the new Observant movement, many Poor Clare monasteries began to reclaim the original Rule of St. Clare with its distinctive hallmark of radical poverty; i.e. no income, rents, or dowries.

The third aspect that characterized the Observant monasteries was the ties between them: there were various activities in advancing the Reform throughout the women's monasteries. The reformed became reformers. Through the institutional links, in groups or individually, some nuns passed permanently or temporarily to other monasteries in order to spread the Reform. They also brought cultural, spiritual, and literary texts that they circulated and transcribed. This led to a true "network," with Santa Lucia in Foligno as the hub in central Italy, that branched out to northern and southern Italy.

The fourth aspect was the many leading women within the Reform. Certain exceptional women stood out with their backgrounds and great skills in the fields of literature, organization, leadership, culture, spirituality, art, etc. Many were of noble family origins and these women became active in driving the Observant Reform. Some activities were characterized by *transcribing* written works, for example, in Monteluce of Perugia, while others were fruitful in *creating* literary achievements, like Camilla, while others sought to form or reform Poor Clare monasteries in the tradition of the Regular Observance.

And so we understand better and arrive at the particular historical context of St. Camilla. Her first spiritual experience was linked to a sermon of Father Domenico da Leonessa, an Observant friar, who preached about the famous little teardrop when she was just eight years old or so. Her teardrop is known, but let's put it in a precise spiritual context. St. Camilla writes, "*My reverend father, when you preached at Camerino the last time,*

I think I could not have been older than eight or ten years old... One Holy Friday, I spontaneously desired to attend your holy and blessed sermon, which I listened to by the grace of the Holy Spirit. I listened not only attentively, but I was totally enraptured, almost inebriated. I was like someone who was hearing things said that had never been heard by anyone before. At the end of your holy sermon you offered a heartfelt exhortation to the people to provoke their hearts to sob and meditate on the Passion of Christ. And you urged them to remember [the Passion] at least on Good Friday and, on account of it, to shed only a little tear, just one. You affirmed with much conviction that only a little tear, just one, would be more acceptable to God and more useful to the soul than all other good works that one could do."

Here the hallmark of Franciscan preaching emerges. Preaching is like a stage, a theater that tries to see, touch, feel, make present, and reproduce visually that which is narrated. It is a preaching that asks the listeners to *physically* enter into the Gospel; in this case, in the narrative of the Passion. Camilla, in this context, is induced to feel compassion for Jesus who is silent before Herod. She joins in the innocence, wonder and simplicity as a child, feeling a deep compassion for Christ who was condemned to death. We can say that her experience was liturgical. She wrote, "I thought those things were happening at that time," almost as a memorial of the Passion of Christ.

These ideas echo the experience of St. Francis who received the stigmata on Mount La Verna in the year 1224. Francis prayed to God, "My Lord Jesus Christ, two graces I beg from you before I die: the first, that I feel in my body and soul as much as possible the pain that you, sweet Jesus, felt at the hour of your bitter Passion." This is a spiritual and physical participation, and Francis says that he wants to suffer in body and soul that which Christ suffered. He then says, "The second is that I feel in my heart, as much as possible, that excess love by which you, Son of God, were willing to bear for us sinners."

To understand this, we must refer to the spirituality of the "spiritual senses," very popular in the Middle Ages. This was a way of referring to mystery. The five faculties were: the body, the senses (seeing, hearing, touch, taste, smell), the heart (emotions and feelings), the mind (intelligence), and the spirit. So we have these five faculties to reach God: the body, senses, heart, mind and spirit. In the Franciscan experience, we do not stop to ask that one or some of the faculties participate in the mystery, but Franciscan spirituality calls for a *total* participation. In 1224, St. Francis asked to feel *all* the pain and *all* the love of Christ.

In the fourteenth century, Franciscan theology was dominated by St. Bonaventure, but we recall the mystics such as Ubertino Casale and Angelo Clareno. But think also of the literary field of Jacopone da Todi. All the literature of this great writer was based on *feeling* that which he wrote: *Santa madre, deh! voi fate che le piaghe del Signore siano impresse nel mio cuore* (Holy Mother, ah! make the wounds of the Lord be impressed in my heart.) But we also recall the artistic field, with Cimabue and other great artists of the period who began to express feeling in their artwork.

We can say, therefore, that the school in which St. Camilla learned the lessons of her spiritual life, was a school in which preaching, theology, mysticism, art, literature, everything was marked in this style. Her spirituality was not, therefore, based so much a method of *lectio divina* and prayer: it was rooted in Franciscan life that was in feeling, sharing, and participating, *with all five faculties*, in the mystery of Christ. Now we can understand better what we mentioned earlier, when the preacher, Domenico da Leonessa, used this method to try to involve the listeners in the Gospel story.

Another episode in the life of Camilla happened when she was about 18 years old. Another preacher of the Franciscan Observance, Friar Francesco of Urbino, arrived in the cathedral of Camerino. He spoke of the joy that the Virgin Mary felt when she received the angel on the eve of the Annunciation. Camilla wrote, "*On the eve of the feast of the Annunciation, Father Francesco of Urbino preached of the divine love that the Virgin Mary felt at the moment of the Annunciation… He stated that there was more sweetness in one spark of love that the Virgin felt at the moment of the Annunciation, than in all worldly loves put together. As soon as the sermon was over, I knelt before the altar and made a vow to the Virgin Mary to keep all my feelings pure until God would ask otherwise of me. But on one condition: that God would allow me to feel at least one spark of the love that Mary felt on that day.*" The preacher is *concrete*, as well as the listener, Camilla, is *concrete*. The presentation of the mystery of the Annunciation is presented in a *physical* way, as well as is *physical* the decision that Camilla made: she promised not to become engaged to any man before the Lord would tell her what her vocation would be.

One of the best-known works of St. Camilla is "The Mental Sorrows of Christ in his Passion." If it is true that Franciscan spirituality tends to participate in and feel the mystery of Christ with five faculties of which we have spoken, then "Mental Sorrows" is simply a profound expression of this. "Mental Sorrows" is a work of great depth and intensity, which was part of a pattern that was already present in Ubertino of Casale and in other Franciscans who had written on the Passion of Christ. She was not, in this sense, therefore, absolutely original. Rather, her originality comes in the way she entered into the experience of Christ's *mental* sorrows.

St. Camilla Battista lived very dramatic human experiences: great pain, strife, hatred, division, and murder both within the Church and in the reality of her family. These experiences touched and deeply wounded her. But all this was a chance for her to reach a profoundly interior spiritual experience. She understood, through a revelation of God, that Jesus Christ experienced not only physical pain on the cross, but especially interior pain. She went beyond the meditation of his physical pain (which was fairly common in her day), to descend into the depths of the Heart of Christ, that same Heart in which she saw her name written in letters of gold: "*Ego te dìligo, Camilla.*" (I love you, Camilla.)

In one of her other great texts, "Memories of Jesus," Camilla Battista enters *into* the mystery of Christ to the point of reaching the highest summits of mysticism, before which our sense as common mortals feels the loss and bewilderment at such audacity. Christ reveals to her the deep meaning of his fully delivering himself to his Father and to us on the cross, and how this mandate is the high road of every person who wants to conform themselves to him. In the work, Christ is speaking to Camilla, "*Recognize and thank God that you do not merit the good so great that [he] would make you conform to me, his beloved Son, by means of the Passion. Because this is the wedding garment that I, your true Spouse, was always dressed in. And you should know that, after good will, this is the most precious thing that God can give you; that is, suffering badly. And you could flee this bad suffering, as I could have fled it. You should know, however, that if you flee it, you will also flee every good thing, because the choice that I made only out of charity and love of suffering was pleasing to my Father.*"

This expression, "*malpatire*" (suffering badly) comes from a work of St. Catherine of Bologna, who, among others, appeared to St. Camilla Battista in a vision. Catherine was an exceptional figure of the 15th century, and she lived a short time before Camilla. But let's listen to the words Jesus spoke to St. Camilla, "*And see that when I finished prayer so enflamed with charity, I countered my enemies, so also you counter them and do not be afraid. I was betrayed by my disciple with a kiss, so if you are deceived and afflicted by the one whom you love, then rejoice. And, remember that I taught you five things:*

The first: when you are offended, be pained for the offense to God more than for your suffering."(The request that Jesus makes to her, is to go completely out of herself, not to think of herself, but to dispossess herself of everything to the point that she no longer feels offended as if the fault was made to her, but were directed at God.)

"*The second: pray to me cordially to forgive that person and free him from the punishment that is deserved, as you would wish that I freed your eye or another bodily limb of yours from a cruel punishment, because your neighbor is [as] a bodily limb of yours and [like] your eye.*" (Camilla, dispossessed of herself is capable of entering so much into solidarity with the sinner, as to experience the same feelings of Christ towards the sinner, so much as to take on his sin as a member of her own body. Underlying this is the doctrine of the mystical body of Christ about which St. Paul wrote.)

"*The third: recognize that you are much more obligated toward the one who does you harm than towards the one who does you good, because those people are the ones who purify your soul; they render it beautiful, gracious, and acceptable to my liking.*" (This is an ever more insistent and increasingly pervasive stripping of herself, through which St. Camilla is deprived of everything, in order to be truly free from everything.)

"*The fourth: consider how great is my charity since, even though you are my mortal enemy because of your sins committed, just the same every injury done to you, I consider done to me. Just the same, I wish that you are pained first for the offense to me. And I wish the same regarding this hate you have towards your enemies; that is every bad thing done to them, consider it done to you.*" (Here we arrive at the summit: the same love of Christ is asked of her. Not only can she not take revenge on her enemies or delight in their sufferings, but she has to be sorry if someone hurt them as if they did it to herself.)

"*The fifth: rejoice for receiving a part of what you deserve. And think that everything is from my permission for your good and do not impute it to sin.*" ("We know that all things work for good for those who love God, who are called according to his purpose." [cf. Romans 8:28]. Whoever reasons in this way perceives everything, good and evil, as an occasion to grow in love and holiness.)

Let's continue our narrative about the mystical experiences that St. Camilla had at the beginning of her journey. We am referring to the gift of the three lilies. "*The first lily is this: 'A hatred so great for the world so that if anyone had asked me, "What do you prefer: either to stay in the world and become Empress of the entire world with assurance of your salvation, or to enter religion with the risk of being damned?', truly, my father, without hesitating I would have chosen at once to enter religion even with the risk of being damned, rather than stay in the world with all its seductions and glories even with the assurance of being saved.*" Camilla had previously spoken of her early years, saying: "*I did not know any other way to get close to God, because, except for that little time of prayer mentioned above, I spent the rest of my time playing, singing, dancing, and strolling in vanities and in other youthful and worldly things that follow. Religious things – like friars and nuns – so irritated me that I could not stand to see them. I often made fun of those who read spiritual books.*" Here her inner landscape has changed dramatically. Now she prefers to run the risk of being damned in Religious life, and the certainty of being saved outside of Religious life. For her, "to enter into religion" does not necessarily mean entering a monastery, but to be with Jesus, sharing his life completely.

"*The second lily was this: a whole-hearted humility because I confessed and sincerely believed with all my heart that there was no worse sinner than I on the earth. And I believed that the greatest mercy God could show me was to save my soul, while the greatest justice that he could administer would be to send me to Hell. And inasmuch as God awarded me his gifts and graces, I considered myself depraved all the more. He always granted me the grace to consider all his gifts debts and not merits.*" These are no trivial little spiritual statements. The saints are not banal! This is true humility of the heart – the truth of one's self; that is, the awareness of one's being ontologically small. How beautiful is this lesson: before God we are nothing because everything is grace, everything is a gift, a gift that requires a restitution. Our Christian experience has meaning only within the deep awareness that everything is grace.

"*The third lily was this: a burning desire to "suffer badly." This desire was so strong that even if he had offered me heaven without suffering, I would not have wanted it. Thus I prayed to God and told him with sweet affection, 'If the great love that you showed me and continue to show me is true and not a joke, give me this true sign: that I might wear that same vestment which your beloved Son wore; that is, to suffer badly in this world.' He announced and promised me so much, that it already satisfied me four times over.*" Here she speaks not only of *accepting* suffering and pain, but of having the *burning desire* to suffer pain, arriving at the point of *yearning* to suffer. Here is the mystic, who is not above the clouds, but who is inside the deepest meaning of things. The mystic is the one who captures the marrow of life.

But why was Heaven for her living with her "crucified Spouse," to love Christ as he had loved her, to feel Christ in total harmony with him? Is this masochism? Are we, perhaps, in front of a weeping woman, bent on her pain? To fully understand the significance of this strange desire, let us take the example of a mother who desires to be with her son who is sick. What would a mother desire: to stand beside her son in the hospital, or stay home nicely rested and relaxed? A mother would suffer terribly if she could not stand next to her son who was suffering.

In Camilla Battista there is not, therefore, a desire to suffer as in the case of the masochist; nor is she attempting to live as a sacrificial victim, nor as a grieving widow. But she has an authentic desire to share everything with the God who loved her first and gave himself completely for her. This is the most beautiful experience of the mystic who, in general, experiences initially the drama of the trial, but when she comes to the profound experience, acknowledges that there is no greater grace than to share everything with her Beloved.

In conclusion, we can summarize what we have stated in four considerations. *The first consideration*: we are part of a history, a tradition. St. Camilla allowed herself to be guided by the great spiritual masters of her time. None of us is born a Christian, like a mushroom that springs up overnight. One must enter into a school of spirituality. Every great saint has always been a good disciple; no saint is self-made. St. Camilla was part of the movement of the Observant Franciscan Reform.

The second consideration: we should have deep gratitude for those who preceded us in the experience of faith. Today, we Christians often live as if without roots, without belonging; however, we belong to a Church, to a people. The region of the Marches, for example, is rich in traditions and holiness. We feel grateful to belong to a wonderful spiritual tradition, also in a country like Italy that gave great spiritual teachers to the whole Church! There is a book written by a professor of spirituality at the Gregorian Pontifical University, entitled: "Italy: nature and grace." The author, Jior Navone, argues that the hills, caves, geography, art, culture, history, made Italy what it is: a land of saints and spiritual masters. Everywhere we turn there is a church, there is a saint, a blessed man or woman; we have a very rich tradition of spirituality and religion.

Third consideration: participation in the mystery of Christ requires a full and physical participation. Physical means a spirituality that is opposed to evanescence or disembodiment. This is the beauty of the testimony to which St. Camilla belongs. Christian spirituality is always concrete, never reduced to ideology, sentimentalism, or transitory.

Fourth consideration: this last point relates to the total sharing, the active participation in the pain, the Passion of Christ. If you love, you cannot desire anything other than staying where your Beloved is. This message runs through and through the history of Christianity from its origins to the present day. It is witnessed by Mary, the women at the foot of the cross, and mystics like Camilla who remained faithfully at the foot of her Beloved. Before the cross, she tapped into the source of grace, through which she found the meaning of her existence, which was in him, where he was – on the cross.

A Woman for Our Times

By Mother Chiara Laura Serboli, OSC
Abbess, Monastery of Santa Chiara – Camerino, Italy

Camilla Battista Varano lived five centuries ago, a fact that might lead one to believe that she lacks a certain modernity. Therefore, one might avoid looking into her life and spiritual experience, believing that she could offer nothing that could speak to our own lives. Approaching her through her writings, one may be surprised, on the contrary, to discover her as a teacher of humanity and faith precisely for the modern person. In fact, Camilla lived in an epoch in many ways the same as our own and her life trajectory was similar to ours. With her modern personality, her experience of God is able to respond to the challenges of our own time.

Though a princess who grew up in the court of the powerful Varano family, immersed in the high culture of the Renaissance, she lived a remarkably "modern" life. She believed deeply in conscience and individual freedoms, which still today seem to dictate our laws. Before her conversion, she lived a life based on pleasure and diversions. As a result of the escapades of her ducal father, Giulio Cesare Varano, she experienced the so-called extended family, which included various siblings, half-brothers and sisters, some his natural children, some not. Like us, she found herself in an age of great movements – cultural, political, and scientific. Absolutism was readily rejected, and relativism ruled. Some were fortunate to enjoy well-being, luxury, and hedonism to the extreme, while others wasted away through neglect and marginalization. In the name of false freedom, there was a distaste for moral rules.

Camilla lived, like us, in a time when it was not always clear which way to go. This intelligent girl, with a strong personality, capable of authentic relationships and thirsty for absolutes, was animated by great passion. Though immersed in the clamor of a thousand calling voices, she was able to recognize a guiding star in Christ and, while remaining malleable to his Word, she allowed the Father to accomplish great things in her. What makes the Saints forever relevant, and therefore also Camilla, is that they knew how to take the Gospel seriously. A Franciscan woman, in the framework of the Observant reform, Camilla was a woman of great evangelical radicalism. A daughter of Clare of Assisi, her eye was fixed on Jesus; only in him did she seek and find access to the mystery of God, of man, and of their alliance. The Word of God was the immediate source of the entire spiritual adventure of Camilla. Through preaching, sacraments, spiritual direction, *lectio divina*, and meditation on the mysteries of Christ, Camilla never sought out anything other than His voice and the will of her Beloved.

In the tradition of Franciscan-Clarian spirituality, Camilla's life was resolutely marked by the encounter with the Crucifix. With Sts. Paul, Francis and Clare of Assisi, she could say that she wanted nothing other than "to know Christ and him crucified."[3] In the disfigured face of the Crucified, she recognized a face full of love. His wounds became for her the tangible signs not of defeat, but of a life more powerful than death. He showed Himself to her as the Lord of life. Her whole person became involved in the relationship with the Cross and nothing was left outside. Like Francis and Clare, Camilla, too, sought to fully immerse herself in the cruel experience of Jesus Christ, as reflected in her work "Mental Sorrows."

The one who loves desires nothing other than to want to be close to her Beloved, wherever he is. Therefore, at the foot of the crucifix is where she sought as a lover to be with her heart's Beloved. For this reason, Camilla chose to make her life one Good Friday, not to live in continual tears as a widow, but to share intensely in the fate of her Beloved. Camilla was not theorizing on the subject; rather, she absorbed herself totally in the contemplation of the suffering of Jesus in Gethsemane, by fixing her gaze upon his Heart in which is beheld the entire history of God and mankind, all the way to experiencing the Passion of Christ as "passion of love." Camilla comes in and teaches us to enter into the mystery of the cross, without remaining as distracted and listless spectators and especially without confusing the feelings of the heart, which are essential in the spiritual life, with a sterile sentimentality, and "recovering it [our faith]," as Pope Benedict XVI said, "from excessive moralistic sentimentality."[4]

Here, at the foot of the cross, she discovered the center, the meaning, the dwelling of the only Love that can quench our thirst. So why should we be surprised that she decided to live there her entire life? Who among us does not wish to pitch his tent there where he found his treasure?

Francis, Clare, and Camilla Battista belong to the ranks of the giants of the Spirit, who, after having long been "shells," made themselves into "channels" of grace, offering even to our own day a school, an exceptional mystical tradition from which we can always draw from.

For us, it is a grace and a joy to live in the same monastery in Camerino that radiates with the memory, holiness, presence, and relics of Camilla Battista. Daily, we welcome those who, upon discovering this great woman, come and knock at our door to enter into the profundity of her spiritual and human life, her warm and vibrant writings, and her intense and dramatic story in order to discover her culture and the eloquence of her holiness and humanity.

Her *Autobiography*, *Mental Sorrows*, and all her other works translated in this book are the filigree of the typical traits of Camilla Battista Varano. She was an illustrious writer and contemplative woman, gifted with great theological acumen who was careful to value God over herself. Free of spiritual trivialities, she was able to describe the sentiments of Christ without being either superfluous, or sappy. Finally, she was able to transmit the Christian experience in a way that was effective in her time, while delivering a message and teaching that is still valid today.

The reading of these writings delivers to us the experience of this great saint who was a light that warms the heart and illuminates the conscience. It involves and calls the Christian experience to become, like hers, full of significance, charm and relevance. If only for a moment, these writings allow the reader to perceive and enjoy the beauty that emanates from her. They have the ability to send forth a feeling of deep gratitude in the reader.

It is important for every Christian to have one or more saints as friends, so that we do not undertake by ourselves "the good fight of faith" (1 Tim 6:12). The saints allow us to count on their example to fulfill in us the Word of Life. Camilla had as "friends" Sts. Clare of Assisi and Catherine of Bologna (1413-1463), and she enjoyed their presence and familiarity in "visions" of them. Even if we cannot expect to experience similar supernatural phenomena, it will be useful to recall an exhortation of the pope, "God's wisdom is manifest in the cosmos in the variety and beauty of its elements, but *his masterpieces,* where his beauty and his greatness truly appear much more, *are the Saints...* The Gospel has suggested to us that God the Father *continues to manifest his plan of love through the Saints.*"[5]

Camilla Battista entered into the "wide-open ocean of the Heart of Christ" by tracing the pathway and handing off to us a map, so that our navigation may reach a safe port, in the awareness of having her, and many other heroes of humanity and faith, as friends and fellow travelers.

On behalf of the sisters of the monastery that safeguards the relics and memory of St. Camilla Battista da Varano, it is my hope and prayer that the English-speaking world may discover her life, and through the intercession and experience of St. Camilla, receive the limitless blessings of Christ.

To His praise, glory and honor!

Mother Clare Laura Serboli, OSC
Abbess of the Monastery of Santa Chiara in Camerino

The crypt of the church of Santa Chiara in Camerino
with the remains of Saint Camilla Battista.

For more information on the community of Poor Clare sisters of Camerino in English, visit: www.saintcamillabattista.it

Or visit their website in Italian:
www.sorellepoveredisantachiara.it
then click "Camerino" or "San Severino" for each community.

The present community of Poor Clare sisters together with some of the friars who participated in the canonization process.

Part of the community of Poor Clare sisters from San Severino from which four sisters departed to re-found the Poor Clare monastery and church of Camerino in 2004. St. Camilla Battista reformed the San Severino community in 1521.

A view of the hill town of Camerino with the Sibylline Mountains in the background.

One of many ruined defensive hilltop fortresses of the Varano ducal family in the environs of Camerino.

One of the halls of the ducal palace in which Camilla grew up.
The building is currently part of the city hall of Camerino.

The cortile d'onore (courtyard of honor) within the Varano ducal palace of Camilla's childhood home.

A portrait of Sister Camilla Battista painted on canvas by an anonymous painter in the 16th century.

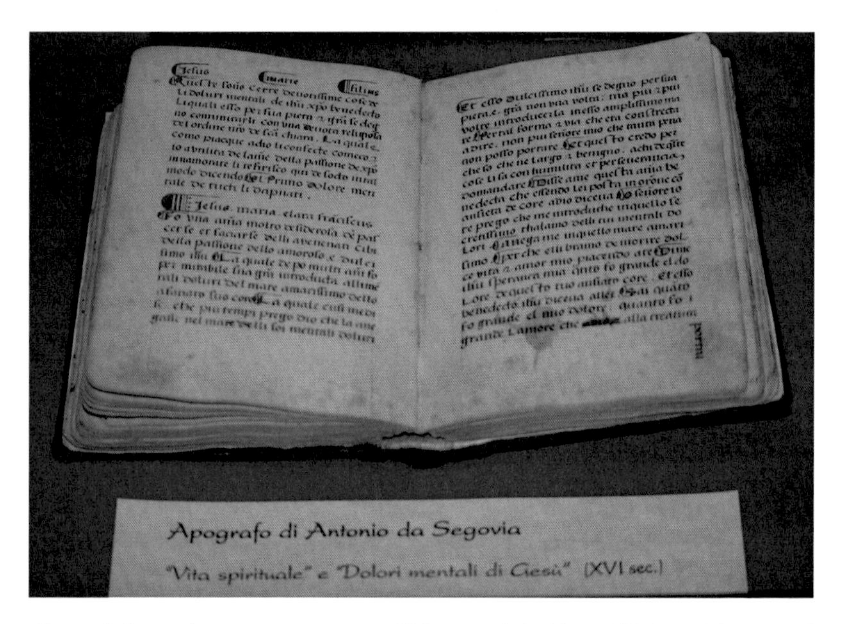

One of the earliest manuscripts of "Spiritual Life" and "Mental Sorrows" transcribed by Antonio of Segovia in the 16th century. It is preserved in the museum within the church of Santa Chiara in Camerino.

The 14th-century courtyard of the monastery of Santa Chiara in Camerino.

The wooden prayer stalls in the monastery of Santa Chiara in Camerino carved by Domenico Indovini in 1489 and recently restored. Saint Camilla prayed in the rear center stall.

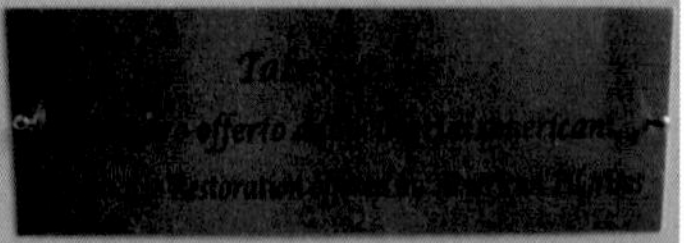

The tabernacle in the church of Santa Chiara in Camerino recently restored through the donations of American pilgrims.

The Public Consistory on February 19, 2010, in which Pope Benedict XVI signed the decree declaring Blessed Camilla Battista Varano in the Register of Saints.

St. Peter's Square on October 17, 2010, the day of the canonization of St. Camilla Battista and five others.

The tapestry of St. Camilla Battista on the façade of St. Peter's Basilica on the day of her canonization.

An Encounter with Saint Camilla Battista

By Bret Thoman, OFS

I discovered Camilla Battista of Varano in 2003 with my wife, Katia, on a pilgrimage to the Marches of Ancona, a bucolic region in central Italy dotted with picturesque medieval hill-topped towns. Under the leadership of the Franciscan provincial minister, Father Ferdinando Campana, OFM, we were taken on a magnificent spiritual journey to the little known historical Franciscan places in his province. He called his region the "*Terra dei Fioretti*" (the "Land of the Little Flowers of St. Francis"), as that great Christian classic was written in the 14th century in the Marches. In the centuries after Francis and Clare, the Marches became the center of Franciscan spirituality, after only Umbria, which it borders to the northeast. We re-lived the stories recounted in the *Fioretti* that took place in the ancient hermitages and friaries like San Liberato, Roccabruna, and Forano, most of which have been reduced to memories and piles of stones.

We did, however, discover some "Little Flowers" that were still quite vibrant. One was a lively community of Poor Clare sisters in the walled hilltown of San Severino Marche. These sisters, many of them young, dedicated themselves to traditional religious cloistered life. They prayed the Divine Office in common, wore the full habit and veil, maintained an enclosure separating them from the public, and observed periods of silence, fasting and abstinence. Yet, these were no drab nuns, as they radiated joy and happiness. One of them recounted a touching story of St. Francis, who passed through San Severino in 1219 with a little lamb, which he tenderly left with a community of penitential women, forebears of the actual community. In our meeting with the sisters in their parlor room that evening, our souls were warmed with their beautifully chanted vespers, while our stomachs enjoyed a scrumptious home-cooked meal, most of the ingredients grown in their garden. They topped the evening off with their angelic singing and some holy joke-telling. Their joy was infectious, and we immediately made lasting friendships with the sisters.

A few months later, four sisters from San Severino left the community to form a new one. Under the leadership of Abbess Chiara Laura Serboli, OSC, they would be re-founding a community in a town called Camerino some 20 kilometers away. The former Poor Clare community there had disbanded after an earthquake in 1997 severely damaged the church and monastery. But this monastery was important to the Poor Clares, the entire Franciscan Order, and the universal Church because Blessed Camilla Battista da Varano had lived and died there, and the crypt within the church contained her remains. The Vatican was studying her cause for canonization, and a declaration of sainthood seemed imminent. So the sisters were setting out to re-found a community, rebuild the church and monastery, and promote the life and memory of Blessed Camilla Battista.

I have to admit that my first impression of Blessed (now Saint) Camilla was skepticism and uncertainty, as I did not initially understand her life and writings. I privately wondered if her five-century-old spirituality based on suffering would be relevant to modern people in the first-world Church today. At the time, she seemed to me a little distant, foreign, remote. Her childhood spent amusing herself among the pleasures and delights of the banquets, entertainments, and conversations in the princely castles of her ducal father's high Renaissance court seemed the stuff of fairy tales. Her adolescent conversion rooted in an odd penitential devotion of shedding a tear once a week appeared to me somewhat peculiar. Although supernatural phenomena are common to some people, such mystical visions, interior locutions, and conversations with passed souls, are outside the scope of my own practical religious experiences. The murders of her father and brothers (likely) ordered from the highest ranks within the Holy See seemed more like the plot of a best-selling mystery novel or a recent cable TV program rather than true life! Yet, after I got to know St. Camilla, she became very special to me.

My "conversion" began one casual afternoon while my family and I were visiting the sisters in Camerino. (At the time, we were living in Assisi.) We were talking with the sisters in the crypt where the saint's relics rest. Her bones are preserved within an artificial plaster cast in the form of her body clothed with the Poor Clare tunic, her face a waxen mask, her head in a veil; a crown and scepter lie at her side. Steeped in Disney princess tales, my then 4-year-old daughter noticed the regal symbols and asked if this sleeping nun was a princess. I was quick to dismiss her question, (which I judged puerile) when Mother Chiara Laura intervened saying, "Yes, she was a princess." Then I understood.

Here was a princess – an heiress to a worldly kingdom with all the honors due such a station. Yet, she had divested herself of all her privileges, voluntarily clothing herself, instead, in the poverty of the penitential Poor Clare tunic. Camilla then became relevant to me: a worldly princess – enamored of the pleasures and delights of the world – abandoned everything to embrace the poor, suffering Christ of the cross. She gave up her worldly inheritance to spend her earthly life at the foot of the cross to suffer with the one she loved in hopes of eternal life. Either Camilla was a fool, or she discovered something in that cross more powerful and valuable than earthly riches.

Yet today Camilla still holds the symbols of regal power – the crown and scepter. Did she remain a princess after all, as the Abbess had affirmed? Or did she abandon her royal status? Indeed, perhaps Camilla, like Pilate, had interrogated Jesus, asking him if he were a king. "Yes," Jesus responded, but, "My kingdom does not belong to this world... it is not here."[6] In response to Jesus's claim, Camilla renounced her worldly kingdom in order to become a citizen of Jesus's heavenly Kingdom. Her status as princess was never renounced; it was transformed.

Camilla followed in the footsteps of Sts. Francis and Clare whose religious legacy she inherited through the Poor Clare Order in the Observant Franciscan Reform. Francis and Clare were born in Assisi some three centuries earlier and just thirty miles away on the other side of the Apennine Mountains. Francis was the son of a wealthy merchant, while Clare descended from a knightly, noble family. Both were privileged and stood to gain much in the world. After their own encounters with the poor, crucified Christ, however, both Francis and Clare renounced their families, inheritances, wealth and honors, and instead embraced poverty to live as penitents in solidarity with the poor. Francis became a servant of the leper – the lowliest person in society; Clare served her sisters in community as well as anyone who came to visit her in San Damiano; Camilla dedicated her life to the cross. The reason that St. Francis renounced his worldly wealth, St. Clare abandoned her honorable status as noblewoman, and St. Camilla rejected the courtly life was because they were seeking to imitate Jesus.

Through the Gospels, each discovered that Christ – the second Person of the Trinity, God almighty whom "the highest heavens cannot contain"[7] – had emptied himself of every heavenly glory because of great love and obedience to his Father. The Incarnation – when God took on human flesh – was an act of divine humility. But the greatest act of love was the suffering and humility that Jesus endured on the cross. "Though he was in the form of God, Jesus did not regard equality with God something to be grasped. Rather, he emptied himself, taking the form of a slave, coming in human likeness; and found human in appearance, he humbled himself, becoming obedient to death, even death on a cross!"[8]

The saints confront us with the absurdity of the Gospel: that Christ, the Word, the second Person of the Trinity, the God-man who is all good and spotless, should lower himself, become incarnate, and die for man, who is sinful. As St. Paul says, "Indeed, only with difficulty does one die for a just person, though perhaps for a good person one might even find courage to die. But God proves his love for us in that while we were still sinners Christ died for us."[9] Thus, Francis, Clare, and Camilla sought to imitate Jesus in their lives by rejecting worldly honors and embracing humility, penance, and poverty. The impetus behind all their actions was Christ himself. In service to and identification with the humble, lesser Christ, they found the Kingdom of heaven on earth.

Identification with Christ in humility, penance, and poverty was life-giving for them in a way that the world was not. Francis said, "May we be able to follow in the footprints of your beloved Son, our Lord Jesus Christ."[10] Clare wrote, "desire to imitate [him on the cross]."[11] Camilla told us, "Look into the most pure Heart of Jesus as into a beautiful mirror. Conform yourself to him, if you wish to have his sweetest friendship and familiarity."[12]

By imitating Christ, Camilla discovered the Kingdom of heaven, one that was quite different from the kingdom in which she grew up. That kingdom was one where people so often sought out ever greater pleasures, diversions, and honors; it was a world where conflict and strife were constant as men sought to increase their territories and worldly gain. God's Kingdom, on the other hand, was one where meekness, humility, and poverty reigned. In the world, people were set on going up; while God's way was one of going down. And the lowest place was the cross. And at the foot of this same cross was where Camilla wished to stay her entire life.

There was a saying in Camilla's day among simple Franciscans that all the theology a Franciscan needed was fully taught in the cross. When 8-year-old Camilla encountered Jesus Christ, she discovered Christ on the cross. He became her Master, mirror and teacher. And the path he taught her reached its highest fulfillment on the cross. The cross is where Jesus said, "*Consummatum est*" (It is finished/fulfilled.)[13] Our Church teachings, Tradition, and Holy Scriptures have long supported the way of the Cross. The Catechism says, "Taking up one's cross each day and following Jesus is the surest way of penance... The way of perfection passes by way of the Cross. There is no holiness without renunciation and spiritual battle. Spiritual progress entails the ascesis and mortification that gradually lead to living in the peace and joy of the Beatitudes."[14] Scripture says, "If a man would come after me, let him deny himself and take up his cross and follow me."[15]

The cross taught Camilla that in this life there is an inseparable, yet mysterious, bond between love and pain. The *Fioretti* recounts how two years before his death, St. Francis prayed on Mount LaVerna for two gifts: to feel in his body the pain which Jesus felt during his Passion and to know in his heart the love which Jesus felt for all humanity. At that moment, a six-winged Seraph appeared and imprinted the signs of the cross on Francis's hands, feet, and side. Francis was at once overwhelmed with joy, but doubled over with pain. The cross that appeared externally on his body was the same cross that had been imprinted internally on his heart some twenty years earlier in San Damiano when Christ from the crucifix told him to rebuild his house, which had fallen into ruin. This same duality of love and pain is what Camilla prayed to have, as well.

Her dedication to the cross and worldly sufferings were the result of her keen knowledge that the cross was the pathway to the Resurrection. The cross purified the soul of all its defects, masks, and vices in order to clearly see God. Without the cross there was no Resurrection; without going down in the world, there was no way to go up to Heaven. The cross was the foundation of her teachings on virtue, forgiveness, and perfect Christian charity, which are certainly relevant in any age.

Thus, in the end, suffering on the cross for Camilla and her spiritual predecessors did not have the final word: the Resurrection did. The cross, though pointing down to the lowest place, was not the ultimate direction the great saints sought. Heaven above was. By embracing the cross, Camilla and the great saints were freed of the things of the world, which allowed them to see created things the way God did. Then they could see clearly that going down was paradoxically the way to Heaven above. Precisely where Camilla was declared to be when she was canonized on October 17, 2010.

So what about her extremism and radicalism? What about the "Three Lilies"? In her first lily, her hatred of the world, did she possibly inherit any dualistic attitudes towards herself, creation, and the world believed by heretics off and on since the 5th century? What about the second lily of believing there was no worse sinner than she? Would psychologists today diagnose her as having a grandiose personality? What about her wishing to suffer badly? She wrote in "Memories of Jesus" of three things necessary for the spiritual life: "great is the benefit of not sinning, very great is the benefit of doing good, the best is that of suffering badly." Most Christians would agree on the first two ingredients – avoiding evil and living a virtuous life. However, is wishing to "suffer badly" a legitimate desire for Christians today? She said that she wanted to make every day a Good Friday to the point of ignoring Christmas and Easter. But why did she wish to be with Jesus at the foot of the cross with John and the Marys, and not burn to be, instead, with Mary Magdalene at the empty tomb? What about being an Easter people of resurrection and rejoicing, not a Good Friday people of mourning and suffering?

Perhaps the answer lies in the results. If, indeed, her writings and life story led her and those influenced by her to a fruitless life devoid of spirit or grace, then we can answer that yes, she was misguided and in error. If, however, her life bore fruit, then we should approach her accordingly. The truth may be complex, even contradictory. Even though Christ was resurrected, he went through the cross to get there. Likewise, Camilla hoped for the Resurrection, but the road she took was through the cross. The cross was a mystery, something difficult to understand, possibly best meditated upon. She wrote in *Spiritual Life*, "These things cannot be easily spoken of, but rather contemplated by the grace of God."

Camilla was a vivacious, passionate, and multifaceted woman; her iron will and temperament were absolute, radical, and intense. She did not allow herself to do anything in half measures, and her personality tended to the extreme. So when she discovered God's great "Ocean of Love" through the cross, she threw herself deeply into the abyss, rather than treading water near the surface or wading along the shore. She wished to be with her lover, her mystical "Spouse" where he was – and she saw him on the cross, which is where she wanted to be.

I do not believe that Camilla's radicalism came from a defective personality or misguided spirituality; rather, hers was a unique calling received directly from God himself. Camilla Battista was a mystic who had a profound encounter with the love of Christ through his cross. In her personal and lived encounter with the great love of God through the cross, she joined the chorus of so many saints who went before and would come after who mysteriously shared intensely in the suffering of Christ. Christ desires all his followers to help him "carry the cross"[16] and participate in his Passion; thus, suffering within the Body of Christ has a redemptive role. This is part of Catholic theology that does not take away from the primacy of Christ in his work of salvation; rather, souls are called to first receive his grace, then to co-operate in his work. As St. Paul said, "Now I rejoice in my sufferings for your sake, and in my flesh I am filling up what is lacking in the afflictions of Christ on behalf of his body, which is the church."[17] Camilla's desire to stay with Jesus on the cross served as a co-operator in penitential intercessory grace.

Perhaps the fruits of her path were revealed when she made the only (possible) reference to the terrible tribulation suffered when her father was murdered by agents of the Borgia family. She wrote, "*Certain prelates and pastors of our souls to whom belong the care of souls ... beat me with harsh words and wounded me with worse deeds and ... took from me a father who was my refuge; ... these prying prelates are guardians of the ceremonial walls of religion, but not the walls of the good and holy life; ...* ***nevertheless, we should not stop honoring these prelates because of this; rather, we must frequently pray for them ... and I will dress in sackcloth and ashes of humility and patience [for them]***." Does not her response echo Jesus's words as he hung dying, "Father, forgive them, they know not what they do."[18] Clearly her encounter with the crucified Lord at the foot of his cross led her to mirror God's radical Gospel of forgiveness and love concretely and as intercessor.

While laboriously translating the writings of St. Camilla over the past two years, I have had the privilege and honor of delving into her spirituality and beliefs. Many times, together with my wife, Katia, we asked ourselves what she meant by particular words and sentences. As a result, I got to know her thoughts rather well. In the process, she soon became like a spiritual director to me. Often, I would come across some statement, idea, or admonition that would seem to be precisely the answer to a particular issue I was dealing with. Beyond that, she has challenged me to deepen my own spirituality. For example, I now carry a small 10-bead rosary with me which I use to say a quick decade for someone I feel has slighted me or who appears to need prayers. And although my spirituality tends to be rather pragmatic, one night a few years ago, I received a special grace while praying for Camilla's intercession during a particularly troubling time.

In addition to having a new friend and spiritual guide in St. Camilla, the sisters of the communities of San Severino and Camerino have become like true sisters to Katia and I. Since meeting them in 2004, we have taken over 700 pilgrims to visit them, pray with them, and discover the life of St. Camilla Battista. The separation of their two communities in 2005 was extremely difficult for them, like "the breakup of a family," as Mother Chiara Laura has described it. Apart from the emotional pain of separation, the sisters faced what seemed like insurmountable financial obstacles in their effort to restore the church and monastery from the damage of the 1997 earthquake. Through the donations of English speaking pilgrims who had visited the sisters with us, we helped them finance the restoration of their five-century-old tabernacle in the church. The main source of funds for the larger work, however, arrived in an unexpected grant from a well-heeled bank in their region. Providentially, the restoration was completed just as the Vatican announced that Camilla would definitively be canonized.

It has been my joy to serve as a sort of "bridge" between English-speaking people and the Poor Clare sisters of Camerino/San Severino and St. Camilla. I hope you will discover in St. Camilla, as I have, countless pearls of wisdom and profound Christian insight. And as you begin her writings, let your reading be guided by her own words: "*Do not allow these few and most devout words to be read except by most devout and spiritual persons. In that way, the matters of God, which should be accepted and read with the greatest devotion, will not be subjected to contempt and abuse ... God is most kind, most wise and most clement and he wants us to distribute his hidden spiritual treasures as he pleases and finds proper. And the manner, the time and the person are not questions upon which he chooses to seek our counsel, because he, amiable truth, does not judge as we do – from the outside – but according to the inner disposition. He sees the disposition of the heart with his holy and loving eye. And so it is written: 'The judgments of God are different from the judgments of men.'*"[19]

Preface

The writings of Saint Camilla were reworked from the original 15th-16th century Italian into modern standard Italian some years ago by an erudite Poor Clare nun in the monastery of Camerino. This English edition of her works was translated from the modern edition while referencing the original. All of the important works of St. Camilla Battista are included in this English translation. She wrote some other works that include letters, prayers, a commentary on the Rule of St. Clare, visions, memories and lives of blessed friars and nuns, etc. These were not included, mainly because they dealt with local personalities, places, and issues of her day.

As a mystic, St. Camilla did not write in prosaic or linear fashion; she wrote to express her spiritual experience of God. Thus, she frequently jumped back and forth between the first and third person in her spiritual colloquies making it difficult to understand who is speaking to whom; some of her writings were addressed to her spiritual father, but at times she switched to God the Father; she frequently changed thoughts and ideas from one sentence to the next, then reverted back. Further, from a grammatical perspective, her old Italian and Latinate sentence structures are quite long and would be considered run-on sentences in English. In the translation, I tried to leave her original language and sentence structure intact as much as possible to preserve its style, but I did make slight changes to make it accessible to the English reader. I also periodically added words in brackets or footnotes for clarification.

Her writings have been approved by the Catholic Church and they contain no theological errors. The exhaustive investigation of her writings by theologians, historians, and cardinals, which preceded the declaration of her heroic virtues, had as one of its tasks the determination of whether or not her writings were in line with Catholic doctrine. Thus, her canonization *can* be understood as an *imprimatur* or *nihil obstat* on her writings. This means that there is nothing contrary to Catholic teaching in her works. Furthermore, at the conclusion of the first phase of her canonization process, a number of cardinals and theologians who were present advocated for Camilla to be proclaimed a Doctor of the Church without delay. Thus, not only have her writings have been declared free of error from within the highest ranks of the Holy See, a nomination of "Doctor of the Church" would imply a very special title indicating that her writings and theological teachings are orthodox and useful to Christians in any age.

This does not mean, however, that they are infallible; nor does it not mean that she was not influenced by certain expressions, historical references, or prejudices. For example, she does express attitudes from a bygone era: she occasionally excuses herself for being an erudite woman; she apparently believes that religious life in the convent or friary is a holier calling than the laity; she assigns guilt collectively to the Jewish people, etc. Thus, a certain critical perspective should be employed while reading. Further, as a contemplative, St. Camilla Battista frequently used poetic language, flowery imagery and symbolism to describe her ideas and visions. Therefore, it would be advisable not to take her account of certain realities literally; i.e. Christ's appearance, descriptions of heaven, hell, etc.

She wrote in old Italian, but quoted Scripture from the Latin Vulgate, as the Bible had not been translated into Italian at that time. However, the excessive Latin appears awkward in the English text. Therefore, in order to make the text more readable in English, I put all her Scripture references in English, while leaving the Latin referenced in footnotes at the bottom of each page. The proper way would have been to leave the Latin in the text and reference the Scripture in English in the footnotes.

Unfortunately, with the exception of the work of the recently deceased Father Paul Lachance, OFM (d. July 31, 2011), at present there are no serious critical studies of St. Camilla Battista in English. There are several noteworthy scholarly critiques of her writings in Italian, particularly by Giovanni Boccanero, a classics teacher from Camerino who did his doctoral dissertation on her writings in the 1940s. Other Italian scholars who have extensively researched her writings include Bruno Giannini and Pietro Luzi. However, none of their commentaries have been translated into English at the time of publication. See bibliography below.

Bibliography:

Paul Lachance, OFM. "Battista da Varona (1458-1524): A Survey of Her Life and Writing as a Poor Clare Visionary." Mystics Quarterly Vol. 20 #1, March 1994.

Pietro Luzi. Camilla Battista da Varano: una spiritualità tra papa Borgia e Lutero. Torino, Pietro Gribaudi Editore, 1989.

Bruno Giannini. La principessa velata: la vita monasteriale della B. Camilla Battista Varano. S. Maria degli Angeli-Assisi, Edizioni Porziuncola, 1991.

Ulderico Gamba. Mistici di tutti i tempi. Pagine scelte, Padova, Edizioni Messaggero, 1995.

Serena Spanò. Battista Varano, in Il grande libro dei santi. Dizionario enciclopedico, I, Cinisello Balsamo, Edizioni S. Paolo, 1998, pp. 259-260.

Bret Thoman, OFS

The Writings of Saint Camilla Battista Da Varano

Latin Couplets Contemplating Jesus Crucified

(Circa 1479)

The first work of St. Camilla Battista was written in classical Latin. It is in the form of elegiac couplets (hexameter + pentameter). The couplets reveal the command that the Renaissance prince's daughter had of the Latin language and meter due to her education under well-known tutors. Her writings are full of extravagant words and phrases as well as numerous references and quotations in the Latin Vulgate Bible and sacred texts that had become familiar to her after her conversion. The work dates from around 1479, when Camilla was young and before she had entered the monastery. The verses may have been used by her to meditate on the Passion of Christ which she mentioned in her Autobiography (chap. IV). The work is an expression of her spirituality in a humanistic form: the contemplation of the face of Jesus that came from a loving and maturing relationship with Christ. If it was written in 1479, this would be her first work, pre-dating *Lauda* (Praises to the Vision of Christ).

The work is presented in its original Latin, followed by the translation in English. Giovanni Boccanero discovered the work during his research, and he divided it into three parts: A, B, and C. Part A alternates between words spoken by Christ (lines 1-4 and 9-12) and reflections of the author (lines 5-8). The second group presents two questions by St. Camilla. The third group is framed by the word "*solus*" at the beginning of each sentence and "*amor*" at the last, in English, "only love".

Latin Couplets Contemplating Jesus Crucified

a) *Huc me sidereo des[c]endere iussit Olympo,*
hic me crudeli vulnere fixit amor.

Langueo nec quisquam nostro succurrit amori,
quem nequeunt dirae frangere iura crucis.

Pungentem capitis Dominum gestare coronam, *5*
fortis amor docuit verbera tanta pati.

Felle sitim magni regis satiavit amaro,
pectus ut hauriret lancea fuit amor.

De me solus amor potuit perferre triumphum:
ille pedes clavis fixit et ille manus. *10*

Si cupis ergo animi mihi signa rependere gratis,
dilige pro tantis. Sat mihi solu[s] amor.

b) *Cum sic despectus rigida super arbore pendes,*
tam dura [m] pateris cur bene Christe necem?

Sponte quidem laxis humeris mea crimina portas! *15*
In cruce Tu moreris, nec crucifigar ego?

c) *Solus amor Christum solio deduxit ab alto;*
Virginis implevit viscera solus amor.

Solus amor sparsit divini semina verbi;
in cruce sustinuit vulnera solus amor. *20*

Solus amor lumen clausi patefecit Olympi;
Invictum potuit vincere solus amor.

Solus amor superas iter est rapientibus arces;
clamat terra(m), fretum, sidera solus amor.

Solus amor nullo claudendus fine manebit. *25*
Prae cunctis igitur solus amandus amor.

a) [Love] ordered me to descend from the starry heavens
Love fixed me here by its cruel wound.[20]

I languish because no one gives assistance to our love[21]
That the laws of the cruel cross are unable to break.

A strong love taught the Lord to bear the stabbing crown 5
on his head, [and] to suffer so many scourges.

[Love] satisfied the thirst of the great King with bitter vinegar,
It was love that opened up his chest with the spear.

Only love could sustain victory over me:
The one attached his feet with nails and the other his hands. 10

If you wish, therefore, to freely repay me the marks of my soul,
love for many. Only love [is] sufficient to me.

b) While you hang so despised from the rigid tree,
why O Christ, do you so serenely endure such a harsh death?

So willingly, indeed, you carry my faults on relaxed shoulders! 15
On the cross you die, shall I not be crucified?

c) Only love led Christ down from the high throne,
only love filled up the innermost parts of the Virgin;

Only love spread the seeds of the divine word,
Only love sustained the wounds on the cross; 20

Only love made light accessible from closed-off Heaven,
only love could conquer the unconquerable;

Only love is the way for the plunderers of the heavenly strongholds,
only love invokes the land, the sea, the stars.

Only love will remain in the end with nothing closed off, 25
Above all things, therefore, only love is to be loved.

Praise of the Vision of Christ

Lauda Della Visione Di Cristo
(1479-1481)

Camilla wrote *Lauda* "Praise of the vision of Christ" in the period leading up to her entrance into the monastery in Urbino. Having made the decision to consecrate herself to the Lord, she began to receive mystical experiences that strengthened her in her confrontation with her father who was against her decision. The "familiarity" which she felt with Christ caused her to desire and ask to see his face, a central point of this poem. According to the Italian scholar, Luzi, St. Camilla has in this period "the first intuition of the memories of Jesus, each says one thing above all: the joy of knowing herself loved by Christ." Luzi compared this poem to the Canticle of the Canticles in its intimacy and intensity.

We left the original 15th century Italian in which it was written in order to appreciate the poem's authentic rhyme and meter.

Lauda della Visione di Cristo

Colloquio che fa l'anima innamorata che languisce de amore cum Iesu Cristo suo diletto sposo.

Quando serà che possa contemplare,
o bon Iesù, el tuo benegno viso?
Credo che me faresti liquefare,
e non vorebbe altro paradiso.
Fammelo un poco, o dolce amor, gustare,
a ciò che lo mio cor non sia diviso
da te, mio ben, mia vita e mia dolcezza,
per la suavità de tua bellezza.

Veder te voglio e fa quello te piace.
E voglime, Iesù, con teco unire.
Tu mio conforto sei e la mia pace;
deh, non me far per tal desio languire.
Si son presentuosa et audace,
perdon ti chieggio, o dolce e car mio Sire.
E si non vol che 'l cor me se disfaccia,
Mostrame, amor, la tua iocunda faccia.

Se pur, Signore, non te costrengesse
nullo respetto a farme sì gioiosa,
se 'l mio grave fallire te l' proibisse,
come che giusta e ragionevel cosa,
mòvante, o bon Iesù, quelle promesse
che fatte m'ha tua bocca graziosa.
Però non me 'l negar, te prego molto:
mostrame el tuo benigno e santo volto.

Quando promette el fedel mercatante
per credito trovar, vole osservare;
quel che promette però el navigante
per le salse onde va de l'alto mare.
Tu so che sei lial, fermo e costante,
e, più che non promette, ne voi dare.
Le tuoi promesse più dolce che 'l mele
attende presto, o mercator fidele.

Praise of the Vision of Christ

A colloquy of a soul in love that languishes with Jesus Christ,
her beloved Spouse.

When will it be possible to contemplate
O good Jesus, your benign face?
I think you would make me melt,
and [I] would not like any other paradise.
Let me taste, O sweet love, a little of it,
so that my heart is not separated
from you, my goodness, my life and my sweetness,
for the suavity of your beauty.

I want to see you, so do what you like.
And you, Jesus, desire that I unite myself together with you.
You are my comfort, and my peace;
Ah, do not let me languish because of such desire.
If I am presuming and bold,
I ask your pardon, O sweet and dear Lord of mine.
And if you do not want my heart to melt,
then show me, my love, your joyful face.

And if, Lord, respect [for me] would not compel you
to make me so happy,
if my major failing forbids it to you,
as would be a just and reasonable cause,
may those promises that your gracious mouth made,
O good Jesus, move you.
But do not deny it to me, I beseech you:
Show me your gracious and holy face.

When a faithful merchant makes a promise
in order to find credit, he waits and wishes to observe [that promise];
That which the sailor promises, however,
goes to the deep seas through the salty waves.
I know that you are loyal, firm and constant,
and you do not give more than what you promise.
Grant me quickly, O faithful merchant
your promises sweeter than honey.

Si me podesse, ohimé, lascia l'acostare
al santo viso, o dolce vita mia,
io so che stretto te vorria abracciare
e per dolcezza forte piangeria.
In vita eterna già non vorria stare,
né paradiso più desidereria;
né altra pace, ohimé, lascia dolente
che stare unita in te sì dolcemente.

Perchè tu se' la vera pace mia,
sei verace om' e ver figliol de Dio;
tu sei el desiato gran Messia,
e sei lo eternale sposo mio.
Tu sei triunfo d'ogni ierarchia
e sei satisfattor d'ogni desio;
tu sei dolcezza, gloria e onore
e d'ogni afflitto cor consolatore.

Però se lo universo io possidesse
e non posseda te, nulla me piace;
se tutto l'oro, perle e gemme avesse
e d'ogni scienzia io fusse capace,
non crederia che mai contenta stesse,
essendo de te priva, o Dio verace.
Però disìo fruirte pura e netta,
umile, ubediente e poveretta.

Se te vedesse non arrìa paura
che me piacesse più creata cosa.
Odo che tanto è vaga tua figura
che l'alma in altro mai non se riposa,
e sente poi d'amor sì gran caldura
che d'ogni pena se fa iubilosa;
e già non sente quando è vulnerata;
vivendo more tutta inamorata.

If you could, alas, let me approach
your holy face, O sweet life of mine,
I know that I would want to embrace you tightly
and I would weep strongly out of sweetness.
I would really not want to be in eternal life,
nor would I desire heaven any longer;
Nor any other peace, alas, leaves [me] sorrowful
compared to being united so sweetly to you.

Because you are my true peace,
you are true Man and true Son of God;
You are the most desired Messiah,
and you are my eternal Spouse.
You are the victory of every hierarchy
and you are the satisfier of every desire;
You are sweetness, glory and honor
and consoler of every afflicted heart.

But if I possessed the universe
and did not have you, nothing [would be] pleasing to me;
If I had all gold, pearls and gems
and I was capable [of knowing] all knowledge,
I do not believe that I would ever be happy
If I were deprived of you, O true God.
But I desire to enjoy you [in being] pure and clear,
humble, obedient, and poor.

If I saw you, I would not worry
that I might take pleasure in any worldly thing.
I hear that your figure is so vague
that the soul never rests in any other thing,
and [the soul] feels such great warmth in love
that every pain renders it jubilant;
And it no longer feels when it is wounded;
While living, it dies completely in love.

Famme sallire a quel soperno stato
D'aver de mia viltà cognizione;
fammete amar d'amor desordenato,
el qual non è subietto alla ragione
e non se tempra quando è consegliato;
né per vergogna refrenar se pòne;
e si cusì t'amasse de bel patto
darebbe a questo mondo scaccomatto.

Tu dolce sei benegno e suave
e sei pieno d'ogni cortisia;
tu sei dello mio cor la vera chiave
e sei tutta la speranza mia.
Benigno Signor mio, non te sia grave
mostrarme la tua faza dolce e pia,
la qual sopra ogni altra cosa bramo,
e per lei veder piangendo chiamo.

Io vo pensando che podesse avere
che questo afflitto cor me consolasse:
ogni mundar diletto m'è spiacere
e stolto parme chi de lui se passe.
Solo una cosa porria possedere
e questo, credo, che me contentasse
che stesse o bon Iesù, nelle toi brazza.
stretta e congionta alla tua dolze fazza.

Questo me privaria d'ogne dolore,
questo me vestiria de gran dolceza,
questo dicendo me s'alegra el core,
questo pensando me dona alegreza;
questo m'azenderia de gran fervore,
questo serà al mio cor somma forteza.
Sol questo me poria cavar de stenta
vivere alegra e far morir contenta.

Let me rise up to that higher state
of having full knowledge of my wickedness;
Let me love with my disordered love,
which is not subject to reason
and is not tempered when it is counseled;
Nor out of shame does it intend to slow down;
And if it loved you according to this good pact
it would give to this world a checkmate.

You are sweet, suave, and good
and you are full of all courtesy;
You are the true key of my heart
and you are all my hope.
Good Lord of mine, do not be grave
in showing me your sweet and loving face,
which I desire above all else,
and to see it, I call out crying.

I go thinking that if I could only have
this afflicted heart console me,
every worldly delight would be displeasure to me
and the one who suffers because of it [the worldly delight] seems foolish to me.
If I could possess just one thing
and this, I believe, would make me content,
if I were, O good Jesus, in your arms,
close and joined to your sweet face.

This would deprive me of all pain,
this would vest me in every sweetness,
only saying this makes my heart rejoice,
thinking this gives me happiness;
This would prepare in me a great zeal,
this will be to my heart the highest strength.
Only this would liberate me from weariness,
and would make me live happily and die content.

Voria sapere, o caro mio Signore,
se 'l mio penare te fosse diletto
voria sapere, o spechio, del mio core,
che utel te serà se pur aspetto;
a me è danno e a te è disonore
se le promesse non hanno l'efetto.
Non te maravegliar se ho gran fretta,
perché par longo el tempo a chi aspetta.

Deh, dolze Signor mio, per qual cagione Voria
el to bel viso e santo me nascondi?
Cognosco ben la mia presunzione,
ma pur te chiamo e tu non me rispondi.
Signor mio dolze, tutte le persone
che in te speran mai non le confondi;
e so che sòl mostrarte a chi te brama.
e dài risposta a chi col cor te chiama.

E tu sai ben, Signor, la fede mia,
e vedi li suspiri che te mando.
Deh, non me usare questa escortisia:
negarme quel che tanto t'adimando!
Non credo già che gran piacer te sia
vederme andar per questo lagrimando.
Sia fatto pure el to santo volere,
ma in ogne modo te voglio vedere.

Se non me vergognasse te diria,
cara speranza mia, un'altra cosa;
forse pietà de me te prenderia,
vedendome de te tanto bramosa.
Ma sappie questo, o dolce vita mia,
che solo in te conven che me riposa;
pur con vergogna el dico e voce fiocca:
basar io te vorria la santa bocca.

I would like to know, O my dear Lord,
if my suffering was delightful to you,
I would like to know, O mirror of my heart,
what usefulness it will be to you if I wait;
To me it is damage and to you dishonor
if the promises do not take effect.
Do not marvel if I have great haste,
because it seems a long time to those who wait.

Ah, sweet Lord, for what reason do you wish
to hide your beautiful and holy face from me?
I know well my presumption,
yet I still call you and you do not answer me.
My sweet Lord, you never confuse
all persons who hope in you;
And I know that you only show yourself to those who desire you;
And you give answer to those who call you with their heart.

And you know well, Lord, my faith,
and you see the sighs that I send you.
Alas, do not be discourteous with me:
To deny me that which I so ask of you!
I do not believe that it gives so much pleasure to you
to see me going around weeping so.
It may be well your holy will,
but just the same I wish to see you.

If I did not feel ashamed I would tell you,
my dear hope, another thing;
Perhaps you would take pity on me,
seeing me so desirous of you.
But know this, O my sweet life,
that only in you it is well that I rest;
Even with shame I say it and with feeble voice:
I want to kiss your holy mouth.

Ormai chi 'l vol saper non cur ch'el saccia:
de te, o bon Iesù, so' innamorata,
e par che tutto el cor me se desfaccia
quando me sento con teco abrazata.
Se non me mostre la tua chiara faccia,
sappi che vivo como desperata.
Veder te voglio, ornai non più tardare,
ché troppo me par dur questo aspettare.

Tutti li sensi perde el suo valore
quando te digni, diletto, parlarme;
le to' parole sónno de dolzore
e fanno per dolceza consumarme.
Quando te veggo, o caro mio Signore,
spander le braza e voler abrazzarme
abasso li occhi e dicote: Non fare!
Tu pur me stregne e non me vòi lassare.

Et io, tapina, per la gran dolceza
perdo la voce e non posso parlare;
vedome condutta in tanta alteza
e la cagione già non so pensare.
Al mio maligno cor quanta allegreza
questo li sia non posso narrare.
Chi l'ha pruato sa non se po' dire
quanto ch'è dolze in tal pena languire.

Più che non posso te vorria amare,
cara speranza mia dolze e benigna;
chi non lo crede lo possa provare
quanta bontà nelle toi braza regna.
Deverìeme de Te tutta infiammare,
ben lo cognosco; ma so' sì maligna
che non me movo per losenghe tante,
anzi più dura sto che 'l diamante.

By now he who wants to know doesn't take pains to know:
With you, O good Jesus, I am in love,
and it seems to me that all my heart melts
when I feel I am embraced with you.
If you do not show me your bright face,
know that I live as a desperate one.
I wish to see you, henceforth, no longer delay,
because this waiting seems to me too harsh.

All my senses lose their value
when you stoop, beloved, to speak to me;
Your words are like sweetness,
And their sweetness makes me consumed.
When I see you, O my dear Lord,
open wide your arms and desire to embrace me,
I lower my eyes and say to you: Do not!
Because you hold me tight and do not want to let loose.

And I, wretched one, out of great sweetness
lose my voice and I cannot speak;
I see myself led to such a height
and I cannot think of the reason why.
To my evil heart I can not recount
how much happiness this brings to it.
He who went through it knows that one cannot say
how sweet it is to languish in so much hardship.

I wish to love you more than I am able to,
my dear sweet and benign hope;
Let he who does not believe it experience
how much goodness reigns in your arms.
I should become all enflamed of you,
I know well; but I am so wicked
that I do not move away as a result of so many enticements,
Rather I am more firm than the diamond.

Par fórsa ad altrui che forte t'ame
per lacrime che stillan l'ochi mei:
so ben, diletto mio, che tu non brame
l'ochi piangenti e li custumi rei.
Cor dritto vol che in verità te chiame
e de costui el vero sposo sei;
e non te piace sol che bagne el petto
de lacrime col cor pien de difetto.

Vorrebbe ben ch'el cor me fiammeggiasse
del tuo amore con perfetta fede,
e tanto io cum fervore te bramasse
ch'aiuto demandasse e non mercede.
So ben, se una sentilla ne gustasse
de quello amor dal qual tutto procede,
virtù, bontà, senno e cortisia,
de questo mondo beffe me faria.

Perché sei dolze sopra ogni altra cosa,
e ben me par crudel quel che non t'ama,
si vol che questa affitta se riposa
non tardar a venir poiché te chiama;.
e mostrali la faccia graziosa,
la qual con tanto afetto cerca e brama.
Vieni, te prego, e mostrate a costei,
ché tutta pace e la sua vita sei.

Vieni, benegno e grazioso amante,
Vieni, conforto della vita mia!
Vieni alle voce mie che sono tante!
Vieni, Signore, pien di cortesia!
Vieni vittorioso e trionfante!
Vieni al cor mio, dolce melodia!
Vieni, ché voglio renegar me stessa,
se tu m'atende la fatta promessa.

It may seem to others that I love you strongly
for the tears that gush from my eyes:
I know well, my beloved, that you do not desire
weeping eyes and such offending habits.
Rather, you want an upright heart to call you in truth,
and of this you are a true Spouse;
And you do not like the one who only bathes his chest
with tears and has a heart full of faults.

I would like that my heart were enflamed
of your love with perfect faith,
and I so fervently desired you
that I asked the help of God and no reward.
I know well, that if I tasted a spark
of that love from which everything proceeds,
virtue, goodness, wisdom, and courtesy
of this world would become mockery to me.

Because you are sweet above every other thing,
and he seems to me cruel the one who loves you not,
if you want to give rest to this afflicted one,
do not delay in coming because she calls you;
And show her your gracious face,
which she searches and longs for you with so much affection.
come, I beg you, and show yourself to her,
because you are all peace and her life.

Come, gracious and graceful lover,
come, comfort of my life!
Come to my voices that are many!
Come, Lord, full of courtesy!
Come victorious and triumphant!
Come to my heart, sweet melody!
Come, because I want to deny myself,
if you grant to me the promise made.

Tu sei cului che pasce cum diletto,
e sei vivente et immortale Dio;
all'alma, che te cerca cum effetto,
te mostre grazioso, umile e pio;
purghi e dirizzi lo umano intelletto
e tutto se' suave allo cor mio.
Tu bene, tu conforto e tu riposo,
tu vita e pace e mio diletto sposo.

Credo, se tutto el mondo me donasse,
el celo e la celeste compagnia
el paradiso aperto me mostrasse
con ogni gloriosa ierarchia
el tuo bel viso poscia me celasse,
nulla per questo me reposaria:
inferno me seria el paradiso
si non e possedesse el to' bel viso.

Famine una grazia, o Signor mio clemente,
e po' fa de me quel che te piace:
infiammame d'amor la ceca mente
azò che sia de te sempre capace.
Tepida sonno, ingrata e sconoscente,
como tu sai, o Signor mio verace.
Deh, dolce pace mia, damme che possa
servirte cum bon cor fine alla fossa.

Null'altra lu mio cor disia
se non d'amarte et esser saziata
de te, o bon Iesù, speranza mia,
et esser del tuo foco rescaldata.
Famme una grazia, si pur vol che sia
de te perfettamente inamorata:
espogliame del mondo el tristo manto
e poi me mostra el to bel viso santo.

You are the one who shepherds with delight,
and you are the living and immortal God;
You show yourself gracious, humble and pious
to the soul, who searches for you with affection;
You purge and straighten the human intellect
and you are all suave to my heart.
You are goodness, comfort, and rest,
you are life and peace and my beloved Spouse.

I believe, that if the entire world were given to me,
and you showed me the heavens and the celestial company,
and Heaven opened up
with every glorious hierarchy of angels,
yet if your beautiful face afterwards were concealed to me
none of this would give me rest:
And Hell would be Heaven for me
if I could not possess your beautiful face.

Give me a grace, O my merciful God,
and then make of me what you like:
Enflame my blind mind with love
so that it is always capable of [receiving] you.
I am lukewarm, ungrateful, and unknowing,
as you know, my true Lord.
Ah, my sweet peace, give me [the grace] so that I can
serve you with a good heart until the grave.

My heart desires nothing else
other than loving you and being satisfied
of you, O good Jesus, my hope,
and being warmed by your fire.
Give me a grace, if you wish me to be
completely enamored of you:
Strip me from the sad mantle of the world
and then show me your beautiful saintly face.

Viene all'aflitta tua dolente sposa,
benegno Signor mio, non più tardare.
Molto l'hai fatta mesta e dolorosa
con questo sì crudel longo aspettare;
nulla per lei nel mondo trova posa,
solo di te se vole aquietare:
Te vole, te disia, te cerca e brama,
Te spesso cum suspir languendo chiama.

Sentito t'abbio al gusto del cor mio
sopra l'argento e l'or desiderabile,
un solo unico ben perfetto Dio,
benegno, grazioso e delettabile;
largo, cortese, dolze e tutto pio
e sopra la scienzia sei amabile.
Infin concludo, parlo e chiaro el dico
che tu sei patre, sposo e vero amico.
Amen.

Come to your aching spouse,
my gracious Lord, no longer delay.
You made her very sad and pained
with this waiting so cruel and long;
She finds rest in nothing in the world,
she wishes to find calm only in you:
She loves you, she desires you, she searches and longs for you,
she often calls you with a languishing sigh.

May I feel you to the enjoyment of my heart
more than silver and desirable gold,
only one true and perfect God,
good, graceful and pleasurable;
Wide, courteous, sweet and all pious
and beyond all knowledge you are lovable.
Finally, I conclude, I speak and say it clearly
that you are Father, Spouse and true friend.
Amen.

Memories of Jesus

Ricordi Di Gesu'
(1483; 1491)

St. Camilla Battista first wrote "Memories of Jesus" between May and June of 1483 while still a young novice in the monastery of Urbino. It was written as a letter by Jesus to her, and is framed around her vocation of *malpatire* or "suffering badly." In it, Jesus reminds her of events while she was living in her father's palace. However, towards the end, the young Camilla addressed some words to herself, breaking up the narration. Therefore, it may seem a bit difficult to know who is speaking to whom, as she switches back and forth without clarification.

Often the saints are filled with doubts, and even St. Camilla Battista doubted the inspiration to transcribe (copy) her "Memories" which she began to do in the monastery of Camerino in 1491. After having begun, she was tempted to abandon the project, as she was judging her handwriting negatively. She also feared that the sin of pride was tempting her. Nevertheless, she went ahead and finished on January, 1491. For two months, she put it aside somewhere, but after a divine illumination, decided to send it to Fr. Domenico of Leonessa, to whom the letter is addressed and dated March 21.

Memories of Jesus

What follow are things I knew before I entered the monastery, which I wrote when I was in Urbino. Take note of them well, because I need to say a *Mea Culpa* because of my infidelity and ingratitude. When last January I was given the strength to write them down, it was very difficult for me because I did not know my motives. Now it is clear to me: it was so that I could show them to you. "So get up and eat,[22] reverend father, the fruit[23] and the work of your hands."[24]
Die 21 *martii* 1491. [March 21, 1491]
Deo gratias. Amen. [Thanks be to God. Amen.]

Spiritus Sanctus, Iesus, Mariae Filius Clara, Franciscus [Holy Spirit, Jesus, Son of Mary, Clare, Francis]

"My sister, often times you have said to me that since the beginning of your vocation, God promised you would experience a great tribulation and you fear you will forget the divine promise when you shall find yourself in those sufferings living like one without hope. Therefore, I decided to write you this letter as a memorial.[25] And I am certain that this will give respite to your sufferings. Remember, first of all, that your vocation was not a result of human words, but it came from the mouth of God against your will. After the desire to do good, you promptly had a desire to suffer badly.[26] Then you became ill right away.

Remember also that since your childhood, God always attracted you to and wished that you meditate on his holy Passion. And he desired for you to live your life similarly to it, as much as your weakness could take. And begin to announce your sufferings to yourself when you are in prayer, and meditate on the moment after the Last Supper, after Jesus gave communion to the Disciples."

And [Jesus] spoke thus: "See, my daughter, that when I was near my Passion, I turned to prayer. I beg you and beseech you with grace to do the same. Because to us[27] for now you cannot do anything more pleasing than this. And as men of the world delight in seeing a person they love accomplish one habit over another more, thus, I knew that to us it gives more delight seeing you in this habit of holy prayer than in any other virtuous habit. And see that while I was in prayer it delighted my Father to show me all the sufferings I would have to bear. It was at this point that I stripped myself of every desire of mine and said, 'May your will be done.'[28] And I was so enflamed with charity in this prayer that I chose to die with so much suffering not for myself, but only for honor to my Father and the salvation of souls. And I returned three times to prayer in order to make you understand and every other person who wishes to truly be pleasing to me that it is not enough to just pray one time, but perseverance in prayer delights me.

And remember that even though I was God and I had come only to suffer, just the same when the hour came, because I was true man, I was forced to pray, 'If it is possible, let this cup pass from me...'[29] And so I say the same to you, my daughter: even though you frequently begged me to allow you to suffer, when I shall give it to you, if because of the many sufferings you begged me, 'May it pass, if possible, etc.', as long as you conclude, 'May your will be done,' do not lose hope and do not think you will be giving me displeasure in this. Because I, as much as I was a man, did the same in order to give an example to you and to everyone. And if the goodness of my Father were so much that, with you continuing in prayer, he bid to show these sufferings of yours to you as he did with me and you were enflamed to wish to bear them not for your sake, but only for honor of God and the salvation of others, as I did, your similarity with me will be so much that my Father will be forced to love you," it seems that he [Jesus] says, "as much as me.[30] And cordially thank God for the sufferings he has prepared for you through his goodness. Feel bitter pain for those that he did not predispose you because of your ingratitude and your little spirit, and you should know that it is out of his charity that he would like to give you every bad thing in order to have a reason to give you every good thing.

Recognize and thank God that you do not merit the good so great that [he] would make you conform to me, his beloved Son, by means of the Passion. Because this is the wedding garment that I, your true Spouse, was always dressed in. And you should know that, after good will, this is the most precious thing that God can give; that is, suffering badly. And you could flee this bad suffering, as I could have fled it. You should know, however, that if you flee it, you will also flee every good thing, because the choice that I made only out of charity and love of suffering was pleasing to my Father. Thus, it is necessary that you do the same if you wish to make yourself similar to me and to be pleasing to my Father. And see that when I finished prayer so enflamed with charity, I countered my enemies, so also you counter them and do not be afraid. I was betrayed by my disciple with a kiss, so if you are deceived and afflicted by the one whom you love, then rejoice.

Therefore, remember that I taught you five things: *The first*: when you are offended, be pained for the offense to God more than for your suffering.

The second: pray to me cordially to forgive that person and free him from the punishment that is deserved, as you would wish that I freed your eye or another bodily limb of yours from a cruel punishment, because your neighbor is [as] a bodily limb of yours and [like] your eye.

The third: recognize that you are much more obligated toward the one who does you harm than towards the one who does you good, because those people are the ones who purify your soul; they render it beautiful, gracious, and acceptable to my liking.[31]

The fourth: consider how great is my charity since, even though you are my mortal enemy because of your sins committed, just the same every injury done to you, I consider done to me. Just the same, I wish that you are pained first for the offense to me. And I wish the same regarding this hate you have towards your enemies; that is every bad thing done to them, consider it done to you.

The fifth: rejoice for receiving a part of what you deserve. And think that everything is from my permission for your good and do not impute it to sin.

See that, after having received the kiss, I asked the crowd, 'Who are you looking for?' and I said, 'It is I.'[32] And the power of my word was so much that they fell to the ground. And the same power by which they fell was given to them to arrest me; that is, by the unity of my will inasmuch as man with that of God: 'May your will be done.' My enemies could not harm me and they could recognize that this was divine power and not human. Thus by divine power it was conceded to them to have freedom over me. Thus, if you shall give your will freely to God in everything and say, 'May your will be done!', your soul, through union with the divine will, shall reach such a form and similarity, that the demons, as long as it will not be given them the power to torment you, shall fall; that is, they shall not prevail over you – and neither created beings. For thus, when you are tormented by demons and creatures, you must know that they received their power from God, as it was with me, his true Son: I was rejected and abandoned by everyone.[33] And to the degree which you will be abandoned, rejoice and thank me all the more. I was presented to different princes with various mockings and torments precisely from the people whom I loved more than anyone. And if you shall receive injuries or shames and reprehensions from different people, rejoice and thank me. I was naked on the cross and I wish for you to be naked on the cross of holy religion; that is, stripped of every love.[34] I was nailed with three nails, and I wish you to be nailed with three; that is, poverty, obedience, and chastity."

He said many other things that I do not remember, but I try to remember that one time when I was praying and that sweet God spoke with me so sweetly and impetuously.[35] He continued to repeat: "Thus I did, and wish for you to do; since your soul was more than full and could not contain more. It heard and did not understand."Then that sweet God relaxed and said, "I would like to say to you many things similar to these, but the vase of your soul is not capable now.[36] Then you understood, not by words, but by illumination of the intellect, that it would become a vase capable of receiving the honey that God wished to insert by way of sickness and tribulation. Remember that I showed you more love when I afflicted you, than when I held you tight in my sweetest arms. Remember when you feel so much suffering, how many times you were called by him daughter, spouse and sister, so sweetly that it made you languish. Remember, poor soul, that God gave you so much of himself, that many times out of great sweetness, you said: 'No more, Lord, no more.' And for humility you fled. Remember how God, to tame your great pride, declared that the signs of love he showed you were not because of the good that you performed, but only because of his charity towards you.

And he gave you this example: when a doctor sees a patient who is in danger of death, he does not opt for many remedies, but takes recourse to the last and strongest one. And thus, as the perfect doctor, he did with you; but not because you deserved it, but because of his charity and in order to free you from that grave and dangerous infirmity. Remember that in order to make you humble, he showed you clearly that these sweet and soave enjoyments could not be earned with human abilities. Rather, he communicated them only by his goodness when and to people who pleased him according to how much it seemed, by his wisdom, that they would be useful to the souls that received them. And because you are proud, he wished to give them to you at the beginning before you did any good, because what were yours were many sins and vices. He did this because if he had given them to you after you had done a lot of good and suffered very badly, you might have fallen into the trap of pride, believing that he had given them to you because of your merits. And thus you should know clearly that when you will have avoided many sins, and you will have done many good things and suffered many bad things, trials and tribulations, without comparison you will be much more obligated to him than before. Because great is the benefit of not sinning, very great is the benefit of doing good, the best is that of suffering badly. And you could not have done any of these things without his grace, 'Because without me you can do nothing.'[37] And you know, having proved it by experience, that you would do every bad thing if he did not hold you back; and you would do no good thing if his sweet hand did not push you along. And you would not bear any pain without sinning, if he out of his charity did not give you strength and the will to bear them. And because of this illumination that he gave you, you are infinitely obligated to him.

To sum up, remember this: God, because of his goodness, made you clearly see that if you never sinned again, if by yourself you did more penances than all the blessed souls, if you cried so many tears as to create another ocean – if it were possible – and if you suffered all the sufferings that one could suffer, these things would not be sufficient to thank me for the minimum benefit that I gave you.[38] Now consider how you could compensate me for your innumerable faults. Despair of yourself and say: 'My Lord, life, and sweetness of my heart, since I cannot thank you for the good things I do or for suffering badly, how will I be able to compensate you for my so many serious faults and dishonest sins committed wickedly against you? Grant me at least this grace, O my Jesus. Write as if I had done every bad thing and had never done any good thing, since truly it would have been and thus it would be. And give me the grace that this little time that I have to live is spent according to your holy will, and after my death send me where it gives you more honor. And if that were even to Hell, I would be pleased, because I want your honor alone to be my glory.'[39] Remember your promises made, the manner and to whom; I will not write of them – you know them. Remember the manner and what was promised to you, and nothing will seem to you difficult. 'Everything soon passes; after pain follows joy; after the storm will come good weather.'[40] This for you will be the favorable weather, the day of salvation. Remember with what ardor you begged me, 'Quickly, promptly, with vigor, my Lord! I can no longer have patience.'" You delay much in giving me the sufferings you promised me. When will you lead me to those abundant pastures of suffering badly, where your chosen lambs become fatted?[41]

"Remember[42] when you are in the torture of the cross that God wishes to give you, and never say: 'O God, why have you abandoned me?'[43] because you know that he prohibited you from saying it. You know the motive. And remember what he said to you: when it seems more that I have abandoned you, I will be closer to you. But with you I want to keep that manner that my Father kept with me; that is, to allow you to feel so much pain as your weakness can bear. Remember that he said that you will fall in a serious error. I do not know if it will be a temptation, deception or falling.[44] He told you not to despair for that, because there is nothing that displeases him as much as despair. Instead, stay in fear [of the Lord] and in humility. It seems to me that, as until now you have largely been in good relations with God, or perhaps it was presumption on your part. So it was necessary to turn the page to the point that it did not seem to you to ever have been with him in love and grace as much as it will seem to be with him in hatred and displeasure. But be strong and constant because the crown is given to the victors.[45] Remember your sincere offer that you made to God; that is, that you wanted to serve him not to avoid Hell, not to merit Heaven, but only because he is Lord who deserves to be served, loved and praised by every creature. Then do it in a way to serve him ardently until death, even if you were certain you would be damned. Remember too that God did not reveal these things to you because of your holy and good life, because when he announced them to you about five years ago,[46] you were nothing other than a devil, a wild snare of the devil, a she-wolf starving for the blood of souls ransomed by the precious blood of Christ, [you were] full of ambition, full of pride, sensual, worldly. Your deeds are not to be written, thus I am silent. This was your holy life before this sweet God called you to his honey-like embraces. Remember this and confuse yourself thinking about his ample goodness and your misery and wickedness. Humble yourself because, adorned in such iniquity, you presume and want to be in his sweet arms like his dear bride, but towards him you are an adulterous prostitute. But what sorrows me the most and compels me to cry over you, wretched soul of mine, is this: after so many sweet embraces, so many sweet words with which he has called you so many times bride and daughter with inexpressible sweetness, as you know, after so many signs of love experienced not by words but by experience, after you felt and tasted him loveable, delightful, advisable, desirable, sweet, gracious and gentle above every other thing, you returned like a canine beast to the vomit; that is, to your previous life and still worse.

This is why you should stay in fear [of the Lord] and say no longer: 'God, protect me from this, and from that other thing I will look at myself'. For this, God made you plainly understand that an ant would be sufficient to break your neck if he [God] were not holding you. And never trust in yourself, even if you returned to so much grace that every day you did miracles. Remember that he made you plainly understand that it is worth more to stand before his Majesty without devotion and tears, that when you are with many tears and devotions, because in that moment, you pay a part of the debt. But when you are with many tears, you leave with a greater debt than when you arrived; learn therefore to have patience during days of sterility and of shortage. Remember that this subtraction is not because of hatred, but for love: for he does not want to give you heaven in this world, as it has been declared to you many times.

I would like to remind you of many other things for your consolation, but I believe that God does not want me to write so that you do not have too much refreshment. With great violence I have written you these things, so that for about one year now I have been considering writing them to you, and never had I been able to do so except now and with great toil. I believe, however, that if God shall grant you the grace to ruminate on them well, he will grant you great consolation in your sufferings.

I do not wish to omit this: Remember that God wants you for himself alone, alone, naked, naked on the bed of the cross. In that most sacred bed he wishes to consummate with you this holy and spiritual matrimony by way of love and sufferings, saying with the beloved Spouse in the Canticle: 'My lover belongs to me and I to him; he browses among the lilies'[47]; that is, he browses among the lilies of many sufferings. These [sufferings] I bore not for my own sake in hope of the prize myself, but only for his pure love that I hope to truly taste before dying, as he firmly promised many times. To whose divine love be praise and glory for all times. Amen."

I knew these things before entering the monastery, after the decisive and irrevocable resolution to serve God in perpetual cloistered life in the Order of the glorious holy virgin Clare. And I wrote them down when I was in Urbino, five months before making my profession on a sheet of paper in sloppy cursive handwriting. And now that exactly seven years have passed since we entered this sacred monastery, I was forced by inner inspiration – I do not know if it was God or the devil – to transcribe them on better paper with more careful, long-hand writing. I resisted this inspiration for several days, because I myself did not know for what motive and I did not recognize any need. But God knows with how much tedium, toils and regret I made this transcription. And innumerable times, after I had begun, the desire came to me to abandon it. While I wrote, it seemed to me that I was writing very ugly letters that were very crooked and confusing to look at. For this reason, I wanted to renounce writing. But after a while it no longer seemed so; because of these contrasts I believed that it was inspiration of God rather than that of the devil.

This text was transcribed [copied] in 1491, the last day of January, in our sacred monastery of Santa Maria Nova, six months after the death of my glorious holy father Friar Pietro da Mogliano. And exactly nine years passed after I took the sacred habit of St. Clare.[48]

Laus Deo. Amen. [Praise to God. Amen.]
"Teaching from your lips is more precious to me than heaps of silver and gold."[49]
"Happy those whom you guide, Lord, whom you teach in your instruction."[50]

The Mental Sorrows of Christ in His Passion

I Dolori Mentali Di Cristo Nella Sua Passione (1488)

In probably the most important writing of St. Camilla Battista, she describes eight different motivations of interior anguish suffered by Jesus. These are the "mental sorrows" that Christ carried in his human Heart, in particular during the agony in the garden of Gethsemane. They are: the damned, the elect, Mary (Jesus's Mother), Mary Magdalen, the apostles, Judas, the Jewish people, and all creation This was a novelty in the 16th century, as there were many writings and devotions focusing on the *physical* sufferings of Jesus. By writing "mental", Camilla does not necessarily mean "of the mind," but rather the interior, most profound part of the human person; it might be better translated "heart" or even "soul." Camilla believed that the "mental" pains were more excruciating for Christ than the "physical" ones he suffered during his crucifixion. The work had many admirers who used it as an object of meditation: Saint Philip Neri of Rome kept a copy for personal use, as did Frederick Borromeo (cousin of St. Charles Borromeo), archbishop of Milan.

St. Camilla Battista began writing "Mental Sorrows" in August of 1488 and finished on September 12, as she attests to in Chapter XVII of her Autobiography. Addressed to her Abbess, Sr. Pacifica Benedetti, Camilla says she began writing down things that she had learned from a nun in Urbino, but in a letter addressed to Fr. Pietro da Mogliano she admits to being the author. In the museum of the Poor Clare monastery of Camerino, the earliest hand-written transcription of the "Mental Sorrows" by an Olivetan monk, Antonio of Segovia is conserved. After the death of St. Camilla, he gave it to the monastery. It is witnessed by a Post Scriptem that designates the author as "blessed." It says, "I, Antonio of Spain, unworthy monk, transcribed [copied] the present book from the original written by the hand of the above mentioned Blessed Sister Baptista da Varano, to whom God mercifully united me spiritually through charity."

While St. Camilla Battista was still alive, this work was published in Naples in 1490, then in Milan in 1515, and later in Bologna in 1521; it seems that she was unaware of each publication. After her death, many editions were published in various languages. Sometimes, however, they were inserted in the classic, "Spiritual Warfare" by Lorenzo Scupoli to whom her work was often attributed. However, in 1750 Gaetano Volpi published an edition in Padua and recognized the author as Blessed Sr. Battista Varani.

Mental Sorrows

First introduction addressed to Friar Pietro da Mogliano[51]

Here follow the mental sorrows of blessed Christ, which, as I have said, he commanded me to write down.[52] But note this: when I returned here to Camerino, I would sometimes speak of these sorrows with my fellow nuns, both for their consolation and my own. And I said that one of the nuns from Urbino had told me these things, so they would not think they were my own. Sister Pacifica many times begged me to put them in writing. I said that I would never do so as long as that nun in Urbino remained alive. When I was commanded to write them down, it had been more than two years since she had spoken of them or mentioned anything about them. So since I had to write them down, I addressed them to her, because she was then my reverend Abbess and I was her unworthy vicar. I pretended, as I had said, that a nun from Urbino had confided to me such devoted things, and for that reason I sometimes say "that holy soul, that blessed soul spoke in this fashion." All of this is to bolster the pretense that readers would not think that I was the true author.

Second introduction addressed to Friar Pietro da Mogliano[53]

The things that follow were revealed to me one day as I was meditating on the sorrowful agony when blessed Christ was praying in the garden [of Gethsemane], where he perspired blood. And as the sun, when it is in the constellation of Leo,[54] has greater heat than at any other time of the year "because it is in its own proper domain,"[55] in such a manner, when blessed Christ prayed in the garden [of Gethsemane], he felt his mental sorrows more intensely than they had been during all his previous life of thirty years, "because at that point it was as if his sorrows were like the sun in Leo; that is, the most elevated point and greatest heat, as if in its proper domain."[56]

It was shown to me that there is much difference between one who contemplates on the physical Passion of Christ and one who meditates on the mental sorrows of Jesus. It is as the difference between a vessel filled with honey or balsam, and that vase which is watered outside a little from the liquid that is inside. He then who wishes to nourish himself on the Passion of the Savior, should not confine himself to simply tasting the edge of the vase; that is, the wounds of Christ and the blood which flowed from his most holy body; in this way he will never appease the hunger which devours him. But let he who wishes to truly be satisfied enter into the vessel itself – as wide as the ocean; that is, into the Heart of blessed Jesus, and there he will find more than enough to satisfy him. This was assured to me.

But when I wrote these things, I did not wish to impede the devotion of those who contemplate the physical sufferings of blessed Jesus; for it is not for everyone to sail on this ocean, especially for us women, since we do not have much ability. Nevertheless God renders capable every person who desires and seeks him in truth. [57]

O my father, how much sorrow do you believe I have suffered in writing these things? Truly, my affliction and sorrow is as the ocean. [58] O miserable and unhappy, the days of my solemnity and joy have been transformed into mourning and tears. O my God, where was I? Where am I now? How can I ever be happy, even though I lost so much good? Who will ever be able to console me? Who will ever be able to give me courage? Who will be able to impede me from weeping and continuously lamenting? O my father, with what words, with what reasoning will you be able to comfort and console me? Who will ever be able to return to me that pure vestment of my original innocence that I have lost, in which God dwelled with so much delight? Who will return to me those loveable, gracious and holy feet? O my God, you have dug out the marrow of my heart and all my spiritual bones! O most clement feet, you make my heart break! I was in love with you like another Magdalene! O God! You had told me that you wished me to be alone in the torment of the cross you wished to give me. Alas, you left me very much alone, because you have taken away and deprived me of pleasure, company and the treasure of your crucified feet, next to which I was prostrate on the ground like a little dog!

I shall not lament, my Lord, that you kicked me away from you, because I deserved it. But I am pained and I weep because you will not allow me to return to lick and kiss them again, as does the little dog faithful to his master and lord. Since you no longer wish, my Jesus, for me to squeeze your holy feet, with grace I beseech you that you truly place me under the feet of the soul of cursed Judas, because in all of Hell, I am unable to find place a more suitable for my malignity, pride and ingratitude.

O worthy exchange of compassion! O miserable desire! For the feet of Christ, I desire to dwell under the feet of Judah. May I be wholehearted toward your laws, that I may not be put to shame.[59]

Mental Sorrows

Jesus Mariae Filius
[To Jesus, Son of Mary]

These are some of the very devout matters concerning the mental sorrows of the blessed Jesus Christ, who by his mercy and grace deigned to impart them to a certain devout religious [nun from Urbino] of our Order of St. Clare. She, in turn, as it pleased God, related them to me. And now I relate them here below in this fashion for the benefit of those souls who are enamored of the Passion of Christ.[60]

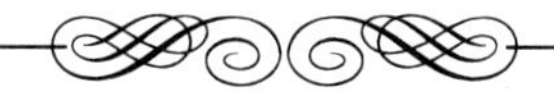

Of The First Mental Sorrow for All The Damned

There was a soul that was very eager to feed on and be sated with the foods, bitter like poison, of the Passion of the most loving and sweetest Jesus. After many years, by a most wonderful grace, she was introduced in the mental sorrows in the most bitter ocean of his impassioned Heart. She told me that many times she prayed to God that he would drown her in the ocean of his mental sorrows and that the sweetest Jesus deigned to introduce her through his mercy and grace not once but many times into that very wide ocean in such a way that she was forced to say, "No more, my Lord, since I cannot bear such pain." And I believe this because he is kind and benign to the one who asks of him these things with humility and perseverance.

This blessed soul told me that when she was at prayer with trembling heart she said to God, "O Lord, I pray that you bring me into that most sacred chamber of your mental sorrows.[61] Drown me in that most bitter ocean, because there I yearn to die, if it pleases you, O sweet life and love of mine. Tell me, Jesus, my hope, how great was the sorrow of your troubled heart?" And blessed Jesus told her, "Do you know how great was my sorrow? It was as great as the love I bore for creation." This blessed soul told me that God had already been pleased at other times to make her aware of his love for creation, to the extent of his pleasure.

And concerning these matters of the love that Christ bore for creation, she told me such lovely and holy truths that, if I wanted to write them, it would take a good bit of time. But since I intend only to speak of the mental sorrows of blessed Christ, as she related them to me, I shall not speak of the rest. Let us return to our proposed subject.

She said that when God told her, "The sorrow was as great as the love I bore for creation," it seemed to her that she was about to faint because she was aware of how great and boundless was this love. On only hearing that word she had to rest and support her head, so strong was the beating of her heart and so weak were her limbs. After she had been that way for a little bit, she recovered some of her strength and said, "O my God, since you have now told me how great was the sorrow, tell me now how great were the pains that you bore in your Heart." He replied sweetly to her, "You should know, daughter, that the pains were countless and infinite, since countless and infinite are the souls – members of my body that have separated themselves from me by mortal sin. And every soul separated itself and split itself from me, their head, as often as it sinned mortally.

And this was one of the cruel pains which I bore and felt in the intimacy of my heart; that is, the separation of my members. And think how much pain a martyr feels when a wire severs his limbs from his body. Now imagine how great was my martyrdom when so many members were torn from me, as many as were the souls that were ever damned. And every member was severed as often as it sinned mortally. The separation of a spiritual member is much more painful than that of a bodily member because the soul is more precious than the body.

And how much more precious the soul is than the body neither you nor any other living person can know, since only I understand the nobility and the usefulness of the soul and the misery of the body, because I alone have made both the one and the other. As a result, neither you nor anyone else can fully appreciate my pains in all their cruelty and bitterness.

And now I will speak only of this: about the souls of the damned. And since in the manner of sinning one manner is more serious than another, so in their separation from me one gave me greater or lesser pain than the other. And therein lies the quality as well as the quantity of my pain. And since I saw that their perverse will would have been eternal, so their pain destined to them is eternal. And since one has committed more and greater sins than another, so in Hell one suffers more and greater pains than another. But the cruel pain that tormented me was that I saw that my infinite members; that is, all the souls of the damned, could never, never, never be reunited to me, their true head. And this 'never again' is what torments in eternity and will torment those poor, unfortunate souls forever, above all the other pains they have or can ever have in eternity. And so grievously did this 'never again' afflict me that I would gladly have chosen to suffer 'again and anew' and infinite times, all these separations in all the forms which were, are, and will be, so that I could have seen not so much all, but at least just one of these souls be rejoined to the wholeness of my other living members; that is, to the members of the elect, who will live forever from the spirit of life that proceeds from me, true life, that [I] give to every living being. And consider here how dear to me is one human soul, if for only one I have said that I would have gladly suffered so many repeated pains an infinite number of times.

And so that you should learn how grievous is the affliction and torture of that 'never again' for those souls who suffer by my divine justice, they, too, likewise would gladly suffer a thousand and infinite pains if only they could hope that they would one day be reunited to me, their true head. And, as the type and quantity of pain was different that they gave me in their separation from me, so through my true justice the pain corresponds to the type and quantity of every sin. And since this 'never again' afflicted me beyond every other thing, so my justice wills that this 'never again' afflicts and torments them beyond all the other pains that they have and will have in eternity.[62] And consider, then, and reflect on how great was the suffering for all the damned souls I experienced and felt in my heart until death."

This blessed soul told me that then that there was born in her soul a holy desire which she believed was of divine inspiration, to present to him [Jesus] the following doubt. With great fear and reverence, so that she would not appear to be probing the Trinity, with the greatest simplicity, purity and trust she said: "O sweet and suffering Jesus, I have many times heard it said that you bore and experienced in yourself, O passionate God, the pains of all the damned. If it pleases you, my Lord, I would like to know if it is true that you experienced those diverse pains of Hell, such as cold, heat, torment, beatings and gnawing of your members by those hellish spirits. Tell me, my Lord, did you experience this, O my Jesus?"

As I simply recall this in writing, my heart seems to melt, as I think of your great kindness in speaking so sweetly and so copiously to one who truly seeks and yearns for you. And then blessed Jesus replied graciously and it seemed to her that such a question did not grieve or displease him, "My daughter, I did not feel those diverse pains of the damned in the manner you inquire about and ask, because they were dead members and detached from me, their body and head. I give you this instance: if you had a hand or a foot or any other member, while that hand or foot were severed or cut from you, you would experience great and unspeakable pain, sorrow and anguish; but after that hand has been cut off, should someone then throw it into the fire, beat it, or give it as food to dogs or wolves, you would not feel suffering or any pain, because it has become a dead, rotten member, and completely separated from the body. But knowing that it was one of your members, you would suffer much to see it thrown in the fire, beaten by others, devoured by dogs and wolves. This is precisely how it was for me with regard to my infinite members, the souls of the damned. And as long as the separation lasted and there was any hope of living life, I felt unthinkable and infinite pains and even all their anguish that they ever experienced in this life, because until their death there was hope of their reunion to me, if they had wished it; but after their death I no longer felt any of their pains, because they were dead members, rotten, severed from me, cut off, and completely excluded from living in eternity with me, their true life. But it caused unthinkable and incomprehensible pain to think that they had been my own members, to see them in the eternal fire, in the mouth of infernal spirits and for all eternity suffering the other diverse, innumerable pains. And this is the interior sorrow that I bore for the damned."

Of the Second Mental Sorrow for All of the Elect Members

"The second sorrow which pierced my heart was for all of the elect. And you should know that in all the ways in which I already told you that I was afflicted and tormented by the damned members, I was likewise afflicted and tormented by all the elect members who would have sinned mortally. And as great as was the love which I eternally bore them and the life to which they were united by their good actions and from which they were separated by sinning mortally, so great was the sorrow which I felt in all those true members of my body.

The only difference between the pain I felt for the damned and the one I bore for the elect was that I no longer felt the pains of the damned after their death, since they were dead limbs and sundered from me by death, while for the elect, even after their death as during their life, I experienced and felt all of their pain and bitterness. In life it was the pains and martyrdoms of all the martyrs, the penances of all the penitents, the temptations of all the tempted, the illnesses of the sick, and persecutions, slanders, exiles, and, in short, I experienced and felt so clearly and truly every great and small suffering of all the elect still alive as you would feel and experience should someone strike your eye, hand, foot, or some other member of your body.

Now think of how many martyrs there were and how many kinds of tortures each one of them suffered and bore and how many were the pains of all the other elect and the diversity of these pains and reflect on this: If you had a thousand eyes, a thousand hands, a thousand feet and a thousand other members and in each one of them you experienced a thousand different pains that provoked at the same time a great sensation of pain, how intense do you think such suffering would be? But my members, my daughter, were not in the thousands, or the millions, but infinite. Nor were the diverse pains numbered in the thousands but they, too, were innumerable, because innumerable were the pains of the saints, martyrs, virgins, confessors and all the other elect. And finally come to this conclusion: As it is not possible to understand how many and how great are the forms of blessedness, glory and reward prepared for the just elect in Heaven, so no one can understand or know what and how many were the mental sorrows which I have endured through the elect members. Because of divine justice, there must correspond to these pains joys, glories, and the rewards; but I felt and experienced in their kind and quantity all the different pains that the elect would have suffered after their death in Purgatory because of their sins, with one suffering more and one suffering less according to what they merited. For they were not rotten members, sundered as were the damned, but they were living members who lived in me, Spirit of life; for I had showered my grace and benediction upon them. Thus I did not experience or feel any of those pains which you asked me about regarding the damned members for the reason I have given, but I did feel them for the elect, because I have sustained and tasted all the pains of Purgatory which they had to suffer.

And I give you this example: if your hand, for some reason, became broken or was somehow else ruined, and after a doctor mended and set it, someone should then put it in the fire, beat it, or give it to a dog to chew on, you would experience great pain because it is a living member that must return perfectly united to the body. Thus I felt and experienced in myself all the pains of Purgatory that my elect members had to suffer because they were living members, and by that suffering they had to be perfectly reunited to me, their true head. And there is no distinction or difference between the pains of Purgatory and those of Hell, except that those of Hell will never, never, never have an end and those of Purgatory will; and the souls that endure the pains of Purgatory willingly and joyfully, even though they suffer, are being cleansed and suffer in peace as they render thanks to me, supreme justice. And this is as much as pertains to the mental sorrow I bore for the elect."

Would that God wished for me to remember the holy words that she poured forth here with unstinted grief, having been able – to the extent of God's pleasure – [to understand] the seriousness of sin, she said that she understood how much pain and suffering she had given to her most beloved Jesus, as she separated herself from him, the highest good, to unite herself to something as vile as the things of this world which provide occasions to sin. But I do remember that she told me, speaking through many tears: "O, my God, many times I have caused you great and infinite pains, whether I am to be damned or saved. O Lord, I never understood that sin offended you so much, I believe that I would never have sinned, not even lightly if I had. But even so, my God, do not look upon what I say, since for all this I would do even worse [sins] than ever, if your merciful hand did not sustain me.

But you, my sweet and kind lover, do not seem any longer to be God, but rather a hell, because these sufferings which you refer to me are so many. And truly you seem more than hell to me. And many times, in my holy simplicity and compassion, I called him Hell."

The Third Pain which The Blessed Christ Bore in His Heart for The Glorious Virgin Mary

And then the loving and blessed Jesus added: "Listen, listen, daughter; do not speak thus right away, for I still have very bitter matters to tell you and especially regarding that sharp knife that wounded and transfixed my soul; that is, the sorrow of my pure and innocent Mother, who because of my Passion and death had to be very much afflicted and tormented, and there never was nor will there ever be such a person pained as she.

And so we have justly glorified and elevated and prized her beyond all other creatures, angelic and human. And this is ever our course: the more a creature in this world is afflicted, brought low and annihilated in himself because of my love, so much the more he is exalted, glorified and prized in the realm of the blessed by divine justice. And because there never was a Mother or any other person in this world more anguished than my sweet and clement Mother, so there is not, nor shall there ever be a person similar to her. And as she was like me in the world because of pains and afflictions, so in Heaven by power and glory she is like me. Of course, she does not possess my divinity, of which there is no participant, except the three of us divine Persons, the Father, the Son, and the Holy Spirit. And so you should know that in all the ways in which I, the God made man, was grieved and sorrowed, so too did my poor and most holy Mother grieve and sorrow, except that I did so in a higher and more perfect way, since I was God and man and she was a pure and simple creature without any divinity. And so grievously did her sorrow afflict me that, if it had pleased my eternal Father, it would have been for me a great consolation if all her sorrows had returned upon my soul and she had remained without any pain; it is true that it would have been as if all my sufferings and wounds had been redoubled with a poisoned and sharp arrow, but this would have been the highest comfort to me, if she had remained without pain. But because my unimaginable suffering had to be without any consideration of consolation, such a grace was not granted to me, although out of filial tenderness I asked for it often with many tears."

Then the nun said that it seemed to her that her heart stopped beating as she thought of the sorrow of the glorious Virgin Mary. And she says that she felt a certain inner anxiety such that she could say nothing but this, "O Mother of God, I no longer want to call you Mother of God, but rather Mother of suffering, Mother of pain, Mother of every affliction that can be counted or conceived. So henceforth I will call you Mother of sorrow. He seems to me a hell and you seem equal to him. So what can I call you other than Mother of sorrow? You, too, are a second hell. No more, my Lord, speak to me no more of the sorrows of your blessed Mother, since I feel that I can bear them no more. This is enough for me as long as I live, even if I were to live a thousand years."

The Fourth Mental Sorrow which The Blessed Christ Bore for His Beloved Mary Magdalene

So Jesus said no more on this subject, since he saw the impossibility [of her bearing it]. He then began to speak to her, "Now can you imagine the sorrow I bore for the pain and affliction of my beloved and blessed disciple and daughter, Mary Magdalene? But neither you nor any other person can understand it, since from her and me all holy and spiritual loves had and will have their origin and foundation. In fact, my perfection of the loving teacher and the love and goodness of her, the beloved disciple, can only be understood by me. Some aspect of it could be understood by someone who has had the experience of holy and spiritual love by loving and being loved. But it would only be a shadow of the true love, for no longer is such a teacher found, nor such a disciple; there never was nor will there ever be another Magdalene. It is justly said that after my beloved Mother there never was a person who suffered more because of my suffering and death. If there had been someone else who grieved more, then I would have appeared to him after my resurrection before I appeared to her.

And since after my blessed Mother she was more afflicted than anyone else, she was the first to be consoled after my most sweet Mother. I allowed my beloved disciple John, during his sweet abandonment on my most sacred chest during that intimate and anticipated Supper, to see my resurrection and the abundant harvest of souls that followed my Passion and death. Just the same, although my beloved brother John suffered pain for my Passion and death more grievously than all the other Disciples, even with the knowledge he possessed, do not believe that he surpassed the beloved Magdalene [in suffering].

She did not have the capability of bearing these lofty and profound things like John, who, even if he would have been able to, would never have impeded my death and Passion because of the immense good that would have flowed from it. But my beloved Magdalene was not like that. When she saw me die, she thought that she had lost both Heaven and earth, for in me were all her hopes, love, peace and consolation. And so she loved me without order and without measure. And so, too, without order and without measure was her sorrow, as only I could know this, I bore it with intense feeling in my soul and I felt for her all the tenderness from her that can be felt and experienced in a holy and spiritual love, since she loved me with complete abandon.

And note, if you wish to understand this, that my disciples, after my death, not having entirely abandoned material things as this holy sinner had, returned to their nets that they had abandoned. But she did not return to a mundane and sinful life; rather, enflamed and burning with holy desire, having no more hope in seeing me alive, she sought me even after my death. She knew that she could no longer find delight or pleasure in anything other than her teacher, whether I were dead or alive. And this is demonstrated true since she, in finding me dead, abandoned and thought little of the live company and association of my sweetest Mother, who is the most lovable, desirable and delectable person that one could have, except after me. And even the vision and sweet conversations with angels struck her as nothing.[63]

And understand that this is true of every soul: if one loves and desires me with true affection, he finds rest and peace in no other sight or presence, but only in me, his beloved God. And, in conclusion, so great was the sorrow of this my blessed, dear disciple, that she would have fallen dead several times, if I, in my almighty power, had not sustained her.

This entire sorrow of hers reverberated in my passionate heart and so for her I was greatly afflicted and anguished. But I did not permit her to be lacking in this pain, because I wished to make of her what I did subsequently make of her; that is, she was to be the Apostle of the apostles, since she announced to them the truth of my triumphant resurrection, as they would later [announce] to the whole world.

I wished to make of her and I did make of her a mirror, an example, a model of the most blessed contemplative life in the solitude of the thirty-three years she would remain unknown to the world, during which she tasted and experienced the last effects of love, as much as they are possible in this worldly life to taste, feel, and experience. And this is everything regarding the sorrow that I bore for my beloved disciple, Magdalene."

The Fifth Mental Sorrow which The Blessed Christ Bore for His Beloved and Dear Disciples

"The other sorrow which pierced my soul was the continual memory of that holy college of Apostles, pillars of Heaven, foundation of my Church militant, sheep without a shepherd. I saw them and I knew that they would have been dispersed and I knew all their pains and martyrdoms that they would have to endure for me. And you should realize that never did a father love his sons, nor a brother his brothers, nor a master his students with such intense love as I loved these blessed apostles, my most beloved sons, brethren and disciples. And although I have always loved all creatures with an infinite love, nonetheless you can imagine that this was a special love which I felt for those who lived physically with me.

And so I tasted a special sorrow for them in my afflicted soul. I pronounced those bitter words for them, in fact, more than for me, 'My soul is sorrowful, even to death,'[64] given the great tenderness I felt in leaving them without myself, their Father and faithful Master. So great was my anguish that it seemed to me another death, this bodily separation from them.

Upon reflection on the words of that last sermon I gave them, no one could have a heart so hardened that he would fail to weep over all those compassionate words that welled up from my heart, which seemed to break out of my heart for the love I bore them. And then I saw that one of them would be crucified because of my name, another decapitated, another flayed alive, and all of them would end their lives in a variety of martyrdoms out of love for me.

To understand how heavy was this pain for me, imagine for a little if there has ever been anyone whom you loved with a holy love and to whom hurtful words or deeds have been done for your sake or out of love for you. O, how much you would grieve that you have been responsible for someone you love being hurt in some way. For such a person you would wish to have only peace and consolation as a result of you.

But I, my daughter, was the cause of their death and not of hurtful words, and not of one death but of all. And of the sorrow I bore for them I cannot give you any comparison. Let what I have told you suffice, if you wish to have compassion upon me."

The Sixth Mental Sorrow which the Blessed Christ Bore for the Ingratitude of His Beloved Disciple the Traitor Judas

"One other fierce, great sorrow constantly afflicted and tormented me. It was like a knife with three poisonous and very sharp points, which continually pierced like an arrow and ran through my Heart saddened as with myrrh; that is, the impiety and ingratitude of my beloved disciple, the iniquitous Judas, most wicked traitor; then there was the hardness and perversity and ingratitude of my chosen and beloved Jewish people; then the blindness, the malignity, the ingratitude of all the creatures that have ever been or ever will be.

First of all, imagine how great the ingratitude of Judas was. I had chosen him to be one of the Apostles and, having forgiven him all his sins, I made him a worker of miracles, a dispenser of everything which had been given to me, and I always showed him signs of my special love to bring him out of his iniquity. But the more love I showed towards him, the greater evil he contrived against me. With how much bitterness do you believe that I concerned myself in my heart over these matters and many, many others?

But when I came to that compassionate and humble act of washing his feet along with those of all the others, then did my heart melt in visceral sobbing. And truly a fountain of tears gushed from my eyes over his dishonest feet. That is why I said in my heart, 'O Judas, what did I do to you that you have so cruelly betrayed me?' O unfortunate disciple!

Was this not to be the last sign of love that I wished to show you? O son of perdition! Why do you thus distance yourself from your Father and Master? O Judas, if you desire thirty denarii, why do you not go to your Mother and mine, who would sell herself to save you and me from such a great and mortal danger? O ungrateful disciple! I kiss your feet with so much love and you kiss my mouth with so much betrayal? O, what bad return you give me! I weep over your perdition, dear and beloved son, and not my Passion and death, since I have come for no other reason.

These and other similar words I spoke to him with my heart as I watered his feet with my most abundant tears. But he did not notice since I was on my knees in front of him, with my head down, as is necessary when one washes another's feet, and also because the thickness of my long hair, as I was bent over, covered my face wet with tears. But my beloved John, since I had revealed to him everything concerning my Passion at that sorrowful supper, noticed every action of mine with care. And he was aware of the bitter weeping I made over the feet of Judas. And he knew and understood that every tear was the result of my tender love, like that of a father who has only one son and at that son's deathbed does him some service and then says in his heart, 'Son, have courage, this is the last affectionate service I will be able to do to you.' And that is just what I did to Judas when I kissed and washed his feet and brought them to myself with such tenderness and pressed them to my most sacred face.

All of my actions and my unusual behavior were noted by that soaring eagle, the blessed Evangelist John, who in his great stupor and wonder seemed more dead than alive. And since he was a most humble soul, he reclined at the last place so that he was the last person before whom I knelt to wash his feet. And then he could no longer contain himself, with me on the floor and himself seated, he threw both his arms around my neck and held me for a long while, like a person who is in agony, and he cried an abundance of tears. He spoke with his heart, not his voice, and said, 'O dear Master, brother, Father, my God and my Lord, now with what strength were you able to wash and kiss with your most sacred mouth those cursed feet of that traitorous dog? O Jesus, my dear Master, truly you leave us a perfect example. But what will we poor little people do without you, who are all our good? What will your poor, unfortunate Mother do when I tell her of this humble gesture of yours? And now, to break my heart, you wish to wash my odorous, dirty feet, full of mud and dust, and to kiss them with your sweet and honeyed mouth? O my God, these new signs of love for me are sure and certain signs of a greater sorrow.' And after saying these and other similar words which would have softened a heart of stone, he put down his feet with great modesty and reverence and let me wash them.

And I have told you these and similar things to give you some knowledge of the intense sorrow I felt for the ingratitude and the impiety of Judas, the traitor. The more love I bore him and the more signs of affection I showed him, the more his dreadful ingratitude afflicted me."

The Seventh Mental Sorrow of Christ for the Ingratitude of His Chosen People the Jews

"Of the Jewish people, ungrateful and obstinate, imagine how the arrow of their incredible ingratitude pierced and wounded me; think for a little how it was grand. I had made this people holy and priestly; I had chosen them for myself as my inheritance above all other peoples of the world;[65] I had rescued them from the slavery of Egypt and from the hands of Pharaoh; I led them with dry feet through the Red Sea and I was their pillar [shade] during the day and their light at night. For forty years I fed them with manna and with my own mouth I gave them the law on Mount Sinai and countless victories over their foes. I took on human flesh from among them and during the time of my life I conversed with them. I showed this people the way to Heaven and did them many favors in that time, such as giving sight to the blind, hearing to the deaf, the ability to walk to the lame, and at the end, life to their dead. Now when I understood that they shouted with such frenzy for Barabbas's release and my crucifixion and death, I felt as though my heart would break.

And no one who has not experienced it knows, my daughter, how painful it is to receive every evil from one who has been accorded nothing but good. And how hard a thing it is for an innocent man to hear the whole crowd shout, 'Let him die. Let him die.' And of the other, who is to suffer the same punishment and deserves to die a thousand deaths, the crowd shouts: 'Set him free! Set him free!' These are matters to reflect upon, not to speak of."

The Eighth Mental Sorrow of Blessed Christ for the Ingratitude of All Creatures

Enlightened by Christ, the Sun of justice, that blessed soul explained the ingratitude in words for herself and for every creature, along with an expression of thanks for all the blessings she had received. She said, in fact, that she then felt in her heart such a profound sense of humility that she truly confessed to God and to the entire heavenly court that she had received more blessings and gifts from God than had Judas and that she alone had received more blessings than the whole chosen people taken together; that she had betrayed him much worse and much more ungratefully than Judas and that she had condemned him to death and crucified him in a worse and more dastardly way than that ungrateful people.

And with this holy reflection she placed her soul beneath the feet of the soul of the damned and cursed Judas and from that abyss she shouted and wept to her beloved God, who had been wronged by her, as she said, "My kind Lord, how could I thank you for what you suffered for me, who treated you a thousand times worse than Judas ever did? You made him your disciple, but you made me your daughter and spouse. You pardoned him his sins but in your mercy and grace you have pardoned me mine as though they never existed. You gave him the stewardship to dispense temporal goods, but to me, an ingrate, you have given countless gifts and graces from your spiritual treasure. To him you gave the grace of working miracles but to me you gave the power of working more than a miracle by bringing me voluntarily to this place [i.e. monastery] and the [religious] habit in which I find myself.

O my Jesus, I have sold and betrayed you not once, as he did, but a thousand – even countless – times. O my God, you know well that I have betrayed you worse than Judas with a kiss, even when under the appearance of spiritual friendship I abandoned you and drew close to the bonds of death. And if the ingratitude of that chosen people was so hateful to you, how was and is my ingratitude for you, since I have done worse than they did and yet I have received more blessings, my true good, than they ever did?

O my sweetest Lord, I thank you from all my heart because, like the Jews from the Egyptian slavery, you freed me from the slavery and sins of the world, and from the hands of the cruel Pharaoh, the hellish demon, who controlled my poor soul as he pleased.[66] O my God, I have been guided through the midst of the water of the ocean of worldly vanities with dry feet. By your grace I have passed to the solitude of the desert of holy religion, where you fed me many times with the sweetest savor of your manna, which seemed to me to taste of every delicacy; that is, all the delights of the world seemed to nauseate me in comparison with the least of your spiritual consolations. I thank you, Lord and kind Father, that many times on Mt. Sinai of holy prayer you have given me the law with your sweet and holy mouth, written with the finger of your mercy on the stone tablets of my most hard and rebellious heart. I thank you, my most kind Redeemer, for all the victories you have granted me over my enemies, the capital sins. The times I have conquered [them], my victory has been by you and through you, and the times that I have lost and still lose is because of my malice and the little love I bear for you, my beloved God.

You, Lord, by grace were born in my soul and you showed me the way and the light and the glory of truth in order to find you, true Paradise. In the shadows and darkness of the world you gave me the power to see, to hear, to speak, and to walk – since truly I was blind, deaf, and mute to all spiritual matters – and you have restored me to life in you, true Life, you who give life to every living being. Who, then, has crucified you? I have. Who has scourged you at the pillar? I have. Who has crowned you with thorns? I have. Who has given you to drink of vinegar and gall? I have."

In this manner she recounted all those painful mysteries with great weeping and tears, according to the grace which God gave her. In conclusion she said to him: "My Lord, do you know why I say that I have done all these things to you? Because 'in your light, I have seen light'[67] and realize that the mortal sins I committed against you have grieved and afflicted you much worse than all those bodily sufferings you endured.

So, my God, it is no longer necessary that you make me know the sorrow you experienced from the ingratitude of all creatures, because, after you gave me the grace of understanding, at least in part my own ingratitude, now I can – always by your action and grace – reflect on how much ingratitude done you by all the creatures together. And in this reflection my spirit practically fails me and I am lost in wonder, my Jesus, at your great love and patience with us, your most ungrateful creatures. Despite our behavior you never, never cease to provide for all our spiritual, material, and temporal needs. And as no one can know, my God, the countless things you have done for your ungrateful creatures in Heaven, on earth, in the ocean, and in the air, so no one can know or understand our most ungrateful ingratitude.

And so, my God, I confess and believe that you alone know and can know how intensely you felt that most bitter arrow of our ingratitude, which pierced your heart as many times as there have been, are, or will be creatures, and as often as each one indulged in such ingratitude. I recognize, thus, and declare this truth for myself and for all creatures: as there has never been a moment, an hour, a day or a month when we do not enjoy your blessings, so there has never been a moment, an hour, a day or a month without many and countless ingratitudes. I believe and realize that this most dreadful ingratitude of ours was one of the cruelest sorrows of your afflicted soul."

These few words on the mental sorrows of Jesus Christ were completed to his praise on Friday, the twelfth of the month of September, in the year of the Lord 1488. Amen.

Conclusion to Sr. Pacifica Benedetti

There are many other matters that she told me which I could relate to the advantage and consolation of my readers, but God knows that out of prudence, I am restraining my hand against the inner impulse especially since that blessed soul is still in the prison of this wretched life. Perhaps some other time God will inspire me to relate such matters which as for the moment I keep silent about out of respect for her.

My dear reverend mother Abbess, I have written and sent you these few devout words for your consolation and prayerful reflection. I beg you by the love you bear to sweet and kind Jesus and to his most holy Mother that you do not allow these few and most devout words to be read except by most devout and spiritual persons. In that way the matters of God, which should be accepted and read with the greatest devotion, will not be subjected to contempt and abuse. For today, because of our own malice, we do not believe what we do not experience of the sweet and infinite bounty of God; rather we ridicule the idea that others can experience, sense and taste this bounty.

But alas, even that is not true because God is most kind, most wise and most clement and he wants us to distribute his hidden spiritual treasures as he pleases and finds proper. And the manner, the time and the person are not questions upon which he chooses to seek our counsel, because he, amiable truth, does not judge as we do – from the outside – but according to the inner disposition. He sees the disposition of the Heart with his holy and loving eye. And so it is written: "The judgments of God are different from the judgments of men".[68]

But we, as persons far removed from such perfection and virtue, glorify God in his saints and with contrite hearts humble ourselves beneath his most clement crucified feet.[69] To them be honor, praise and glory from me and from every one of his lowliest creatures "now and forever and ever."[70] Amen. Amen. Amen.

Finis. Finis [End. End.]
DEO GRATIS [Thanks be to God]

"For the fruit of noble struggles is a glorious one."[71]

"As your lips have instructed me, I have kept the way of the law."[72]
"I have labored only a little, but have found much."[73]

Prayers

Preghiere

St. Camilla wrote various prayers, some of which have been included in this English translation. Not much is known about this first prayer to Jesus before the Eucharist, which has been attributed to her. In the original Italian, she used "voi" (the more formal second person plural) when addressing Christ, whereas she had used "tu" (the familiar second person singular) previously. It is possible that it was added in the late 16th century by someone copying the work when it became more customary to use the more formal second person plural as a greater sign of respect towards the divine holiness.

Prayer to Jesus before the Eucharist

May the Lord Jesus Christ be blessed together with the glorious Virgin with all the saints, who are and may be of help to me so that I may worthily receive this holy Sacrament to their glory. Cure, O my Lord, all my infirmities and strengthen my weakness, so that I, with the help of this spiritual medicine, will be totally healed, and I pledge myself completely to your holy service. May your spirit, my Lord, enter into my soul so much that I might transform into you, so alive with charity, humility, obedience, poverty of spirit, mortification of the body and scorn of the world that you taught me with the example of your life and so that I unite myself so much with you that I can never distance myself in all time. Amen.

Prayer to God
(1490)

This is the first of two prayers written during a three year period of interior suffering (1488-1490). It contains certain themes that recur in other works.

O sweetest, most gracious God, Father of infinite mercies, I am the lost sheep from among the hundred, who for almost three years had wandered off lost as a vagabond through briars and thorns[74] where I fed on poisonous vinegar. Now, sweet God and merciful Lord, with all my heart I desire to return to you, source of true peace. Take me and carry me once again on your merciful shoulders, O faithful and "good shepherd who lays down your life for your sheep."[75] Bring me back, O my good Jesus, to the corral of your infinite mercy and pity, and "do not hide your face from me."[76] O my sweet Jesus do not permit me to be shipwrecked in the very harbor of consecrated life, after you helped me so much and you struggled so hard to take me away from the stormy ocean, which is the snares of the world.[77] Remember, my Jesus, how much I cost you; remember, merciful God, the great price you paid for me, a sinner, on the bitter cross! Remember, my good Redeemer, what I wished to do and not what I have done. I am like the tax collector who, out of great shame stands off at a distance and would not even raise my eyes to Heaven, but I keep my eyes fixed on the ground and "beat my breast praying, 'O God, be merciful to me a sinner.'"[78] O merciful Lord, receive into your open arms this lost daughter who wandered to a distant country where she squandered her inheritance on a life of dissipation. I no longer deserve to be called your daughter, nor slave, nor servant, because I have persecuted the souls redeemed by your precious blood.[79] Come towards me with your grace, clement Father, and embrace and squeeze my afflicted soul with your sweetest arms, as you once did in the days of old, and visit this inconsolable soul. Give me, my Lord, the kiss of your holy peace and put an end to this deadly war from which I have suffered so much for the last three years. [80] And if I do not deserve it in any other way, I would willingly give my life to obtain peace, my sweet Lord. Deliver me from this dangerous life! Deliver me, my God, from the snares of this world! Deliver me from the loathsome prison of my miserable body. Draw me towards you, O merciful God! Draw me to you! Leave me no longer in this exiled world. I cannot remain here any longer. Everything persecutes me:

infirmities, demons, other creatures, and interior tribulations. Everything pushes me away and cries to me, "Escape, escape! It is no longer for you to remain here." Receive me to you and in yourself, my sweet God, because I am ready to gladly come, with a joy I cannot express in words. You see it; you know it, my merciful Lord. Send me where you wish most until Judgment Day, provided I not be eternally separated from you, true and highest good, as I have deserved. I shall consider it grace and mercy and I will say, "Praise and glory to you, merciful God, who live and reign forever and ever." Amen. Amen. Amen.

Prayer to Jesus Christ

This prayer, along with "Prayer to God," was written during a period of interior suffering, and allows it to be dated between 1488-1490. As in the other prayer, there are expressions often used by St. Camilla Battista. This prayer to Jesus Christ is less dramatic than her prayer to God, because St. Camilla does not ask to flee from the trial, but she abandons herself, like Jesus himself in the moment of Gethsemane.

O sweet Lord Jesus Christ, so many times I have given you vinegar [in exchange] for the continuous honey that you have given me! So many sins in exchange for so many gifts! So much evil for so much goodness! Oh so many times, while I made use of your created things or simply enjoyed them (and I still use them) while not having anything of mine that is not yours, I have offended you with your things. Oh so many times, while accepting your wages, have I marched under the banner of the devil and of the world. Oh, give me now the grace of returning to you good grapes and no longer wild grapes; good ones, not bad ones, gratitude and not ingratitude. And [give me the grace] that I may always feel pain when I may do otherwise or when I think something against your Majesty. And for that to happen may I give love for love, blood for blood, life for life, so that as I scandalized the heavens and the earth with my life, may the divine Majesty be always praised, blessed and glorified and my neighbor edified so that my life in the future may be holy and virtuous. Amen. For so many infinite benefits that I received from your Majesty, my sweetest Lord, lover of my soul, I shall give back to you my heart, loving you and recognizing you as my Master. My heart will be in Heaven, where it will always praise your holy name; it will always be your guest, it will do always your will, it will always be drawn near to your holy body, it will support every injustice, it will not consent to any sin and it will always be yours forever. Amen.

Prayer to the Virgin

In this prayer, various episodes are recorded that caused the Virgin Mary joy or provoked suffering during her life. After a long list of titles honoring the Mother of God, St. Camilla lists the seven sorrows of the Virgin in the tradition of the Servites of Mary (another mendicant Order from Florence). The titles are uninterrupted in almost perfect succession; however, she then lists the "joys" from the crown of the seven happinesses recorded by the Franciscan friars, although both groups contain variations. The author refers to Mary in the formal second person plural "voi", as in the prayer to the Eucharist, instead of the more familiar second person singular, "tu" which she usually uses. It could be the result of a 16th century editing change.

Virgin of virgins, Mary, Mother of the highest grace and mercy and kindness, Queen of Heaven and earth, full of grace, daughter of God, Mother of Jesus Christ, Spouse of the Holy Spirit, Queen of the angels; Empress of Heaven, star of the sea, lady of the world, glory of the saints, joy of perfect Christians, honor of women, joy of men, house of the Holy Spirit, flower of the virgins, counsel of widows, hope of sinners, fountain of mercy, way of salvation, door of paradise, stairway to Heaven, pillar of the world, epilogue of every perfection and kindness, to you I commend myself and I beg you that through that sword that St. Simeon prophesied to you, when you offered your Son in the temple, that you would be pleased to free me from all my present and future evils. I beg you, holy Mother, for the second sorrow that you received because of your sweet Son, when you lost him in Jerusalem among the multitude of people, searching for him for three days, so I beg you holy Mother, that you pray to your blessed Son, that he may give me a true contrition before my death and a true confession and satisfaction of my sins. I beg you, Mother of piety and of mercy, for the third sorrow that you had for your blessed Son, when you were told that he had been taken and put to death; so I beg you, glorious Mother, that you free me from all my invisible and visible enemies of my soul and of the body. I beg you, most benign Mother, for the fourth sorrow that you had, that you pray to your dear Son that he remove from me every lukewarmness and he enflame me with his love. I beg you, sweet holy Mother, for that sorrow that you had for our blessed Jesus, who would honor to visit me in the hour of my death and that he would receive me with mercy. I beg you, sweet Mother, for the joy that you had when the angel Gabriel greeted you and for the joy when the Holy

Spirit came to you and for the nativity of your sweet Son and for his holy circumcision and for the devoted adoration of the holy magi and for his holy baptism and for the temptation and for the cold and for the heat, and for the toils and for the hunger and for the thirst that your sweet Son endured and for how much he did for us, and for the miracle when he transformed water into wine, and for his holy preaching, and for his holy miracles, and for his holy and blessed Passion, and for our redemption and for the teachings given to the Disciples, and for the prayer that he made in the garden, and for the sweaty blood vanished from him, and for the insults and offensive words that were said to him, and for the slaps and for the jokes and derisions that were done and said to him, and for the many beatings that were given to him, and for the multitude of the scourges that he endured on his holy body, and for the flagellation on the column and for his crucifixion, and for the drink of vinegar for his burning thirst, and for the seven words that he said on the cross, and for the opening of his side, and for his precious death, and for his burial, and for his holy resurrection and for his admirable ascension, I pray to you, O Mother of highest piety, Mother of mercy, O sweet Virgin blameless Mary, hear my pleas and prayers and look at my tears and my miseries, because my sins are horrible and I do not know who to run to, if not to you, glorious blameless Mother of our sweetest Lord Jesus Christ, since you were the cause of salvation of our humanity. Therefore, O sweet Mother of highest charity, incline the ear of your pity to my pleas and be good to me, and in all my needs be my help. O precious gem, O sweet Virgin Mary, intercede before the divine throne, with your pleas and prayers, O holy Mother. Pray to your Son Jesus Christ, our Lord, that he will make me pleasing to him and that I may grow in his love and in his praise and glory. To the Lord Jesus Christ and to his blameless Virgin Mary be always honor and glory world without end. Amen

Introduction to the Considerations of the Passion of Our Lord

Introduzione Alle Considerazioni Della Passione Del Nostro Signore

Follows is the Introduction to the work, "Considerations on the Passion of our Lord," which were published by Matteo Pascucci in 1680. Pascucci himself affirmed that the Considerations were not written by Camilla Battista da Varano, but by Blessed Enrico Susone, a German mystic. It is thought that she collaborated with Bl. Susone on the Considerations, but the work was not hers. Nonetheless, it is believed that the Introduction to the "Considerations" was written by Camilla most likely as a guide for the sisters in the monastery. Some scholars believe the "Considerations" to be the exercise referenced by Camilla in chapter IV of her Autobiography when she said, "It seems that it [the Considerations] was written just for a person who did not know how to meditate."

We have translated only the Introduction to the "Considerations" since it was likely written by Camilla Battista, while the text of the "Considerations" is excluded. It is not known when she wrote it.

Introduction to the Considerations on the Passion of our Lord

Any soul servant of Jesus Christ, who wants to imitate him and have him as a model and example of his actions, is required to operate in the same spirit that he, the Son of God, operated, whose sovereign and excessive charity led him to die for us on the cross and to suffer bitter pains. And he who sees this and demonstrates due gratitude, as is expected, melting in sweet and bitter tears, will not only be washed from all his vices and sins, but will be enriched and adorned with every virtue. And thus, with worldly affections taken away from himself, he will fall in love only with our Savior Jesus Christ, and because of his ardent and seraphic desires, will be completely transformed into him. Also, he will be visited often and illuminated with supernal gifts and graces, freed from many temptations, troubles and sorrows; he will be placed in a spiritual peace and consolation, growing always in love for God. And this will happen easily if he strives to reflect, meditate and devoutly ruminate on this pious and devout exercise of the Passion of Jesus Christ in the way that is written below [in the Considerations] and according to how it was revealed and taught by Jesus Christ to a soul who greatly desires to be perfect.

This soul, at once thinking of the Passion of the Redeemer, before the crucifix after the morning and piously sorrowful and lamenting that he he did not manifest to him that compassion that he wanted and [believed] was due him, was suddenly rapt in ecstasy of mind and illumined by the supernal light. Presented before his mental eyes were some considerations of the Passion and sufferings of Jesus Christ and his blessed Mother. And it was also revealed to him that every day while kneeling prostrate on the ground, he strove, as far as possible, to conform himself, through pious affection of compassion, to the loving Jesus, with an effort to be present with his mind to those below mentioned things, as if with the eyes and ears of the body he saw, heard and felt them in his person. So it happened that that soul, with such effort, though he lived it in a trying and irreverent time in the past, through this continuous exercise, reached such devotion and love towards Jesus Christ and he received from him so many graces and illuminations that his doctrine and his life were an example and encouragement of holiness and devotion for many.

And he who does not strive at least one or two hours per day or night, to do some exercise of devotion, to remember to be grateful to such a faithful Redeemer, truly he deserves the title of undevoted and ungrateful.

While only a drop of blood to repurchase you was sufficient, he [Jesus] wanted to pour out everything for us.

Oh, how happy is he who sees and knows that firey love and charity with the mind's eye. Oh, how many blessings are received by the one who puts his effort to meditate on this and thank him. Oh, how many graces he obtains, because he never ceases to take in the precious balm of that blessed grape that was pressed from the winepress of the cross.

But how it is to weep and mourn that in these present days few are those who seek such things. Indeed, it seems that Christ Jesus is, so to speak, cast out and rejected by every Christian heart, as the Lord himself once appeared to a devout person lamenting and went away pained in search of someone else to give his grace to, yet he found none who wished to receive it.

But note the following teachings, O faithful soul who desires to set out on this safe path. The first will be that you must think and ruminate, not for just an hour or two, but continuously on the Passion of Jesus Christ, this being the most spiritual and devout exercise that a servant of God can do to quickly achieve perfect charity. Indeed it seems that there is no other way or door that leads to get close to God in a short time.

But these things should be prefaced. And first of all: confidence should be connected with fear [of God], because although the creature who takes this path may in the beginning find himself dry, arid and undevoted and with many battles from the devil, believe me, if you remain firm and constant in this enterprise, the continuous exercise will grow every day into grace and in the end you will find what you wanted.

The second thing required is a profound humility: the soul should deem himself unworthy not so much in understanding, but in thinking about the profound mystery (that is the Passion of beloved Jesus) should firmly believe that he does merit to bring about such a noble treasure in the heart. And he knows that it is a singular gift of God to even think about it, even for a short time.

The third thing that is required is a concern to look at the grace granted in prayer, warning not to waste it in some other way, without seeing, hearing, or speaking about mundane things, but above all it should be warned that not only when he is praying, but when eating, drinking, working, sitting or walking, or whatever he does in the world in the presence of others or alone, he may strive continually to look to Christ with the eye of the mind and constantly bring him into memory, always imagining to see him on the cross, or on the pillar, or in the sepulcher, or in any other place that better teaches him the devotion. And when he realizes that this thought is not in his mind, he returns right away. And although in the beginning it is hard, if he strives for some time, with divine grace he arrives at this goal that, even if he would like, cannot be removed from his heart. But blessed, blessed, blessed a hundred times blessed is that soul who always brings loving Jesus Christ to the eyes of his mind.

The fourth thing required is that he reads from the beginning [the Considerations], he inserts some "Pater Nosters" on the Passion, or other prayers and thinks about that in order. And when the mind begins by itself to conceive devotions without speaking, then it no longer needs to use words, or other devotions, but it works with the mind, if it can, and where it finds pastures it stops, while it lasts, without passing beyond. And when he fails with the mind, then he speaks again with words.

The fifth necessary thing is that if, after obtaining devotions or tears, the mind sometimes remains dry, harsh and cluttered, then thank God and be serene because this is necessary and not to be despaired, because, with patience, he will eventually notice the grace return double.

It should finally be noted that the following prayer: "Hail, sweet Jesus," will benefit to say from time to time with various genuflections, while bowing to obtain the goal proposed by the Divine Mercy.

Prayer: Hail, O sweetest Jesus, full of grace and mercy! Blessed be your harsh Passion and cruel death and blessed be the blood of your wounds! I beseech you to have mercy on my sinful soul.

Novena to the Virgin

Novena Alla Vergine

Follows is a Novena dedicated to Mary to be used in preparation for a Marian feast. It is composed of nine parts, one to be used each day for nine days. It is a beautiful and detailed devotion utilizing traditional images and biblical themes of Mary and Jesus.

It is not known when she wrote it. However, it is thought that she used it for her personal devotion and possibly for that of her sisters. It echoes many themes from her Autobiography and "Mental Sorrows," in particular the vocabulary, expressions, and phraseology used. She frequently uses the word *dolce* (sweet) when referring both to the Mother and Son with various usages such as sweetest, sweetly, sweetness, etc. It appears 104 times and is a sign of the affectionate devotion of St. Camilla Battista towards the Virgin Mary.

Novena to the Virgin

First Day

On the first day, contemplate when the blessed Mother of sweet Jesus was brought to the Temple, until the Annunciation of the angel. First of all, think of the profound humility she had in her heart and in her ways of doing things, as she considered herself the vilest not just in the Temple but also in the entire world.[81] Think of the great silence that she had, because she did not speak except out of great need, as she was not idle, but she always did some good action when she was not physically occupied in prayer, because with her mind she was always as in heaven. But when she was in the Temple to pray, that is part of the night, in the morning and after dusk, she prayed with such fervor and fiery desires of divine love, that when she finished praying, it seemed that rays of splendor emerged from her virginal face which caused every person who noticed her to strive to do good and refrain from evil.

Consider also her inner purity, not so much in the external glances of her eyes or her most exemplary manners, but also for her vow and firm resolve to keep her virginity. Being of marriageable age, the priest of the Temple wanted to give her in marriage, but this deeply disturbed her. However, sensing God's will, she agreed to take Joseph as a husband, as God had commanded, and to wed with much fear of God and zeal for sincerity. And because of this, she gave herself more fervently to prayer and deepened her humility. Thus transformed completely into divine love more than usual, the angel Gabriel appeared to her greeting her in a new way; that is, "Hail Mary, full of grace, the Lord is with thee."[82] Because of this greeting, she was totally amazed, responding to the words of the angel in such a prudent manner, as is narrated in the Holy Gospel.

Now think with how much humility and fear she accepted these mysteries; that is, the conception of the Son of almighty God through the work of the Holy Spirit. But you, devout soul, think of the new fervor and love that was in that furnace that was her heart, since she had been given so much and such a divine Son, and while in those nine months she held him in her womb, her love and desire grew more and more that it seemed that for millions of years she could worship this little God-baby conceived in her own nature; that is, in her pure and virginal blood, as well as many times she seemed to languish out of love and to desire to give him her milk and hold him gently in her holy arms.

Second Day

On the second day, think in what high state, in what deep abyss of love the blessed Virgin was in during that most sacred night in which she gave birth to the only begotten Son of the eternal Father. And after giving birth, how reverently she worshiped him and then took him in her arms and squeezed and kissed him with such love and tenderness that her soul practically melted out of the great sweetness of love. Just the same, fortified by the Majesty of God the Father and her sweet Jesus, his Son, and the Holy Spirit, and the angelic hierarchies that were present there, she sweetly wrapped him in swaddling clothes and gently laid him in the crib in the midst of two animals; that is, the ox and the ass, fulfilling in him all the mysteries that had been prophesied about him.

Watch then how she gently nursed him and while suckling him, it seemed he sucked out the innermost parts of her heart for love of his sweet Mother. O Queen of heaven, how did you not die out of love, seeing yourself nursing sweet Jesus!

Watch again how she later accompanied him on the eighth day when she had him circumcised, as God commanded according to Jewish law. And she had great compassion because of the grief and pain he suffered at that tender age. Thus, she wept bitterly and caressed him, saying kind words and giving hugs.

Then contemplate with how much joy she greeted the three crowned kings who came with their gifts. Pray then to this sweet Queen that she will concede to you the gift of being able to spiritually offer every day the following three gifts to her Son. The first is holy love of God and neighbor: this is what is meant by the gift of gold, the most noble metal and the most worthy virtue there is; and also because without charity no other virtue is sufficient for any spiritual profit. With humble prayers, induce this sweet Virgin to give you the second grace of offering her divine Son, Jesus, the gift of perfumed incense; that is, holy and devout prayer and devotion, having in both your mind and heart, through abundant devotion and meditation, all the mysteries of her sweet Son, Jesus. Then pray to her with all your heart that she gives you the third grace of presenting to her firstborn Son, Jesus, the mortification of all your senses, which is what is meant by that strong and bitter myrrh.

But if such a mortification seems too unbearable, listen to the teaching presented to you by sweet Jesus, Lord of heaven, who said with these words: "O my soul, if you wish to mortify your eyes, observe my meek and resplendent eyes that out of love, at the moment of my Passion were blindfolded with a fetid and stinking bandage to make me suffer and humiliate me. Additionally, if you delight in listening to vain and useless things, and if you enjoy the praises of men and it is too heavy for you to be blamed and vilified with calumny, think of the insults that my ears heard. You should know, therefore, that I was called the son of a laborer, and they believed I was born of Joseph who was a carpenter, but they did not consider that my origins were so great and eternal such that Scripture says: "Who can describe his origin?"[83] I suffered as well in being called a drinker of wine, seducer of people, blasphemer of God, and other injuries and slanders were uttered against my ears. And when you want to stop the temptation of gluttony, think how I was given vinegar and gall to drink, as had been prophesied to me by the holy prophet David: 'And they gave me poison for food! And for my thirst, they gave me vinegar.'[84] By listing all my pains and sorrows that I have come to suffer for love of you, it certainly shouldn't be too heavy to stop all your thoughts for my love by turning your gaze to me, your sweet Lord."

Returning to my first argument – that of the sweet Madonna, think and consider how for forty days she remained in that so vile and despised place in order to fulfill the commandments of the law. And finally, think when she presented her sweet Son Jesus in the Temple, with how much joy she brought him in her arms seeing herself mother as well as virgin, and placing him into the arms of the holy prophet Simeon. And this venerable old man, upon seeing the Queen of heaven, said to her with a prophetic spirit, "A sword will pierce your soul";[85] that is, this Son of yours will be like a knife that will go through your soul, and from that moment on, she no longer rejoiced. Therefore weep with her and be saddened with her until the time of the great event comes; that is, the bitter and sour Passion, and then every pain, every sob and every lament will be removed.

Third Day

On the third day, think how the Virgin was forced to flee with her Son, little Jesus, to go on a pilgrimage, because Herod wanted to kill her Son. And since she gave birth at night during winter, already her pains, afflictions, and wearinesses were beginning by going to Egypt, as the angel had commanded her. Think for a bit how she endured the cold and how she lacked every [material] thing because she was poor, and she did not have sufficient clothes, nor medicines, nor ornaments to cover herself. I am not speaking of food, because she had a little bread and water, and when she found some fountain she quenched her thirst, and this was all the food and delicacies she had. For her Son, no food was necessary, because he was so tiny that he was suckling milk, and he ate this alone.

She arrived in the great city of Egypt, all worn out and tired from the trip. Not having friends or relatives there, it was sometimes necessary for her to put herself to work in the service of some person in exchange for lodging. There she lived as a pilgrim and a stranger[86] in much poverty and need. She spent seven years there. Then, following the command of the angel, she returned to her country. And whereas earlier, the Virgin had made the journey with great tenderness with her sweet Jesus who suffered no trouble in walking as he was carried on his sweet Mother's chest or sometimes by Joseph, now on the return trip sweet Jesus made the entire journey, and his sweet Mother felt great compassion for his effort considering his young age and that he was of delicate nature.

Finally, reflect how, having arrived in their country without clothing and without comfort, she lived in a poor and small house with her Son and with Joseph, with great charity and humility, not by going here and there with friends or relatives, except to the Jewish ceremonies and the solemnities of the Temple according to the commandments of God. And once in particular, while going to the great feast in Jerusalem with Jesus and Joseph, on the return home, God so willed and allowed that sweet Jesus was not with her. This highly distressed her, and she returned immediately to look for him. And not finding him, she wept bitterly. Then on the third day she found him among the teachers, and all joyous and serene she went to her Son saying, "Son, why have you done this to us?" [87] as if to say, "O Son, why did you do this, that your father and I went to look for you with such grief and pain?" Then sweet Jesus said to his dear Mother, "Why are you looking for me?" And then the sweet Mother took her beloved [Son] and hugging and kissing him with great tenderness led him back to his poor home, where he stayed with her until he came to the age of twenty nine or thirty years.

Fourth Day

On the fourth day, contemplate how the sweet Mother remained with her loving Son after the happy passage of holy old Joseph from this life, her one and only comfort and good company. But what did I say? O most merciful Virgin, you were not already alone, but accompanied by everything in Heaven; with you was the Father, with you the Son, with you the Holy Spirit, with you were the holy angels who were contemplating the abyss of your humility.

O sweet Mary, with how much respect and love you served him, with how much sweetness you contemplated him! O Queen of Heaven, how [wonderful] it was to see both of you at the poor table with only a few fragments of bread and a small glass of water! O sweet Mary, with how much respect you served him. Thus, I believe that when he went to rest, with sweet love you covered him with the few clothes you had. And when he got up, you were equally prompt in handing him his cloak, and with the same sweet love and respect you served him his needs in his sweet humanity.

Think again and say with your mind: O holy Virgin, how many times while he slept did you contemplate him and he in turn, I think, showed you the rays of his divinity many times out of consolation and especially when he prayed. How you were so pleased and happy while going somewhere together with such a sweet presence, and how you were in pain when your Son Jesus went away from you! Finally, I thank you for all the services you have done to my sweet Jesus.

Fifth Day

On the fifth day, think of the consolation of the Virgin when Jesus began to preach, since the eternal Father did not want his beloved Son to be hidden from people, but that he should reveal himself through sermons and even miracles, which caused him to endure hardships in going from city to city. Many times she went to hear him preach and with great love and respect she listened to his sweet words.

Also think how many times she saw him suffer great sacrifices that grieved her heart. Meditate also when she saw him persecuted by the Jews who despised his preaching, miracles, and all his other works. And out of great contempt for him they called him a seducer of the people, a deceiver, demoniac, a blasphemer of God, and they insulted him in many other ways, injured and persecuted him, for which this sweet Mother felt unbearable grief knowing well who he was. And the more she knew of his wisdom and innocence, so much more compassion she had for him. I think that many times the eyes of the Queen of heaven became fountains of tears when she considered the offenses received by the paternal Majesty for the insults that were delivered to his beloved Son.

Finally meditate on much pain and grief the Mother felt in seeing the actions the Jews took to kill sweet Jesus. And therefore consider that she never had anything in this world other than grief and pain for the sake of her Son, Jesus. Just the same, the Son bore everything out of love of us in order to atone for our sins. So it is necessary to know how this Queen of heaven suffered so many sorrows, afflictions, hardships, needs and distresses for our cause; we, out of gratitude, should repent and cry bitterly while we remain in this world, to express great and deep compassion to both the Son as well as to his Mother.

Sixth Day

On the sixth day, contemplate with pain in your heart and sadness in your mind, and with abundant tears the great spectacle, the grand reproach that the afflicted Mother experienced while her Son, Jesus, hung from the tree. And meditate well on her pains, sobs and wailings more in her heart than her voice, because many times she could not speak because of the grief she felt. And because of intolerable pain and tears of blood that sprang from that angelic face that sometimes it seemed that her sweet loving heart had broken. And those few chosen ones who were standing nearby; that is, John, the Magdalene and her sisters, sometimes wept more for the Mother than for the Son. And when for a brief moment she came to her senses, she said in a faint voice and an anguished heart, "Now what has become of my beloved Son, Jesus, is he alive or dead?"

The onlookers tried to aid and comfort her with words as best they could, and they led her near the cross with difficulty, so that she might have the strength to utter a few words before the good Jesus died. And while the Virgin was standing next to her Son hanging from the cross nailed with three very large nails and completely full of pain and anguish, his face soaked with bloody tears, all sorrowful, she barely recognized that this was her sweet Jesus. He demonstrated that the water [of tears] was already finished, and her heart seemed completely divided in half.

And she began to speak as best she could to her beloved Jesus, saying words such as these, "O my sweet Son, you have demonstrated well your great love by praying to your heavenly Father for those who crucified you. And by your ineffable mercy, you gave Heaven to the good thief, while to me your distressed Mother, you do not say anything. O my Son, former Counselor of my soul, now you are like a very sharp knife to me. O my Son, whom I carried in my womb for nine months with so much love, and I fed you with my milk with such loving kindness, and how many times I wrapped you in swaddling clothes when you were a baby, and how many times did I clutch you to my chest with affectionate hugs, now I cannot even touch the end of your foot! Oh, how unfortunate is this day for me and you, my Son! Thus all the joys and pleasures that I received on the day of your birth when I heard the multitude of jubilant angels singing, 'Glory to God in the highest and on earth peace to men, etc.'[88], today I heard the crowd of people shouting, 'Away, away, crucify him!'[89] While on that night the angelic messenger announced to the shepherds, 'I bring you tidings of great joy,'[90] today John came to me to say that you had been captured and tied up like a thief. That night I saw the farm animals, the ox and the ass kneeling before the crib almost in adoration, today I saw that crowd of Jews tormenting and mocking you, and bowing and kneeling to the ground they scoffed you, saying, 'Hail, king of the Jews'[91] after having crowned you with thorns, and having put a reed in your hand as a royal scepter, and after having blindfolded your eyes with an unclean and smelly rag, they seated you on a common and contemptible chair. And even after so many mysteries that were so sweet and gentle to me, I lifted you from the crib taking you in my arms, and I nursed you holding you tight to my chest with gentle love. Today, my Son, you were given gall and vinegar to drink, and I cannot find you anywhere. So I can rightly say with the prophet that I am greatly distressed and humiliated for you, O sweet Son of mine, afflicted for the pain I see you enduring, humiliated because, having lost you, my only hope, I no longer dare to go among the people because, whereas before I was honored by many people out of respect for you, today I am despised by all the people and cast out because I lost you, sweet Jesus, my Son." Thus, the Virgin, sweetly lamenting her suffering, spent that most bitter day in tears and lamentation.

Finally, reflect how he was taken down from the cross and placed in the lap of his afflicted Mother. And then she renewed all her cries, all the laments and bitter sobs. And the sweet Mother, observing the entire body of her Son, saw it all bruised and battered. And she was in such unbearable pain that she was unable to express one word seeming almost dead. Then Joseph and Nicodemus, out of compassion for the Mother, took the body of Jesus, and placed it in the tomb according to Jewish custom. And then the so afflicted and sorrowful widowed Mother, upon returning to Jerusalem, was accompanied by John to Mount Zion, and Mary Magdalene went along too, and even the sisters of the sweet Mother did not want to leave her but they stayed too full of tears and sighs.

So you, O devout soul, while you make this pious meditation on sweet

Mary, weep and sigh with her and the other women who were with her until dawn on the following Sunday morning.

Seventh Day

On the seventh day, contemplate the immense joy that the Queen of heaven had while she was in prayer contemplating the mystery of the Resurrection. And she began to feel a joy of mind such that she seemed to see that glorious soul retake his precious body. And feeling united in divine love with the paternal Majesty, she begged with sweet lament that his clemency would reunite Jesus's soul with his body without delay. And being completely raptured in such a thought, she melted in sweet tears upon seeing her beloved Jesus. And suddenly he appeared to her all glorious and serene and full of splendor, surrounded by the multitude of angels, saying in a soft and cheerful voice, "May God save you, my dear, sweet Mother." And upon hearing his beloved voice and seeing his venerable demeanor so bright and full of divinity, she at once reverently worshiped him. And hugging him gently, the sweet Mother said, "You are welcome back, my sweet child, etc."

And now with the eyes of your mind, consider all the affectionate deeds and sweet colloquies that the Queen of heaven made with her resurrected Son. Think then when she saw him ascend to heaven. Observe her angelic face wet with sweet tears out of emotion of his departure. Then sweet Jesus asked the blessing of his sweet Mother, and she took his precious head with reverence and passionate love and held his chest and hugged him gently. And very moved out of love and tenderness they remained for a period of time close and embraced in this way together while good Jesus sustained her as his sweet Mother. Then he said, "My dear and beloved Mother, please let me go, because the eternal Father is waiting for me." At these words the gentle Mother left her child, as a wise person who was desirous of the triumph of her Jesus. And then her sweet Son, after giving his blessing to those few who were present there and all were crying for emotion of love, once again embraced his Mother. And in this last embrace made by the Son to his Mother, he pulled to himself her heart and in such a way that he had her take part in the rays of his divinity, that the sweet Son Jesus recalling his most sacred arms back towards himself and starting slowly to rise so sweetly above, his sweet Mother barely noticed, because she was so engrossed that she almost seemed to rise up along with her Son.

The good Jesus worked in this delicate way; that is, he rose up so gently, even for the elect who watched his Ascension. And when he was so high that they could no longer see him, he flew in the blink of an eye to the throne of his Majesty. And immediately he sent the angel to comfort them, who sang with joy and gladness saying, "Men of Galilee, why do you stand looking up into heaven?"[92] And the Queen of heaven, upon hearing the angelic voice, seemed to awaken from a sweet sleep, and filled with infinite joy, upon considering the glory and the triumph of her sweet Son Jesus, she returned to Mount Zion and waited with great love and desire for the coming of the Holy Spirit. And reflect that the Queen of heaven had this desire more for the Apostles and all the faithful who were there and would come than for her, because she was now filled. And because of the fullness that she had, her soul, burning like a furnace, was more and more lit up with the desire to approach the divine love.

Ten days after the Ascension, the Holy Spirit descended upon the Virgin Mother and on those who were enclosed there at that Holy Cenacle, deep in prayer and divine contemplation. And they felt so enflamed as a furnace of fire and coming out with great fervor, not fearing death nor scourges, they went preaching all over, converting people to the true faith according to the command from their divine Master and what their sweet Mother reminded them. As the holy Apostles ordered her, obedient and humble above every creature, she remained where they put her, especially John the evangelist, because good Master Jesus had assigned her as his Mother. And he, truly obedient, never abandoned her, and he served her in all her needs, although she needed little because her life was so celestial.

Eighth Day

On the eighth day, reflect with your mind how the Queen of heaven lived for fifteen years after the Pentecost until the Assumption. In this time, she exercised every spiritual action of prayer, meditation and contemplation. And she prayed for all the faithful who were confirmed continually in grace and holiness. She also prayed for the faithless and nonbelievers whom the paternal Majesty wished to illuminate and convert to the faith of his only begotten Son.

Then think about how she continually meditated on all the mysteries of her loving Jesus and she retraced in her mind all the places where human redemption had been worked out, particularly in the places of his most bitter Passion, and mainly in the garden [of Gesthamane] where he was so cruelly captured, then where he was so brutally whipped at the column, where he was crowned with thorns, where his beautiful eyes were blindfolded, where his divine face was marred, where he was beaten with rods on his precious head above the rough and prickly crown of thorns, where finally the innocent one was sentenced to a cruel death on the cross, where his dear Mother met him with the cross on his shoulder at the Golden Gate, where he was crucified between the two thieves. And at this point, reflect how her heartfelt cry was renewed with immense compassion for the human nature of the innocent Jesus so much that it seemed that it was the day when she saw him on the gallows of the cross.

And you, devout soul, cry along with the grieving Mother, considering that blessed Jesus endured so many outrages and punishment for your sins. And consider that the Mother wept so bitterly in reparation for what we are not able to do; that is, to weep bitterly for our defects the cause of which resulted in so much suffering to the Son and Mother. Think finally how the Queen of heaven was searching with her mind the other mysteries, and coming to the last; that is, to the Ascension, and contemplating the triumph, the infinite glory and the Majesty of her Son, this thought involved her in so much love and sublime contemplation that it seemed to her that she was before the Holy Trinity already admitted to the divine embraces.

So, her place of prayer could rightly be called heaven, because her face returned from that conversation more splendid than the sun itself, so much that the Apostles were afraid to show her to those who were not very well experienced in the faith for fear that they would worship her as a goddess. And when she had to talk or speak as a teacher of those who were converted to the true faith, she was the only refuge and comforter of all the elect who, for the sake of her Son Jesus, bore hardships and tribulations. And she did this with much love and gentleness that she seemed all passionate for love of God and for the salvation of souls, and she would have wanted to die for them if it had been necessary.

And reflect how her heart then became a fiery furnace because of this exercise; she burned of a continual desire to be personally reunited with the paternal Majesty and with her beloved Jesus and the Holy Spirit to enjoy the splendor of the Father, the sweetness of her Son, and the love of the Holy Spirit, world without end. Amen.

Ninth Day

On the ninth day, having passed fifteen years now, contemplate how the Queen of heaven, the Spouse of the eternal Father, the Mother of sweet Jesus, the abode of the Holy Spirit, was alight with a new desire and a stronger than usual burning love to be reunited with her only Son. All languishing with love, she seemed almost beside herself she was so enflamed. And the eternal Father, upon seeing the burning desire of his spouse, watched her gently. And even her sweet Son Jesus heard the voice of the beloved Mother who said with the silent language of her heart, "O my sweet Son, now it is time for you to come to me, because I can no longer stay without you, now how can you be without me, since I am your Mother? Remember, O dear Son, that in the thirty-three years you were in this world no creature loved you more than I did, and no creature was more sorrowful over your labors, sorrows, pains, sufferings, insults and cruel death as I who suffered with you so many pains up until this point. By now it is time for you to put an end to my sighs and wishes."

And so affectionate were those outbursts taken to Heaven by divine love, the Holy Spirit said to the Father and the Son: "My spouse melts like wax in the fire of love, let us send for her." And then by command of the Holy Trinity, the prince Gabriel came down and told the Queen of heaven that the Holy Trinity was waiting for her with great desire, and that she should be consoled because soon her Son would come for her, and that if she wanted something, she should say it as the Archangel would promptly report it [to the Trinity].

Then the sweet Mother, low to the ground in deep humility, thanked the Father, the Son and the Holy Spirit for such grace and, having greeted the Archangel Gabriel who had brought her such a sweet notice, dearly begged him to ask her Son out of grace and virtue to gather together the Apostles at the time of her passing, because she very much wanted to see them gathered together. And her just request was granted. And think how this desire would not have given pleasure just to her, but also to the Apostles. She was very certain that her Son would come in person, so she had asked the grace to give them the joy of seeing their dear Master wrapped in glory.

And being all assembled in the house of the Virgin in a very short time by virtue of the Holy Spirit, and after having learned the reason of this miraculous return of theirs, they all cried over the departure of such a Mother, and some kissed her hands, some her feet, some merely looked upon her sweetly as they were not able to speak for the abundance of tears, some expressed themselves with sobs as if saying, "O Mother, do you really want to leave us orphans? And if you do, to whom will we turn in our distress? You were all our refuge, and so on," and other expressions of affection that I do not relate, but I leave you to imagine, devout soul.

And that sweet Mother, seeing them so afflicted because of her separation, could not contain her tears of compassion for them. Just the same she consoled them with sweet words and sweet promises from her Son and their Master. And being immersed in these discourses, suddenly the Savior appeared, accompanied by a host of angels and saints of the Old and New Testament and, saluting his sweet Mother and the Apostles who were present, said as he often did, "Peace be with you."[93] And all fell prostrate to the ground, and they worshipped him, and with much happiness and great joy, they prostrated themselves at his feet, kissing them with great reverence and tenderness of love. And he let them do what they wanted in order to give them some consolation with his sweet presence. And in this way for a brief moment the sweet Jesus contemplated his sweet Mother with eyes of love.

Now imagine, devout and contemplative soul, and observe a little the sweet Jesus who comes to his sweet Mother, and opening his sweet arms, he throws them to her neck and embraces her close to his most sacred chest while emitting rays of divinity. And in these sweet and gentle embraces, he drew the soul of Mary out of her body, and the holy angels who were present there saw the soul of their queen so resplendent in the arms of sweet Jesus, and began to sing with sweet melody. And think how the Redeemer commanded the Apostles to bring the body of the Mother to the valley of Jehoshaphat, and they waited there until the third day. And so it was done.

On the third day sweet Jesus came, accompanied by all the hierarchies of angels and all saints of the Old and New Testament with prince Michael, and brought the soul of his sweet Mother, and among sweet melodies and angelic singing he rejoined it to her body and filled it with glory and bliss so much that only her body; that is, that of the Virgin, seemed paradise to behold. Then the good Master gave his sweet blessing to all the holy Apostles, who all wept with emotion at the departure of their comforter.

And you should know, devout soul, that the Savior began to go up slowly in the sky and this was for consolation of the Disciples who were all soaked in tears. And the angels and saints, singing and rejoicing, went with the Savior and the Virgin, and so entered in the heavenly court. And having placed her at the right hand of her Son, Jesus, as mentioned above, there was again a great celebration and joy among the Holy Trinity and the seraphim enflamed with divine love. She was then crowned with a sublime crown, and the divine spirits, according to their order, offered her songs and sounds full of sweetness.

Think also how she lit up all of Heaven as a new light, and how the Holy Trinity exalted her above all the choirs of angels, and above all the saints. And think also that this exaltation was not only as a place, but strength; that is, this Queen in virtue and strength has more power than all the angels and saints combined. And secondly, she was exalted in her ability of divine love, because she is more able to contain divine love and the Holy Trinity that all the nine choirs of angels and saints that ever were and ever will be. Finally consider that she was exalted inasmuch as her splendor. For you should know that if it were possible that all the holy angels and saints who are and will be were alone in one place and the Madonna were alone in another place, she would exceed the splendor of all these angels and saints, who each one in itself shines seven times brighter than the sun, and the multitude of angels and saints is so much that only the divine Majesty can count, nothing will surpass this Queen in splendor, without any comparison.

Think again how she was made treasurer of all God's treasures, and she is the one who dispenses all graces. Think also that she was made advocate of sinners, and that she prays for all and beseeches forgiveness of our sins and with tender love opens her arms before the sweet Jesus saying these words, "O my sweet Son, I try to move your innermost parts, which were born from mine, so that you have mercy on the sinners for whom I was chosen Mediatrix by you." And the sweet Mother makes many other sweet and loving prayers for us, before her sweet Son Jesus, loving everyone as her own children.

But you, devout soul who are bowed down before the Queen with the affection of your heart, embrace and hold her holy feet tight with sweet and abundant tears, saying, "Sweet Mother of mercy, I will not depart from these holy feet until such time as you give me your holy blessing, and, although I am unworthy, remember that in order to save me, you were made the Mother of God and that your sweetest Son was hung on the tree for me, so that you can not certainly deny me this grace."

Spiritual Life – The Autobiography of Saint Camilla Battista

La Vita Spirituale (1491)

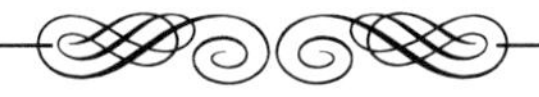

The "Spiritual Life" also known as the "Autobiography" of St. Camilla Battista was written as a letter in the form of a confession directed to Father Domenico of Leonessa, who was born in San Severino Marche. As a child, he moved with his family to Leonessa, which name he took after becoming a friar. Seven times he was elected provincial minister of the Observant Franciscan friars of the Marches region. He was a preacher, and propagator of the *Monti di Pietà*, a sort of credit agency that lent money to the poor at little to no interest. He died in Urbino in the Marches on April 20, 1497.

Most of what we know of St. Camilla comes precisely from this work. Camilla narrates how she went to Father Domenico of Leonessa, who had been a type of spiritual director for her since she was 8 or 9 years old. She begins her spiritual life by describing her conversion initiated after hearing the friar's sermon when he exhorted his listeners to shed a little tear. She then narrates how her spiritual life developed, grew, and deepened while at her father's castle in Camerino. She details her relationship with Jesus, her receiving the three "lilies," and her struggle to become a nun and leave her father. She then describes her entrance into the monastery in Urbino and her transfer to Camerino. Finally, she describes various visions (including one of St. Clare) and spiritual ecstasies, and concludes with her desire to transform every day into a Good Friday.

A recurring theme throughout this letter is her suffering. Almost like a refrain, St. Camilla quotes a verse from Lamentations 1: 12, "is any sorrow like my sorrow," eight times throughout the work. This letter was written between February 27 and March 13, 1491 at the end of a three year period of intimate suffering during which time St. Camilla felt an intense spiritual desolation, the dark night of the soul, as St. John of the Cross described it.

This work has been studied by scholars of the Italian language for its literary merit, especially by those studying women's writings in Renaissance Italy.

Spiritual Life – Autobiography

"To Jesus, Mary

O Christ the most pious King,
Possess our hearts
So that we can continually praise you
in the right way."

Inspiration to Write the Letter

My dearest reverend father, I am letting you know in this letter that during this entire month of February,[94] I have been in great torment and mental anguish. The reason is this: I experienced an intense, strong, and fervent inspiration [to write this letter]. But I countered [the inspiration] with great and forceful resistance, as I had a doubt that it might be a temptation from the devil, which I feared could transform my spirit into pride and greed, having received from God such a power over me because of the sins and iniquities that I committed.

Finding myself afflicted and deprived of any help or human counsel, I took recourse to my usual weapon of holy prayer. I prayed to God and his sweetest Mother with all my heart and love, that he would enlighten me in the great darkness in which I found myself because of my sins, and that I would know whether or not it was his will to write. Truly, my dear father, I can tell you in good conscience that during this entire month I have been almost outside of myself, as a result of praying unceasingly to God that he would help me in such great agony.

I was unable to find peace while sleeping, waking, praying, or saying the Holy Office. But today, the second Sunday of Lent on February 27, after having received Eucharist, I finally resolved to obey and begin to fulfill this inspiration. Otherwise, I could find no rest. I hope by the grace of God that I have chosen his will, and it seems to me, through his goodness and grace, that it is so rather than not.

However it is, in what I shall write I cannot bring to light [of my own power] anything other than confusion and shame in front of you and of God. It is precisely this, more than any other consideration, that persuades me to obey this inspiration, even though many other useful and necessary considerations have come to me. My dear father, the inspiration I had is this: for the well-being of my soul and in order that you may better understand what I am going to say and the importance of what I have already told you, it is necessary that I tell you and clearly explain to you that which I have never said nor explained to anyone. I am speaking of my spiritual life – how it began, and how it has continued until this moment. I wish to do this, although it is difficult and bitterly painful for me, as God knows.

My dear father, until now I have spoken incompletely by letter or in person with you when I have given you some indication of the pain that breaks my heart. But now the time has come, to my uncertainty, for me to bear my entire soul and manifest the hidden sore that for almost three years has been consuming my poor, afflicted soul. This has been and still is a sharp knife that has pierced my heart. This was and is that spear of that powerful soldier [i.e. Longinus[95]] that has penetrated the recesses of my own heart.

O my dear father, do not be displeased and do not grow weary of listening to me. Like another Magdalene lying at the feet of good Jesus, I shall throw myself at your good paternal feet, full of tears, all full of shame and blushing. I shall humbly tell you the story of my most unhappy happiness. It seems to me that I can say with complete sincerity "most unhappy happiness," because as a result of my sins, unfaithfulness, and ingratitude, happiness has changed for me into vinegar and poison. But my dearest father, I earnestly beg you to try to look and see with paternal and sympathetic understanding "if there is any sorrow like my sorrow."[96]

Camilla Asks Divine Favor to Write

Now speaking about such a great topic; that is, about God and the things he secretly worked in my soul through only his goodness and grace – makes my heart tremble. Thus, I recount and write with great fear and trembling. And since I know that what I am and what is in me are nothing other than falsehood, deception, and lies, I therefore invoke and call the good spirit of blessed Christ with pious and heartfelt love to assist me during my recounting.

I know that in fact only he is the true and simplest Spirit, without any darkness, and he loves truth and purity. May he give me the grace and the gift to be able to tell you with simplicity, my father, of the graces and particular gifts that I received unworthily and without recognition from most clement God, Father of all mercies.

And I wish to do so in this manner: to say as little possible rather than add even one syllable too much. In fact, I wish to show you these things as they are *sub titulo at sigillo confessionis* [under the seal of confession]. Therefore I say, *Confiteor Deo omnipotenti et tibi, pater* [I confess to almighty God and to you, father].

The Beginnings of Camilla Battista's Spiritual Life

You should know, sweet and dearest father, that my entire spiritual life had its origin, beginning, and foundation in you, and from no one else. I am quite sure this will surprise you and perhaps be quite difficult for you to believe, because I know you know nothing of it, nor did I ever believe or think of relating such a thing to you or to anyone else. But listen to what happened and you will see that with God all things are possible.

My reverend father, when you preached at Camerino the last time, I think I could not have been older than eight or ten years old. You can calculate my age if you remember when you preached there. On the 9th of April I will be the age of our Lord Jesus Christ, as I was born in 1458. Subtract the years gone by since you preached here from thirty-three, and what remains corresponds to my age then. [97]

One Holy Friday, I spontaneously desired to attend your holy and blessed sermon, which I listened to by the grace of the Holy Spirit. I listened not only attentively, but I was totally enraptured, almost inebriated. I was like someone who was hearing things said that had never been heard by anyone before. It seemed to me that such things had not yet happened, but were happening just then. You can understand my age and how innocent and naive I was from this: when you said that Jesus was dragged before Herod, and that he would have freed him if only he would have spoken, I immediately had so much compassion that I prayed to God to give me the grace that this Jesus Christ would speak and respond, in order not to be killed.[98] But when I heard that he did not desire to speak, I was overcome by a great pain and I kept on saying within my heart in order to remove the suffering I was feeling, "Woe to him; why did he not respond? It seems as if he himself wanted to die." That's how it was, my good Lord, but I did not understand it. I have told you this, my father, so that you would know how old I was when this sweet God began to want to take possession of this ungrateful soul of mine.

At the end of your holy sermon you offered a heartfelt exhortation to the people to provoke their hearts to sob and meditate on the Passion of Christ. And you urged them to remember [the Passion] at least on Good Friday and, on account of it, to shed only a little tear, just one.[99] You affirmed with much conviction that only a little tear, just one, would be more acceptable to God and more useful to the soul than all other good works that one could do. As those holy words went out of your mouth by the virtue of the Holy Spirit, by that same virtue they were engraved so deeply in my tender child's heart that they could never leave me or have been forgotten.

So when I had grown a little older, on remembering your holy sermon, I made a vow to God that every Friday I would shed at least one tear for the love of the Passion of Christ. And my entire spiritual life had its beginning from this, as you will be able to understand from the following. Therefore, don't be surprised if I told you that my spiritual life had its origin and beginning in you, but "praise God with me and let us give thanks to our Creator together from whom come this and every other good thing."[100]

The Difficulty in Observing the Vow

Having made that vow, I strove as much as possible to keep it, although every Friday evening before going to bed, I struggled very much to shed that tear. And religious things seemed an abomination for me to read, nor could I suffer to hear them read. That is why I struggled so much before I could shed that poor little tear. But with the help of God, when a tear fell from my eyes, do not think I waited for a second, because I would quickly get up and run away with little notice. Sometimes, because of my vivacious temperament – laughing and chatting all evening long – it was not possible for me to shed even one. But then I would feel unhappy for that entire week, and I feared that some disgrace would happen to me.

During Lent I went to confess to Father Pacifico of Urbino. After the confession he asked me whether I had made a vow, to which I answered that I had not. But after reflecting briefly, I remembered and said that I had made one, but sometimes I could not keep it, even though I always desired to fulfill it. He asked me what the vow was, but I did not wish to tell him, as

I felt embarrassed because it was a good thing. Yet, after resisting a little, I told him. He responded, "My child, I will not release you from this vow; on the contrary, I wish for you to keep it. But if, after every effort, you are not able to succeed, you must not believe that you have sinned."

After persevering for a long time in this vow with great difficulty, as I just described, it pleased God that I happened to find a meditation of the Passion of Christ divided in fifteen parts. It seems that it was written just for a person who did not know how to meditate. At the end of each chapter, it prescribed the recitation of a Hail Mary, then the next part began with these words, "I thank you, my Lord, for having done this and that for me..." It was a very long event. Just the same, I took that little book and tried to read it, all the while devoutly kneeling before the crucifix every Friday. And so I have done for many years. In those fifteen Hail Marys and mysteries, I always attempted to shed some tears for each mystery. Precisely when I said the Hail Mary, God granted me the grace more often than not to shed more tears than I desired.

One Friday night I was occupied until the eighth hour of night[101] when my father, the lord [the duke], gave me permission to go to bed. As it was very late and that meditation was very long and everyone else was already in bed, I was strongly tempted to neglect it that evening. More than four times I struggled between saying yes and no. At last God helped me to victory, and I made my usual devotion. If you knew, my father, the danger from which I was set free through that prayer about one hour after going to bed, you would be astonished. If you ask me about it, I will tell you, but now I shall skip over it so that I do not tire for writing too long. Blessed be the soul who does not neglect the good begun because of temptation! I say this from experience, because I was tried. To keep it brief, let us go back to where I was distracted.

From this continual reading of the Passion, I obtained such a profound partaking in it that I no longer wished to just read it, but to meditate on it. I wanted to reflect on it for a certain period of time not just on Friday, but each day, and not following the written meditation by rote, but in the manner God deemed to inspire me. And so great was the gift of holy tears God was giving me, that many times I desired to be able to recite a rosary without weeping, for the sake of the people who were around me, given the shortage of places suitable to prayer. I did this for three consecutive years before I resolved to give myself up wholly to God.

However, the devil's malice tried to deter me in every way possible from this meditation that made me weep. And he caused the people whom

I could not avoid in the house to believe that I was weeping for some silly foolishness or another. And all that gossiping and whispering behind my back pierced my heart. Yet by the grace of God I took it lightly and never allowed myself to be deterred from doing what I desired. I turned my back on them and turned my heart to God and minded my own business. "Think good or bad of me," I said in my heart, "I will consider it little."

And so I continued for those three years through an ever fervent devotion towards the Passion of Christ. On Fridays I always fasted on bread and water alone. I had also made a vow to abstain on that day from some of my faults and sins, yet sometimes out of my weakness I violated this vow. Also on that day, many times I scourged my entire body and I would get up every night to say a rosary. And whenever I did not get up out of negligence, I said two of them instead of one. And now that I am a nun, I don't get up, nor do I do any good [i.e. any such ascetic practice]. Moreover during those three years, I used to fast on only bread and water on all the feasts of our Lord and of our Lady. There were some weeks in which I fasted three days on bread and water or either two days consecutively and it happened more times, but at present I no longer fast. But I did all these good works not only to win a prize in Heaven, rather much more on earth.[102]

But at the end of my long, devoted, moving prayer when I desired to quit and distance myself from God, my soul was enraptured in such great tranquility and peace that I cannot even begin to describe. Because in that brief time of prayer, perhaps the duration of two Hail Marys – sometimes more, sometimes less – my body stopped breathing as if it were dead, but my soul was completely tranquil and peaceful. For this reason, many times I said to God with all my heart, "My Lord, if you desire that in order to be in contact with the world I should separate myself from you even in the slightest, then before that should happen, send me not one, but one thousand plagues." I intended simply to say, "If you know that I could lose this little devotion that I have now..." I did not know any other way to get close to God, because, except for that little time of prayer mentioned above, I spent the rest of my time playing, singing, dancing, and strolling in vanities and in other youthful and worldly things that follow. Religious things – like friars and nuns – so irritated me that I could not stand to see them. I often made fun of those who read spiritual books and I was very concerned with looking nice and reading worldly things. In those three years [1476-79] my heart was imprisoned. I prayed so much to God to give me the grace to set it free, but with my prayers I was never able to obtain such a gift. Listen, however, to how I was delivered. O God, you are very good, because in a thousand ways, you always help the soul that sincerely seeks good.

The Beginning of The Voice that Calls

In order to lead me out of darkness towards the true light, God ordered in his mercy a blessed soul to come to preach in Camerino. He was a true trumpet of the Holy Spirit, Father Francesco of Urbino, who now rests in peace. His words and teaching were like thunder and lightning that struck my soul, because during that entire Lent he preached continually these terrible words, "Fear God!" His sermons filled my soul with such a fear of God, a knowledge of the wrongs and injuries I had done to him, and such a great fear of Hell that, had I not already known that despair displeases God more than any other sin, truly, my father, I would have despaired of ever obtaining mercy. All my hope and comfort during that pain was in just one word: mercy. I never spoke to anyone of my anguish, but I wept bitterly all day and night as my penance. Because of fear of Hell, I intensified my prayer and meditation on the Passion of Christ. And while before, I considered and wept just once a day, now I would reflect and weep twice – morning and night. On Friday I committed this folly: either I ate three or four mouthfuls of bread and drank a sip of water, or I took nothing at all. And at night out of reverence for the Passion of Christ I did not sleep because I did not even lie down in bed. And I could truly say, "I sleep, but my heart stays awake."[103]

While persevering in my vow and praying frequently for the above mentioned [fear of Hell], I began to hear certain voices within my soul. They seemed to be coming from far away, but not so far that I could not hear them clearly. These voices told me that if I wished to avoid Hell, which terrorized me, I ought to flee the world and enter a monastery. At the same time I received an illumination, which allowed me to understand clearly that if I chose to remain in the world, I would have damned myself, because of my worldliness.[104]

These voices seemed to me more bitter than vinegar since I was naturally inclined to worldly things, and my temperament went contrary to what they were telling me. My strong repugnance to the idea of entering a monastery resulted from my sin and from my desire to abandon myself to the muck and mire of the world. I had many reasons that would in no way allow me to agree to this plan. I could not decide in favor of it, because I did not feel that my heart was free from certain passions, from which one must be free if one truly wishes to serve God.

Letter Exchange with Father Francesco

Through the inspiration of almighty God, true and only lover and freer of souls, it came to mind to secretly write a strictly personal letter to this preacher for the zeal of others' salvation – not mine. This I did without hope of receiving any response, though it was useful not to others, but to myself. I do not remember if I had written words in that letter that could have made him think good or bad about me; I only concluded the letter thus, *Memento mei in tranquilla sublatione mentis tuae* [Remember me in the serene elevation of your mind.] I said this because I believed that every servant of God felt at the conclusion of their prayer that peace of which I spoke to you above – so much more Fr. Francesco who seemed to me an angel of God and not a mere human.[105]

Father Francesco was inspired by God to answer me by secret means, as was necessary so that a scandal would not be created.[106] He told me that he would do everything possible both in public and in private regarding what I had written him. Then he added these holy words, "My daughter, I beg you to strive to keep your heart and body spotless, like the holy virgin Cecilia, until God shows the way you are to follow him; and do not allow yourself to be conquered by worldly, sensual passions that pass through your mind. Strive to overcome yourself in this. Farewell."

Having read these words, I felt as if I were going to faint, because they did not seem to me simple words, but very sharp arrows sent by God to pierce my heart. That friar had never seen me nor spoken to me: how could he have known my imprisoned heart so well? When I came to my senses, I said to God, "You, Lord, have spoken to me through the mouth of this friar, because I know that he knows nothing about the state of my soul. You tell me that I should overcome myself if I wish to be free. Thus I resolve to do it."

And truly, my father, it only took overcoming myself just three or four times in avoiding seeing what attracted and delighted me, that I was freed of that passion.[107] This is why I felt such great affection and love for Father Francesco. Perhaps a bit too much, but it was necessary, because the false and worldly love that I felt changed into holy and spiritual love. The great benefit I received from his words compelled me to this.

Interior Struggle with Her Religious Vocation

Just as in former times, when God urged his people, freed from the slavery of Pharaoh, [108] to sacrifice in the wilderness, so much more was he soliciting my soul to embrace religious life. But my maliciousness slowed my fulfilling such a precept and would not consent in any way to the divine voices. Rather, while rebelling strongly, I found other excuses, not the least of which was worldly love. Then I added quite a particular excuse, "Who would ever be able to separate me from the powerful hands of my father?" His hands kept me close and tight because he was so fond of me, and it seemed it would be impossible to free myself from him, regardless of my decision. O my God, my God, what did you wish to do with this false and harlot soul of mine? [109] What did you need from my deeds, my sweet Jesus, you who so forcefully sought me out and desired me? What gift have I brought you? How could I reward you, my Lord?

Here I shall say nothing of the many attempts God made to try to wrest me from my powerful father's hands, because, my reverend father, it breaks my heart, and I am unable to recount them without great suffering. Thus, this most patient and wise God, seeing the hardness and obstinacy of my heart, sought to soften it in another way. On the eve of the feast of the Annunciation, Father Francesco of Urbino preached of the divine love that the Virgin Mary felt at the moment of the Annunciation. He spoke with such fervor and affection that he appeared as a seraph. He stated that there was more sweetness in one spark of love that the Virgin felt at the moment of the Annunciation, than in all worldly loves put together. As soon as the sermon was over, I knelt before the altar and made a vow to the Virgin Mary to keep all my feelings pure until God would ask otherwise of me. But on one condition: that God would allow me to feel at least one spark of the love that Mary felt on that day.

I persevered in such supplications day and night with much fervor and desire. But since my impure soul was not ready for a treasure as precious as this spark of divine love, God sought to purify me in the following way. The preacher wished to preach on Holy Saturday, even though it was against custom and in opposition to his superiors, since there were many events happening in the cathedral on that day. Few people were present since the sermon was unscheduled, but there was one person for whom God willed this sermon!

The friar asked everyone to forgive him for preaching on that day, but said he felt called to do it in order to calm his conscience. Since the next day was Easter, he wished to clarify some things that rendered receiving communion illicit. He said many things, but what struck me were these words, "Anyone who confesses without a true promise to avoid all occasions of mortal sin cannot receive communion." Then I said within my heart, "Poor me! I have almost always received communion that way, because I have never had the willingness or the readiness to let go of my vanities and foolishness until now. This evening when I confess, I will state this sin." And so I did.

Father Oliviero who heard my confession asked, "How long have you been confessing and receiving communion in this way?" I answered, "Almost always." He replied, "My child, I do not wish for you under any circumstance to receive communion tomorrow. Reflect well on your sins and return in one week for a general confession." And so I did, though I felt a lot of shame and confusion in front of the others since I was not able to receive communion on Easter Sunday with them. I feared they would gossip saying, "She must have done something very bad." Thus I felt the truth of that proverb, *Chi non dà quello che duole, non può avere quello che vuole* [He who does not give that what pains, cannot get what he wants.]"[110] Thus it happened to me that time. Having made that confession, by the grace of God, I felt deep contrition for my faults for almost all of Lent. It is true that I was not scrupulous of every little thing out of neglect and ignorance, as I am now; but what I did not do then I did later on, as you will see. But it was enough then for me to do as much as I knew and understood.

On the octave of Holy Saturday I confessed to Father Oliviero in St. Peter's Church in Muralto. I received communion, and then I spoke with my devout Father Francesco of Urbino, to whom I had never spoken before. He asked me if I wanted to become a nun, to which I said no. This seemed to sadden him. Then he said, *Iam facta es sana, noi amplius peccare. Vade in pace.* [Now you have been healed, do not sin anymore. Go in peace!][111] So I returned home feeling quite comforted.

After my soul had been purified in the aforementioned way, divine goodness began to hammer me more forcefully and those voices were no longer distant as before, but were very near. They were so clear and evident that sometimes I covered my ears with my hands to avoid hearing them, because I did not wish in any way to consent to them. But it was useless, because I constantly heard them, as they spoke to my soul and not to my body. Therefore every time I went to prayer, it seemed to me as if I were going to war. And it truly was, for is there any greater battle than this?

But this never caused me to avoid going to prayer as I was accustomed to. But once when the benign Spirit of God forced me more powerfully, and I resisted with equal strength, he threatened me saying, "Do what you wish, give yourself to the world, you will never get any good from it." Think, my dear father, how this pained me. And I thought and kept on reflecting, but by no means would I persuade myself or consent to becoming a nun.

While persevering in prayer, one Friday if I'm not mistaken, a strong conflict came to me during prayer. It was a battle in my soul between yes and no. As a result of the great agony, my entire body began perspiring. In the end, my will – which has always been strong and sound – in that moment spontaneously and freely sat like a judge on the bench in court to judge the cruel struggle. It uttered its sentence against me. With much love and courage I decided to serve God so fervently that, if for this it would have been necessary to suffer martyrdom, I would have chosen it right away, rather than repent of my decision.

In that moment the inspiration to become a nun in the monastery of Urbino was infused inside me; never would I have wanted to go elsewhere.[112] As it is a great comfort to an afflicted and martyred body to be laid on a soft bed full of flowers and roses, so my resolution gave rest to my martyred soul. Then I remained in a deep peace, very calm, serene, rested, and happy.

O my God, I beg you, guard me and be near to me, because hereafter I shall say nothing but angelic and divine things. My sweet Lord, give me the grace, that with this rotten mouth and poisoned tongue of mine I shall be able to relate and show, to my confusion and shame, the wonderful graces you granted to me – a sinner. So that you, my father, may tell me not once but a thousand times, "These things are very good for you, my daughter, this and every trouble you have. "What more could God do to you that he hasn't already done?"[113] And that is the truth.

After the Great Decision

Now that I had united myself to the divine will through my resolution [to enter the monastery], in a short time the floodgates of Heaven opened above me and the flood of the abyssal divine mercies totally filled my sinful soul. Then God, benign Father, embraced his prodigal child, and he received her sweetly in his paternal arms embracing her benignly. Then with his mouth, he gave her the sweet kiss of his holy peace, not just once or twice, but many times.

O heart of stone, why don't you break? What are you doing? Why do you still delay? It seemed that God, most high and true good, could not get enough of embracing my unworthy and adulterous sinful soul in his most holy and sweet arms. It is quite true what I say, even if many times out of holy humility, I fled and humbly prayed to him that he would leave my soul alone, and he would free it from his holy arms. In fact, sometimes I stopped praying. But it did little good to flee or pray, because he would not leave me until his clement Majesty liked. And sometimes it would take much time for my soul to recover after finishing prayer.

I will not write here of the sweetest, most loving words full of heavenly food and honey, full of exultation, cheerfulness and joy, that could soften and make a heart of stone fall in love. For as the prophet says, "In my heart I treasure your promise, that I may not sin against you."[114] But truly and surely I could repeat those words of the Canticle, "My soul failed at this flight,"[115] and the words of the prophet, "How sweet to my tongue is your promise, sweeter than honey to my mouth!",[116] and that one, "Your servant loves your promise; it has been proved by fire."[117]

In those moments, I no longer remembered the fear I previously had of him, nor did I remind him of any sin that I had committed. I truly understood from his words and by experience that in myself those words of the prophet had been fulfilled, "None of the crimes he committed shall be remembered against him."[118] Thus I submerged myself and went down totally into divine love.

Jesus Showed Himself as Father, Friend, Spouse

Thus I learned on my own, "The fear of the Lord is the beginning of wisdom; prudent are all who live by it."[119] As the fear is great, so is the delight of love that follows. And since the reverence that I had for God was great and without measure, so too was love's sweetness great and unmeasured. Then I loosened the rein on love which my heart with great energy had mightily restrained for years because of concerns for worldly honors and caution. I let it go wildly and furiously, and cast it all on my sweetest and most blessed Bridegroom, Jesus. I called him that because that is how he showed and proved himself in my soul. Sometimes he was like a most benign Father; sometimes he showed himself in the most familiar and practical terms that he seemed like a very dear friend and companion; but mostly he was as the sweetest Spouse.

When God shows himself in the form of a Spouse to a pilgrim soul, I believe – by the little experience I had – that this is the sweetest way that God can communicate or give himself in this earthly life. If that sweetest joy had lasted long, I would never have desired to die, because it seemed to me that I was already enjoying everlasting life and heaven in this world. And I do not believe there is any difference between Heaven and this delight, except what there is between the full payment and an advance deposit. Whereas one is sure and lasts forever, it is certain that the other could be lost and forfeited. But alas, the difference to which I am referring is not little, but infinite.

Therefore I saw myself so enormously loved at the depths of my core and I knew with certainty that in me there was nothing but iniquity and sin, because when one finds Jesus Christ, the Sun of justice, then it is possible to see oneself with clarity. I marveled greatly and felt amazed. Therefore one day I told him with great humility, "O Lord, I know that the demons dare blaspheme you, but now I believe that they will more greatly dare to call you a lover of iniquity." I beg you, my Jesus, do not let yourself be called thus on account of my love. For I am nothing other than deep iniquity and you take such great delight in me that what else can they call you except a lover of iniquity? Then my sweet God kindly responded, "You should know, my dear daughter, that I am not at all a lover of iniquity and I do not take delight in that. On the contrary I delight in the innocence, in which you were born and which is still yours." I was ignorant of spiritual expressions and I did not understand what this innocence meant.

But when I became a nun at Urbino, I found some words in a book referring to a soul to whom God had granted a certain grace. I asked, "What does it mean, 'I restore you to your original innocence?'" And those true servants of God explained to me what the phrase meant, "I forgive you your sins including both guilt and punishment." Then I realized that all my sins had been forgiven. Until then I had thought that this innocence was a beautiful gift given to the soul, but I didn't know of what it consisted. And blessed Christ added, "Actually, I take delight in myself and not in you, because I myself have placed this innocence into your soul; it is mine, not yours. I rejoice and love myself, not you." And here he thoroughly let me know that he did not love nor delight in anything but in himself in Heaven and earth – by putting his love in people. Because nothing outside of him and without him is lovable or pleasing either in Heaven or on earth. Thus he set me free from my pride and vanity.

O my father, this is such a topic that the more I say, the more I would have to say. And even if I ever spoke such a lot, I would have said nothing. It is enough that you clearly understand in what peace and tranquility, in what sweetness and love, in what confidence and awareness I found myself in that holy spiritual jubilee. In fact, I often found myself in divine conversations in the sweet arms of the celestial Spouse, in the love and awareness of the benign eternal Father, in the grace and consolation of the Holy Spirit.

O most gracious weather, serene and soave, how you have become stormy, dark, and tenebrous. O incomprehensible peace who passed over every reasonable aspect, how you have been transformed into deadly war. O indescribable sweetness, how you have changed into gall and vinegar! O love, how you rip out my soul, you have changed into such cruel hatred! O friendship, O unimaginable familiarity, how you have changed into discord and enmity! O sweetest arms, how you have let me fall from such a sublime height into the depths of Hell! Alas! It was a terrible fall! It's no wonder that you broke all your bones, my poor soul.

Now weep, now sigh and say, "Bitterly she weeps at night, tears upon her cheeks, with not one to console her of all her dear ones."[120] "All my intimate friends hold me in horror; those whom I loved have turned against me!"[121] "O, that my head were a spring of water, my eyes a fountain of tears, that I might weep day and night over the slain of the daughter of my people!"[122] "The garlands have fallen from our heads."[123] "My eyes shed streams of tears because your teaching is not followed."[124] Let Heaven and earth weep for me; let all reasonable creatures join in my sorrow. Weep, my dearest father, if you haven't a heart of stone, for your inconsolable daughter. "Look and see whether there is any suffering like my suffering."[125]

This has been and is still that hidden wound which broke my heart long ago. Now I show it to you, I reveal it to you, as I can no longer conceal it; I can no longer cover it. Aid it, if you can, otherwise, treat it with compassion, which will relieve me a little. I can no longer bear it, I can no longer suffer this wound. The pain is wearing me to the bone. I am as one inebriated from sorrow and bitterness, and I am almost uncontrollable. I do not know what to say and what to do, so if I err with some word, forgive me, because it is written, "To the measure of her boasting and wantonness repay her in torment and grief."[126]

The Gift of the Three Lilies

Now let us return to the story already begun. As promised, I shall recount in all truth and simplicity, as I have done so far, the order of my spiritual life – how it developed until the time of my tribulation. By the grace of God, "he who is a flower of Sharon, a lily of the valley"[127] and "who browses among the lilies"[128] left me three fragrant spring lilies[129] in order to give me a sure sign that he himself had been working in my soul.

The first lily was this: a hatred so deep for the world so that if anyone had asked me, "What do you prefer: either to stay in the world and become Empress of the entire world with assurance of your salvation, or to enter into religion[130] with the risk of being damned?", truly, my father, without hesitating I would have chosen at once to enter religion even with the risk of being damned, rather than stay in the world with all its seductions and glories, even with the assurance of being saved. And all this is owed to the deep hatred I felt for the world. But it no longer seem to me the world, but what it really is – a kind of temporary hell and an anticipation of the eternal Hell. And it really is so, even if there are those who do not believe this. [131]

The second lily was this: a whole-hearted humility because I confessed and sincerely believed with all my heart that there was no worse sinner than I on the earth. And I believed that the greatest mercy God could show me was to save my soul, while the greatest justice that he could administer would be to send me to Hell. And inasmuch as God awarded me his gifts and graces, I considered myself depraved all the more. He always granted me the grace to consider all his gifts debts and not merits. And in fact, it really is so; he – the most lovable Truth – taught me so.

The third lily was this: a burning desire to "suffer badly."[132] This desire was so strong that even if he had offered me heaven without suffering, I would not have wanted it. Thus, I prayed to God and told him with sweet affection, "If the great love that you showed me and continue to show me is true and not a joke, give me this true sign: that I might wear that same vestment which your beloved Son wore; that is, to suffer badly in this world." He announced and promised me so much, that it already satisfied me four times over. Soon after, I became ill with a sickness from which I never healed and have had now for thirteen years.[133] But I bore it so willingly that perhaps it will not even seem believable. However, for a year now it seems I can no longer bear it, while before I was very happy. But in this I do not glory in myself but in the Lord, "my soul, be at rest in God alone, from whom comes my hope."[134] And while I was like another Job afflicted in my body by a cruel and mortal disease, I sang psalms and thanked God in my heart.

After seven months during which I was in danger of death, I got up from bed. Father Gregorio[135] (whom I've heard died) taught and directed me to meditate on Christ's life by reciting beads of the Virgin Mary. This took me three hours. The sweetness and consolations I received in that prayer were so many, that I did not know how to stop, nor was I able to. Everything was honey, sugar, and sweet and tasty manna to my mouth. Everything I meditated on did not seem to me to have already happened, but was as if I was physically present to the words and maternal gestures of the glorious Virgin Mary and the child Jesus. It was as if I were accompanying them on their tiring journeys. But while contemplating the Transfiguration of Jesus, such high and great gifts were promised me, that now I cannot even hear the word "Transfiguration" mentioned without rejoicing in my heart.

And following the words of the prophet, "Taste and see"[136] after having tasted Jesus, a desire so great came to me to see him, that all my prayer was nothing other than a continual longing to behold his most serene and loving face. And all the plants, flowers and roses seemed to recall his beauty; and when I saw the starry sky my heart would burn within, saying, "The heavens declare the glory of God; the sky proclaims its builder's handiwork."[137]

O my sweet Jesus, if the works of your hands are so beautiful what will it be like to behold your splendid face? Show yourself to me, let yourself be seen, my good Lord! Why do you let me yearn so? You alone are all my life, my only hope, and all the love of my heart and soul. Why do you hide your most holy face? And [I said] other similar words. Then I no longer fled from him, but eagerly ran after him, "Your name spoken is a spreading perfume."[138] I told him, "More delightful is your love than wine,"[139] and "how much more delightful is the fragrance of your ointments than all spices,"[140] and "Let him kiss me with kisses of his mouth."[141]

Therefore, after having let me suffer six months because of this desire, he pleased me in the following way. I asked to see his glorious face, but he turned his back on me. Therefore I said jokingly, "This Jesus Christ turns everything backwards!" But if my wish were truly granted "backwards," that time I was truly satisfied "right-wards," because I was left feeling satisfied and very happy. Hear now how he showed himself to me.

One day while I was praying, I clearly felt that he was in my soul. Before leaving me, however, he said, "If you wish to see me, look at me." And as when a person turns his back and distances himself from another, going his own way, thus he did in my soul. When I began to see him, he was already far from me – more than six paces away, and he was walking ahead across a large hall. At the end of this hall there was a very small door, similar to the door to a room. I continued to watch him until he bent his head (for he was very tall) and entered that little door. Then I no longer saw him, the room, or the door.

Thus I saw him from behind, not facing me. He wore a dazzling white garment – such a whiteness that cannot be seen in this world – reaching the ground. It was hemmed at the bottom with a border a thumb high with golden letters, which I could not read because they were too far off. And though he was walking fairly slowly, he did not stop. His slender waste was tied with a belt, which was solid gold and two thumbs high. He was a head taller than other men. His hair was rather tightly curled and was long and seemed golden, reaching almost to his belt. I could not see all of his head to discern if he wore a crown, a diadem, or a wreath of flowers and roses; he did not want me to see this. I think he wore something on his head so beautiful that I didn't deserve to see. But it was so beautiful to see his full blonde hair on his wide, well-proportioned shoulders, creating a striking likeness to shade on white vestments. It was all quite wonderful!

During those two and a half years in which I still remained in the world with resignation, I received many favors and gifts from God, which I will not recount here. In fact, it is better to say less than more, or to say too much of something little – doing so makes me feel more at ease. But you must know, my dear father, that during that period I came to know all my afflictions and future tribulations, as you will soon clearly see, in order that I might be prudent and patient. Poor unhappy me, I was neither one nor the other, but I behaved like a wild sheep. Therefore I can't help complaining and saying, "All you who pass by the way, look and see whether there is any suffering like my suffering."[142] "Those accustomed to dainty food perish in the streets; those brought up in purple now cling to the ash heaps."[143]

Entrance in the Monastery at Urbino

Then came the fullness of time, for "there is an appointed time for everything"[144] in which I was afflicted and tested to see whether or not I was [made of] gold or lead. I suffered disease, temptation, threats and prison, but with the help of God in everything, I answered it all in the proper manner, by refusing pleasures and joyfully embracing diseases and threats. In accordance with his promise, God willed to completely set me free from the worldly slavery of Egypt and from the hands of powerful Pharaoh. For those two and a half years his heart was hardened, and he said with his own mouth that if he hadn't feared God's punishment, he would never have permitted me to enter a monastery. [145]

Having thus plundered Egypt, full and rich with treasures and spiritual graces, with dry feet – that is, without any weariness and regret – I crossed the Red Sea. I mean to say that I left the vanity of worldly pomp and the comforts of the courtly life. Such [worldly] things seem red in color; that is, beautiful to look at like the color red, but in fact they are not beautiful at all, because they are nothing but smoke and kindling wood that does not last long.

And looking back at the Sea, I saw Pharaoh submerged with his entire army in that Sea; that is, the devil with all his snares, vices and sins. And I was thus placed in the desert of holy religion [consecrated life], in the sacred monastery of Urbino, and it was precisely you, my father, who were present as a witness. I was truly so happy when I saw myself leave the world free of its snares, such that I could have sung with the prophetess Miriam, "Sing to the Lord, for he is gloriously triumphant; horse and chariot he has cast into the sea."[146] It is possible that others could leave the world with as much heart and fervor as I did by the grace of God; and they could possibly do so with even more [fervor] than me, but I don't think so.

Do not be scandalized that in some ways I have claimed for myself the image and dignity of the chosen Jewish people – so full of so many benefits and divine gifts; it's just that I cannot come up with a better comparison to myself to describe the innumerable benefits I received from God – all the more considering my immense hardness and ingratitude.

The Vision of The Name of The Heart of Jesus and Other Graces

Until now I have told the story of my spiritual life when I was a lay person, in which I tasted just a spark of divine love, which I sought through the intercession and merits of the glorious Virgin Mary. It was truly just a spark when compared to the essential fire of love that exists in everlasting life. Just the same it was so much that I could no longer bear it, nor contain it any more, and neither did I want it anymore. Over and over I said, "No more, my God, no more!"

Now I will recount what took place after I took the Poor Clare habit. As [in the plains of the world one finds the song of the birds, the splendor of flowers, the secret refuges of animals], as Ubertino of Casale said,[147] so in the holy monastery of Urbino I found the sweetest songs of holy prayers, the beauty of good examples, the secret treasures of divine graces, and of heavenly gifts. And as I was moved and urged by the Holy Spirit, I felt the holy desire to enter into the "interior of the desert";[148] that is, the very secret sorrows of Jesus's Heart. Then with all my heart I refused every sweetness of divine manna, not out of rejection, like that chosen, ungrateful Jewish people, but out of holy humility. For I considered myself most unworthy of that gift, which for me would have become more a debt than a merit. With an upright and pure heart I prayed to God that he would feed, satisfy, and fill me with only the most bitter, poisoned foods of his Passion, because my soul hungered and thirsted only for those. I longed for, searched for, and ardently desired only those things and nothing else, in harmony with the beloved Spouse of the Canticle, "my beloved is a sachet of myrrh lying between my breasts."[149] Then I resolved to spend all my prayer time meditating on Christ's Passion; and I no longer wished to meditate on or think of anything else. I concentrated all my soul's energy on entering into the most bitter ocean of the spiritual agony of Jesus's Heart, in which I would have desired to drown, were it possible.

It is no wonder that I had the desire to enter inside your heart, O good Jesus, because when I was still in the world you showed me that my name had been written in golden letters on [your heart]. Oh, how beautiful were those large golden letters written in ancient script on your vermilion heart: *Ego te dìligo Camillam* [I love you, Camilla].[150] And you showed me all this, O good Jesus, because I marveled that you loved me so immensely. Then apologizing, you said that you could not do otherwise, because you were carrying my name written in your heart and, raising your glorious arm, you let me read the above words. O my poor soul, why can't you derive a little comfort in remembering the great love and affection of your beloved Christ? But I know you will say it is not possible, because all these recollections are not consolations to me, but stinging arrows that pierce through my heart. Therefore I can't help saying, "Come, all you who pass by the way, look and see whether there is any suffering like my suffering?"[151]

Now returning to my story, I continued in such desire and prayer for those two years and maybe six months, in which I remained in Urbino. Then I returned to Camerino. During that time, by the wonderful grace of the Holy Spirit, I was introduced to the most secret nuptial-bed of the Heart of Jesus, true and only ocean, most bitter and poisonous, unfathomable to every human or angelic intellect.[152] Many times I would have sunk and drowned in that ocean, if the mighty hand of God had not helped me, because I would have been able to stand much less such bitterness than the sweetness of his divine love. Then I said, "No more, no more, my Lord, I cannot bear it any longer. I am drowning, because this love has neither end nor bottom!"

Then he seemed no longer a paradise to me, but his whole being seemed a cruel hell. I say this because many times out of holy simplicity and compassion, I called him "Hell," and didn't give him any other name, as I couldn't find any other name so suitable. I will say no more about this here, because I will tell it elsewhere. However, I do not wish to omit this: although I was shown only as much of Jesus's mental sorrows as I could bear, and, by the grace of the Holy Spirit, as much as my soul was capable [of bearing]; still, when facing the reality of them, I understood them only as much as a grain of sand would be when compared to the sky or the entire earth and, on the contrary, much less, if it were possible at all to understand them.

During the two years I was in that blessed monastery of Urbino, through the divine influence of the Sun of justice, my soul was flowering and blooming marvelously in holy desires pleasing to God and I could truly say that "flowers appear on the earth."[153] But more than any other flower, one in particular branched out and flowered with such sweet perfume – that spring lily that had already been planted at the beginning of my conversion in the sterile soil of my soul; that is, the burning desire to suffer badly. In that holy time, this lily, more than all the others, was blessed, ploughed, and weeded by the royal hand of the true King Ahasuerus,[154] blessed Christ Jesus, and irrigated, sprinkled and soaked with the waters of his spiritual sufferings.

Even though in those years I was frequently very near death, I often begged God saying, "O my Lord, when will you lead me to those rich pastures, to those pleasant gardens of suffering badly, where your chosen beloved sheep graze? O my Lord, you delay too long in giving me what you promptly and generously promised. My Lord, I can no longer be patient because of my many sins. Do not regret giving me what you promised. Do not deprive me, my Lord, of such a great gift."

Then followed the great distress of my bitter religious profession which greatly troubled the Franciscan Order and also the world – friars and nuns, nobles and laymen.[155] Here, out of prudence, I will not write what happened, for I do not wish for others to suppose that I am telling it with some other personal aim in mind. However, I do not wish to be silent on this: it is true that there was some disturbance because of my profession on earth, but be sure, my most beloved father, that there was a great feast and joy in Heaven among the angels. I do not say this out of conjecture; because I knew with certainty that it was so in Heaven. Not that I believe that such a feast was on account of me, rather I am sure that it happened for the future good of this blessed monastery of Camerino that would rise up after my profession and for the glorious and angelic rank of virgins, snatched from the world, who would live there. Therefore it was right and just that the devil caused disturbance on earth, while the angels rejoiced in Heaven.

And note this: in that same year of my tribulation, by divine will you were elected provincial minister [of the Observants] for the first and last time. Most wise God willed by his goodness and grace that as you had been the cause and beginning of my salvation, so you were present in the middle and at the end; that is, in the middle of my tribulations and trials and at the end of what I have been doing from September until today. It was fitting that you, and no one else, were the provincial minister in that period, so that the one who from the beginning had been the cause of such great good should participate in that great disturbance among the friars and nuns, lords and noblewomen.

Now it is certain and quite clear that, as you were not outside of those troubles and tribulations, so God willed that you should also take part in all the good that has been and shall ever be done in this sacred monastery of Camerino. And although as provincial you tried hard to prevent it from being founded, God chose precisely you – willing or unwilling – with your authority and presence to accompany us here by giving the beginnings of life to this sacred monastery. Stay away from Camerino if you like, but nowhere else in the world have you obtained such good fruits and done such good as here in Camerino. It is actually the devil, knowing the spite you have done him here, who persuades you to hate this town and want to escape it. I tell you these few words with filial sincerity. [156]

After I was transferred to this monastery together with the other reverend mothers, through the authority granted to you by the pope, I was not unaware, but was rather fully conscious that his divine Majesty was pleased that I return here, in order that I should have greater serenity and consolation. And God wished to give me another clearer, more noble sign, and it was this: it was not the first Friday, but if I remember correctly, it was the second after we had entered this monastery. Sister Costanza, whom you know, was spinning by the fireplace and I was sewing. She began to sing that Laud[157] that says, *Anima benedetta, dal alto Creatore* [O blessed soul of the highest Creator…] and I began to sing with her. When we came to those words that say, "*Resguarda quelle mane... resguarda quelli pei... resguarda quello lato…* [Look at those hands… look at those feet… look at that side…], I could no longer bear it, and I fainted and fell into the arms of the nun who was near me. The nuns thought it was just a physical ailment, because they were accustomed to my fainting-fits. But this time it was spiritual, because at that moment my soul was enraptured in the contemplation of the mystery of Jesus taken down from the cross into the sad, maternal arms of his afflicted Mother. I was taken [spiritually to the scene], and I heard the sweet and sorrowful sob of the grieved Mother; I heard the loving disciple, the Magdalene, shout loudly in a heartfelt voice, "My Master!"; I heard the beloved disciple, John, weeping bitterly and groaning quietly, "My Father, Brother, Master!"; and likewise I heard the laments of the other devout women.

I remained in such a state from just before Compline till the first hour at night,[158] and I would have remained like that the entire night, had I not made a great effort to recover my senses, such that I would not be a burden to my sisters. In fact, while I was in that state, sometimes I heard the nuns quite well, other times very little. But when the glorious Virgin's voice became louder, I heard nothing at all of this entire world. And then it seemed to me that my soul was almost separated from my body, while my eyes shed tears when I heard what was said and done around me.

When I recovered my senses, I felt so tired and afflicted that for fifteen days it seemed as if my body had risen from the tomb, so changed was I and my face transfigured. Before that happened, I thought little or nothing of the mystery of Jesus taken down from the cross – when the Virgin Mary kept her beloved dead Son in her arms, but instead I usually meditated on Jesus's crucifixion or his agony in the Garden of Gethsemane; these had attracted me more than all the rest. But since then I have always been devoted to the mystery of Jesus taken down from the cross.

That episode left its mark on me; for more than two years, I could not bear to look at a crucifix, nor could I stand to see ladders, hammers, nails or pliers; in fact, I cannot remember having seen those things at all during that period. This was the sign that God gave me to let me know that my return to Camerino pleased him. But now I say: "Come, all you who pass by the way, look and see whether there is any suffering like my suffering?"[159]

Remorse for Not Having Confessed to Blessed Peter of Mogliano

As the Hebrews were baptized in water and fire, according to the apostle,[160] so my soul was baptized first in the waters of tears of repentance and devotion, then in the divine seraphic fire. Now hear how God wished to baptize and purify my soul from its faults, in the tribulations mentioned above, in order to give me new gifts and favors. The year of my tribulation, during which I was bitterly afflicted, ended. God disposed this for my merit and crown for no other reason but because, as I have said, he wanted this monastery to be founded under the name and Rule of the Poor Sisters of Saint Clare, as it currently is. [161]

Then by the grace of God, our pastor and provincial minister, Father Peter of Mogliano, was elected – that glorious and holy soul – truly blessed by the miracles he worked while alive and continues to work after death. Upon coming to our monastery, after completing several tasks, he told me in the presence of several other nuns, "Sister Battista, prepare yourself, I wish to hear your confession before I leave." I answered promptly, "No, no, I do not need to confess." He replied, "I feel an inspiration and I wish to hear your confession. I feel that you should." And since I kept on saying no, he sent the other sisters away and repeated, "Come here. I feel this inspiration. Why do you not wish to confess?" I responded, "Because I do not want to; I do not feel I need it." He seemed a little displeased and said with a sigh, "I do not like this response; think better of it." And he departed.

O my father, he was very kind with me, though I acted like a donkey! Perhaps just a day passed after he had departed Camerino that my heart was already in anguish. I said within myself, "What an obstinate and ignorant donkey I was to answer Father Provincial in that way. I wish to truly confess to him as soon as he returns." So I wrote him begging him to forgive my gross blunder. In a few days this desire to confess to him grew so much that I could no longer find peace. So many things I had never formerly confessed (owing to my broad conscience) were now made evident to me, that I couldn't do anything but plead to him by letter to return. But like a wise old fox, he delayed in order to increase my determination, as he told me afterwards. His delay lasted from the provincial chapter meeting to the feast of the sacred Stigmata of Saint Francis.[162]

Meanwhile, by the grace of God I was given such great sorrow and contrition for my sins that I wept bitterly for both those confessed as well as those not yet confessed. I suffered immensely for having offended the infinite divine Goodness and I felt such a great hatred for myself that I wished with all my heart that, after my confession, Father Provincial would feel a deep hatred and detestation also for me. And as I desired to be detested, God promised me that I should, instead, have love. And so it happened.

Having made my general confession with great honesty, illumination, and contempt for myself, he was so satisfied and pleased that from that point on he always loved me with a holy spiritual love, more than any spiritual daughter that he ever had in the world; and I am certain of this. After that confession, I was left more pleased and happier than he, and my soul was at peace.

The Apparition of Saint Clare

A few days later, a nun of our Order appeared in my soul, not only during prayer, but almost continually.[163] She was very beautiful and was dressed just like one of us with a black veil on her head. I saw her as clearly as I had ever seen anything plainly with my own eyes. I enjoyed seeing her more with the eyes of my soul than if I had seen her with the eyes of my body. I rejoiced and felt much love at her beautiful and joyful face. I felt a great joy in both seeing her and feeling so loved. But I was surprised and I wondered why I did not recognize her. However, she seemed to delight in my bewilderment, as if to say, "Do you not recognize me?"

When she appeared to me interiorly, my soul instinctively threw itself on its knees before her, although my body was seated at table, or by the fire, or by the grill. But she gently wished me to rise. However, I did not want to because I felt that her reverent appearance deserved that I remain kneeling before her. She seemed to emit rays from her eyes, they were so beautiful; indeed, all of her was beautiful. I did not know why I celebrated and felt so joyful at her presence, nor why she was so kind and gracious.

The vision lasted a long time, around fifteen days without exaggerating. She seemed to be around forty years old. Then she disappeared and I never saw her again – neither before nor after. During those days I never had the slightest idea that she was Saint Clare, our glorious mother and standard-bearer, because I had the desire to see her not in this world, but in the next.

But hear, my father, what this little sheep of yours was thinking. Out of principle I was always against nuns from other monasteries [transferring and] being received here. I thought she was a nun from some other monastery whom God wished to transfer here, and for that reason he showed her to me so that I would not be against her, but would be receptive and favorable. So I said in my heart, "Who could ever be sad or discontent should this nun come to our monastery? Her presence alone will make us all happy."

After she vanished from my mind, I was left with such great love and devotion toward our glorious mother Saint Clare, that I had no doubt that the nun was her. And if by the blood of Christ I shall ever go to Heaven, I would recognize her among a thousand thousands and I shall embrace her and tell her, “My sweetest mother, you were the one who visited me in the world.”

Alas! What was I then and what am I now? Therefore I say again, “Come, all you who pass by the way, look and see whether there is any suffering like my suffering?”[164]

Two Angels Hold Camilla Battista’s Soul at the Foot of the Cross

“Wonderful are your decrees; therefore I observe them.”165 Under the firmament there are no clearer or truer witnesses than God’s. And to you, father, who search for him so sincerely, I know they are much appreciated. For this, O Lord God, I will not refrain from singing of your praise to my old devoted father, but I shall give an account of it to your glory and to my confusion, not to unbelievers and foolish men, but to you, because I know that he who has been tried believes. And I beseech and beg you, angels, about whom I must say a few things, to help me so that I may truthfully recount the generosity and kindness you showed my ungrateful soul.

A few days after our glorious mother, Saint Clare, vanished from my soul, two golden winged angels came to me wearing the same dazzling white garments as the one I had seen blessed Christ wearing. One of them seized my soul from the right side, and the other from the left. They carried me up and placed me at the sweet crucified feet of the human Son of God. And they kept me there almost continually for more than two months, so that I seemed to walk, speak and do what I wished without a soul. My soul was there where those two angels kept it, and they never left it. I do not remember if I had ever previously had a desire to stay continually at the feet of Christ.

After this time passed, they let my soul return to my body as before, but I remained with such great love and devotion towards the seraphim that I did not desire to think or speak about anything else but the seraphim. And I always begged them with sweet affection that one of them would visit me, as he had the prophet Isaiah. After having prayed to them for many days, and with no one coming, one morning before the first hour prayer,[166] I turned to plead to the sweet Mother of God. With holy impatience I said to her, “My sweetest Mother, most benign Queen, I know you are Empress of the angels and all obey you as their true Lady and Mistress. I beseech you, my sweet Madonna, that you command a seraph to visit me, as he visited the prophet Isaiah. You know, my Lady, how much I long for it."

And without begging too much, she gladly promised to send me one. I was so delighted at this promise that my heart exulted. After a few days passed, one night after morning lauds I began to pray. I felt a strong desire to meditate on the love of God for his creation. This wasn't my usual meditation, nonetheless I let my mind go where God led it and I began to think of ordinary things that mattered little. But suddenly I was indescribably drawn to exalted and sublime thoughts and I entered such a deep and profound ocean that I would have turned back more than twice if I could have. They weren't words or visions, but rather an interior illumination that I cannot explain with words. But for your consolation, beloved father, I will say a few things. These things cannot be easily spoken of, but rather contemplated by the grace of God.

First of all, I saw that if another god was similar in every way to our most benign and clement God and did all things out of love, as our God did for us, two things would still remain indebted and could never be repaid. The first is this: the act of love, by which he loved us first, not us him, will always remain a debt that one can never repay. The second is that another god might suffer for a god like himself, equal in everything to his infinity; but our God has suffered for us, most vile nauseating worms, for our sins; this, too, remains a debt that cannot be paid.

The second thing: I saw that every love that we could offer God is nothing but the worst hate; any praise of ours is unpraiseworthy;[167] and all our thanks, compared with what is owed our holy God, is blasphemy.

The third thing: I saw with certainty and clarity that the glorious Mother of God, together with all the angels and human beings, are not sufficient to thank divine charity for the creation of the smallest flower that exists on earth created by God for our usefulness, considering his infinite excellence and greatness and our immense nothingness and insignificance.[168] Now, my father, think how humbly I regarded myself when I considered all the benefits and graces I had received from God, much more than flowers and plants! Then truly I lost all trust in myself and in all my good deeds. Then I refused with all my heart all God's gifts in order not to add debts on top of debts and ungratefulness to ungratefulness, such that if Christ should have appeared to me, I would have closed my eyes in order not to see him.

Then, with my head bent to the ground, I asked the grace of his divine Majesty to place me perpetually and continuously at the most clement feet of his crucified Son, and that the time I stayed there should be imputed to blasphemy and fornication, because I was sure that I would have committed these and every possible evil had his merciful hand not held me. Further, I asked that after my death he would send me where I would most honor him; and though it might be to Hell I would have been quite happy, because I wished only that his will be fulfilled in and through me. In this were all happiness, reward and my glory. I saw his immense love as the ocean so profound and exceeding all bounds which God bears to his created [people]. When I recovered my senses, I could not contain myself, and I kept saying, "O madness, O madness!" No word seemed any longer true or appropriate for such great love.

Then I was conceded those most gracious feet, which for five years I possessed with so much continual contemplation of them and with so much peace that surely, if I were to speak to you of it, O my father, it would seem hard to believe. Now I am deprived of them and have become like a widow; now I am stripped of such a rich vestment, now I am deprived of the treasure of my heart. O crucified feet, O only hope of my soul, how is it possible to live without you, that were the life, heart, and treasure of my soul? O my Jesus, give them back to me, and then send me to Hell and I shall be happy! Then in that hour I am sure I shall weep, embrace, and kiss those very holy wounds so much, that my heart will burst and be consumed in my miserable body.

O feet, through which it pleased me to touch, embrace and kiss all feet! O sweetest feet! How you have embittered the sweet experiences I spent over you, that is all my devout tears full of love and devotion! O merciful feet! I never thought this spot would be forbidden or taken away, since it was not even denied to adulterers or prostitutes! Alas! And a thousand times alas! I am so much unhappier, much more miserable than all other sinners! O most clement feet! If it was not for my fear of tiring those who are listening to me I would spend all this Friday weeping and sighing, as I am doing now.

Do not be surprised at this, my father, because, as gold shines more brightly than all other metals, this affliction oppresses and torments me above all others. I think it is because I possessed this grace longer than others. Therefore "my harp is turned to mourning."[169]

Why Camilla Battista Cannot Yet Leave this Life

Those most lovable and sweet feet made me lose my train of thought, but by the grace of God, I will continue and finish the garment which, only by his grace and inspiration, I began to sew and weave. When the light I just spoke of disappeared, a blaze so great remained in my soul, that I dare say with utmost truth that my soul was strongly enflamed and scorched by this ardent spiritual blaze, as every material thing is enflamed and scorched in earthly fire. That blaze lasted, if I remember well, more than three months. Such a fire was a desire to leave the prison of this body to be with Christ. And this desire was so great that perhaps you won't believe me, but God knows that I tell the truth: it was such a violent, burning desire that to be in my body made me feel the pains of Hell. On the contrary, the pains of Hell seemed to me a relief compared to what I was feeling. Never again would I like to experience it, except when about to die. For should I die with that longing, death would no longer be death, but going to a wedding *pulsantibus organis* [accompanied by organ music].[170] Then I could say most sincerely with the Apostle, "I long to depart this life and be with Christ";[171] and with the prophet David, "Lead me out of my prison, that I may give thanks to your name. Then the just shall gather around me because you have been good to me."[172]

Then I clearly knew that it was one of the seraphim that had visited my soul, according to the promise made to me by the sweet Mother of God, their sweetest Empress and mine. Violently afflicted in my soul and body by this burning desire, I wept and sobbed bitterly and begged God to free me from the misery of my body and of the world. Thus one ordinary day while praying and weeping loudly and begging God for this, it seemed to me that blessed Christ showed me a great compassion and held my soul to his most sacred Heart with his arm, telling me over and over, "Don't cry so much!" And with the other hand he dried the eyes of my soul, because those tears were spiritual, not from my body, though I also wept very much corporally.

Nonetheless, those sweet words of blessed Christ did not dry the eyes of my soul; on the contrary, everything liquefied into tears and still more and more I begged him to set me free from this corporal prison. In the end he said, "I cannot, not yet." And he showed me in different ways that his powerful hands were bound and tied. Then he said, "These are the prayers that the nuns and friars are offering up for you so that you may not die. Have patience!"

I do not remember whether what I am going to say now happened before or after what I said above. Once, while feeling so much spiritual fire that I could hardly bear, I foolishly turned to lament to the seraphim. Nearly repented of having begged them to visit me, I said to them, "O sweetest spirits, I have long been praying that one of you would visit me, because I believed that those to whom you came would have paradise, because you are so close to God. How is it then that after you came to me I now suffer the pains of Hell? I do not understand how your nearness to God can be a benefit."

Then in a sweet and familiar way they spoke to me as if to a dear family member or friend and said, "What gives you pain, gives us pleasure. You have a burning desire within, but because you are living in your body, you lack the presence and fullness of him who is present to us; that is why you feel a great pain in proportion to the desire you feel. But we have the burning desire completely united with the real presence of him whom we desire. Therefore our delight is great, in proportion to the greatness of our incomprehensible longing." They declared that they were so intimate with God that he never stayed, nor could stay without them, nor they without God. They said that they – the seraphim – were also in such harmony with the cherubim (and the cherubim to them) that one could never visit a soul without the other. And they said, "It is true that cherubim have the greater influence in some souls, while seraphim in others; but in your soul we seraphim have pre-eminence. Therefore you have more fire than light."[173]

And so it was the truth! Though that illumination I had received, as I said above, was great and incomprehensible, yet I had received three times more fire than light. Now I clearly understand that the two angels, who held me so long at the feet of the cross, were a cherub and a seraph. This is the fire by which I said I had been baptized and purified through the sincere general confession I made to my holy Father Peter of Mogliano, now in glory.

Decision to Transform Every Day to Good Friday. Christ Orders Her to Write 'Mental Sorrows'

"Behold the bread of angels, truly the bread of children."[174] I say this because after the visitation of the two angels, I had a great hunger for the sacrament of communion that could not be quenched. For almost two continual years I received communion every Sunday. But my longing was to receive communion every day, if that had been possible.[175] And when I thought of staying without it more than eight days, I felt I would pass out, so great was my sorrow.

For three years[176] before my tribulation began, I felt as if I were in a sabbatical year – my spirit was filled with angelic peace. Then all the ways to Sion; that is, to holy Heaven, were freed up, peaceful, and traversable for me and I ran along them without any obstruction. I owed all this to my holy desire and devout prayer. Then, truly my father, I had (or I thought I had) a heart more angelic than human, more heavenly than earthly. I do not think I ever had any other presumption than this: if anyone then had told me, "You will arrive at this situation," that is, at the point I had reached and which you now know, I would never have thought it possible. It is true that I had this presumption and vanity in my heart, but I do not know of any others.

Then I made this holy reflection in my heart by the grace and gift of the Holy Spirit: that every day of my life I wished and still wish to be only Good Friday. Then I would always weep for the most bitter Passion of Christ, in order that at my death he might appear to me risen in glory. From that time on, I no longer wished to interiorly recognize Easter nor Christmas, nor any other solemnity that the Church celebrates. I did not even know how to add anything more to the rite of Good Friday than that to which I was already accustomed. Indeed it is true that for a while now, my mind is forced to think of all the feasts the Church celebrates almost against my will, since I am invariably attracted to the Passion of Christ following the promise I made that my entire life should be a Good Friday.[177]

So the last things are connected to the first; that is, on Good Friday my salvation was initiated through your holy sermon, and now on a Good Friday of my continual meditation, I conclude the revelation of the story of my spiritual life to you, who were present at the beginning of it. On "coming up from the desert"[178] of this world, full of delights I embraced my passionate Spouse, separated from him in body, but not in soul. As the time of my unhappiness and spiritual desolation came near, just as "He who knows all things before they exist still knows them all after they are made,"[179] I was warned in the following way. But I, ignorant, did not understand.

One day, as soon as I had begun prayer, I was told, "Go and write the mental sorrows of my Passion that you know." I excused myself and said, "My Lord, I do not even know how to begin, because I would not wish in any way that people would think these things are my own [invention]." I was told, "Begin in this way: once there was a soul very willing to graze and be nourished, etc." And two pages were read out like that.

I quickly got up and obeyed the command. The words came so fully that I never needed to think of what I had to say. And so it happens even now: every time I am going to write, I feel no little fatigue, but then the words come plentifully without thinking. O, what bad news was that command to me, when it seemed Jesus wished to say, "I see that the vase of your soul must suffer not a small corruption, but a huge one. So now emit the balsam of my mental sorrows and spread it in others, because it is of no avail to you, because of your corruption." This is why I write. But I strongly doubt that what I am doing at present is not the same, but much worse, almost as if God were saying, "So, because you are lukewarm, neither hot nor cold, I will spit you out of my mouth."[180] O God, spare me this bitter judgment.

This happened in August [1488] when my cruel battle had already begun. But I was ignorant of the devil's crafts and, because of the great peace of my soul, I did not foresee any trouble. On the contrary, I thought that everything was tranquil, peaceful and safe from enemies.

The Two Years of Tribulation and the Death of Blessed Peter of Mogliano

In the eight days following the feast of Saint Francis, I was so cruelly beaten and trodden by my enemies, that I clearly recognized that they were not friends, nor were their inspirations good. On the contrary, I saw and experienced that they were mortal enemies of my soul. Then God opened my eyes a little bit and I saw myself in the middle of the battlefield encircled all around by powerful foes. And I saw that I could escape from their clutches only by divine power. Any other route would have been impossible.

Then I was wounded by a serious suffering. Not knowing what else to do, I fasted on bread and water during the octave of Saint Francis and begged God and the saint to help me. One night in a dream, all my future tribulation was shown to me in an image. "On the poplars of that land, we hung up our harps."[181] At this point all my happiness ended and every evil began. Then the well of diabolical wickedness which had been kept closed for ten years was thrown open, and the poisoned dragon came out. Its jaws were wide-open, and it roared against me with such force and furor that it seemed that it wanted to swallow me alive. In its evil will it would have devoured and swallowed me, but the almighty hand of God, who never forsakes anyone who hopes in him pulled me out safe and sound from its roaring jaws. This was, as you know, by his goodness alone, not by any merit or prudence of mine. Then I was stripped of my every rich and precious vestment. My eyes were gouged out, my hair was shorn and shaved of all its spiritual force,[182] and "they stripped and beat me and went off, leaving me half dead."[183] In these two years [1488-90] during which I was afflicted, I never had any human help or comfort, except for the three times I had the opportunity to speak with my holy and glorious Father Peter of Mogliano.

When he was elected provincial minister, I rejoiced much saying, "Now I'll meet with him often. The devil may do what he likes, because now I will be helped with such wisdom." O my holy father, you came to Camerino, but your beloved daughter could not speak a word to you, for death suddenly took you from me! The thought of this loss overwhelmed me. This death, in fact, made me so upset that I was almost desperate. I firmly proposed within my heart to never again open myself to anyone because of this anguish, if God, through the merits of Father Peter, had not revealed clearly with whom.

O my father, you did not wish to leave me an orphan, because you saw what was necessary for my salvation! First of all, in fact, when you were almost in Heaven, you at once freed me from the power of my enemies, and led me unexpectedly to the way of truth. Then God inspired me, by the intercession of Father Peter, to put all my trust in you, as I previously had in him, and as a result refer to you how my tribulation had developed, having me understand that it was necessary for my salvation. And it was indeed so, as you know. Only God knows, and no one else, how bitter this inspiration was to me, against my entire will.

But after I had related to you my story – I tell it not for flattery, but with utmost sincerity – I remained so satisfied and content that I would not be open with anyone in this world but with you, my father. For different reasons I hoped that I might be allowed to rest and have some spiritual respite after this serious battle that had already been going on for two years. But alas, my father, this was not true. On the contrary, after your departure I was more cruelly afflicted and beaten down than ever. I rebelled strongly, blaming God for my every vice, sin, or error. I complained of him for many things, I blamed holy Scripture of being deceitful, which is the biggest iniquity, and other things which I'll pass over. I believe, most devout father, that when you hear these things, it will seem to you that my poor soul was among the pains of Hell after you left six months ago. And in fact it really seemed to me to be hellish and diabolical. But above all it broke my heart not to be able to say a word to anyone, as you know, or receive the least comfort in such great need and necessity.

O my father, where were you? O my father, during this time I have longed, I could not speak to you, nor can I now, nor you to me. O ill-fate and misfortune! How great it has been from beginning to end. Therefore, throughout this painful story, I have always sown those words of lament and suffering, "Come, all you who pass by the way, look and see whether there is any suffering like my suffering?"[184]

O my father, I speak to you alone: please reflect and see whether there is suffering like mine. O, if God gave me a voice so powerful as to be heard in all the world, I would cry out loud and say, "O all of you servants of God who pass along the way of his divine love, do learn at my cost and be humbled" because we may talk to and with God, with the Virgin Mary and all the angels and saints and yet miserably fall into the ruin of mortal sin, as I did. Learn from this unhappy wretched soul "that has arrived in the ocean of divine love and of spiritual sweetness, but now a strong storm has submerged it in the depth of the abyss and of Hell."[185]

Will and Entrustment to Her Confessor

As the proverb from Ecclesiastes says, "all rivers lead to the sea,"[186] it was just and right that, as the saving waters of my salvation which had their beginning and origin in you by the grace of God, my father, by the divine design after passing so much time, should return to you. "The rivers keep on going."[187] "I planted, Apollos watered, but God caused the growth."[188] The astuteness of Satan has not uprooted the plant, and there is still some green; that is, the interior life, generosity, and willful inclination towards good. God has taken care of me so much to keep me unhurt, pure and immaculate in the body, so that for his grace and not for my faculty, I am still chaste and I can say with the Mother of God, "I have had no relations with a man."[189] So, dearest father, give thanks with me to the creator, who deigned to look after me as friend and bride.

I believe without a doubt, my father, that writing this letter – something I have never before done and that is new for my soul – will bring either great good or great wickedness. With all my heart, I beg God and his glorious Mother to grant me the grace that it contains this purpose: that it may be my last will and testament. If God should wish, I indeed make my will regarding what I possess, which is my soul and body; since for love, desire and affection, I certainly do not possess anything else in this world.

I leave my body to the earth; may God grant me, by his grace, that it may soon dissolve into dust, in accordance with its vile matter. I leave my soul in your charitable hands, my most beloved father, because you are, after God, the only hope of my salvation. And if, by the precious blood of Christ and your prayers, I shall find a place of peace and mercy, I will not forget you.

Vale, Pater optime, in domino Iesu meo, quem pro filia tua exorare memento. [Farewell, dearest father, in Jesus my Lord, remember to pray to him for your daughter.]

In monasterio Sanctae Mariae Novae, Camerini, die 13 martii (6), anno domini 1491.
[In the monastery of Santa Maria Nuova, Camerino
13 March, 1491 AD]

Sora Batttista

I am infinitely grateful to you, my sweetest Lord, who have given me the grace of telling your truth in all sincerity and simplicity. Thus I beg you to grant me the grace that this story be believed with simplicity to your praise and glory, and to my shame and confusion.

I proposed to obey the inspiration to write about these things of my spiritual life as they seemed to me to be of divine inspiration. So I decided in my soul to tell you them out loud, but I was obliged to write them.

I had thought, then, to give them to you with my own hands; but it is necessary, instead, to send them to you wherever you are. I do not know why or for what reason. May God wish for me to discern correctly.

Instructions to the Disciple

Istruzioni Al Discepolo
(1501)

Instructions to the Disciple was written around 1501. St. Camilla wrote it as a letter, commonly believed to have been addressed to a Franciscan friar named Giovanni Pili da Fano (John of Fano), who became the spiritual father of Saint Camilla. After begging her, his "daughter" became his spiritual "mother" and she openly recounted to him the spiritual secrets of her heart in this letter. John of Fano was the provincial minister of the Observant branch of Franciscans within the region of the Marches of Ancona. During the 1520's the Capuchin reform movement began near Camerino, when several Observant friars began re-establishing a more prayerful Franciscan way of life rooted in the hermitages. After initially persecuting the Capuchins, John of Fano ultimately entered the new Order himself in 1534.

Saint Camilla offers her disciple ten instructions and counsels, almost like a Decalogue. She is well-versed in her knowledge of the Bible and she quotes Scripture directly and indirectly. Nonetheless, the "Instructions" are not a heavy theological work and she does not flaunt her erudition. Rather, she writes as a mother who opens up her heart and spiritual life to her disciple out of love, because she authentically desires to see him excel in spiritual progress. The "Instructions" are a great tool for anyone who desires to delve deep into the secrets of God and discover practical methods for living a more profound spiritual life. They include plenty of authentic and sincere pearls of wisdom and spirituality due, no doubt, to the personal experiences of the author.

It should be noted that in the past there was some doubt among scholars as to whether or not the "Instructions" were actually written by

Saint Camilla Battista; however, most scholars now attribute this work to her.

Note that, as in other works, St. Camilla sometimes speaks of herself in the third person. She writes of "that nun" as if she were someone else, but in reality she is speaking of herself. Other times she speaks of herself in the first person.

Instructions to the Disciple

Camerino 1501

Domine Iesu Christe, qui corda servorum tuorum nosti, respice devotionem huius animae et da mihi peccatrici gratiam tuam, et ut impleatur voluntas tua per os meum, ad honorem maiestatis tuae, atque ad spiritualem utilitatem devotissimi filii mei.

[O Lord Jesus Christ, you who know the hearts of your children, look at the devotion of this soul and give me, a sinner, your grace, so that my mouth will conform to your will, to the honor of your divine Majesty and the spiritual usefulness of my most devoted son.]

Introduction

Many times, beloved soul of God, for your consolation you begged me write to you about the spiritual life and of the wonderful graces that God gave this nun, whom you revere with great devotion. To you she seems like God on earth; that is, through her, God works in you for your salvation. Since I love you with all my heart, I wish to satisfy, with divine grace, at least in part this pious and holy desire of yours. That nun, in fact, confided to me all her secrets.[190] This I know with certainty: under no circumstances should you seek to be esteemed by men; rather, seek to be pleasing only in the eyes of God. I beg you, therefore, to keep this writing a secret between you and me. If you do differently, you will displease her greatly.

Before setting sail in the ocean – where I feel your prayers draw me – I wish to share with you some holy thoughts. If you honor them, you will be blessed!

The Usefulness of Prayer

I wish that you, devoted soul, be a friend to holy prayer. That nun came to know God and herself by entering through the door of prayer. Through prayer, she developed friendship and familiarity with almighty God. He revealed to her his secrets and he gave peace and serenity to her soul. He gave her friendship with the angels, an unwavering faith in the Trinity, a firm, certain hope in her salvation, a strong, constant love of God, and an ardent desire of salvation for others. Prayer so intoxicated that nun so that she could say with the Apostle Paul, "The world has been crucified to me, and I to the world."[191] I mean to say that I loathe the world so much that it seems to me a temporary hell. I do not wish to please him in any other way! For I know that that nun feels a great joy when the world has a negative opinion of her and considers her far from God, when in actuality she is close to him. This is a result of the uprightness of her humble heart. All this because her soul rooted itself in prayer in the Passion of Jesus. I wish for you, too, to do the same so that you will be able to say with her, "All good things together came to me in the company of wisdom."[192]

Here I will not write anything else of holy prayer, as I already spoke to you of it in person. Just do it, since you already understand this. What you cannot reap, take with force; when you cannot pray with your mind, pray with your mouth *et sufficit tibi* [and it will be enough to you].

Spiritual Optimism

I wish that you, soul blessed by the Lord, imitate your mother in this virtue that God conceded to her: in all things that you hear and see, learn how to retain the good: *piglia la rosa e lascia star la spina* [Pick the rose and leave the thorn alone.][193] If there are even one hundred reasons or one thousand teachings in the Holy Scriptures that authorize you to judge evil, but you had only one reason to think well, hold yourself to this one thing and ignore the hundred and the thousand. This is how she, whom you love so much in God, has always acted. Her heart has been more faithful to this tenet than to any other. Under no circumstance could she persuade herself to think badly of her neighbor. Only with great difficulty and after a very trying experience could she surrender to the evidence.

This tenet gave her a great, hopeful boldness *in cospectu Altissimi* [before the most high] who never rejects her pleas, "Light dawns for the just, gladness for the honest of heart."[194] If your heart is good, if you always work with honest intentions *erga Deum et proximum* [before God and men], in short time you will gain two sweet fruits: first, holy illumination of the intellect; and second, the joy of angels in your upright heart. The joy I speak of is a joy that neither the world nor all created things could ever give. These are the peacemakers who, in their contemplation, will inherit the earth of Jesus's humanity nailed to the cross. "Blessed are the pure of heart who will see God"[195] with the light of their intellect even in the present life. This I wish for you, blessed soul: that you may eternally enjoy God in Heaven with your beloved spiritual mother. This mother of yours, in the desert of this present life, among innumerable dragons, walks by the grace of the Holy Spirit according to this surest path. Always search for the good in everything, even among undeniable evil, believe me, as I love you with sincerity of heart! Many men and women, as a result of thinking and judging without fear of consequence, fall into grumbling and gossiping. The servants of God thus lose so many graces, so many divine gifts – how many I cannot even imagine. Flee, flee from this infernal plague! Flee this vice! Again I insist: flee from it promptly!

Believe me: the judgments of God are quite different from those of men. Your mother was judged the wrong way many times and on many occasions. *Deo perimittente* [God permitted] it for her good, so that the treasure of grace would be most purely conserved in her. Thus, she learned, at her expense, that the judgments of men are erroneous. So do, soul devoted to the Passion of Jesus Christ, like your mother. The spirit of wisdom will rest within you.

I wish that you, blessed soul, follow this counsel of mine: serve the Lord, not as a slave out of fear of temporal or eternal punishments, neither as a penitent sinner who looks for a reward; rather, as a noble child. Give to God love for love, penalty for penalty, blood for blood, death for death. These are the short but sure paths, hidden from human eyes, but which are perfectly known and acceptable by God who knows and sees all things. Before the soul begins to walk, alas, before it even knocks on the door of God's mercy, he opens to it the treasure of his eternal wisdom. Before it asks, more than it can desire is granted. The soul would not even know what to ask of God who already gives it in his infinite, incomprehensible goodness. Our loving crucified Lord Jesus is infinitely full of largesse, most kind, and quite generous. He loves much and takes pleasure in those who conform themselves to him. He renders the heart free, magnanimous, and very large, so that the King of eternal life can easily pass within. God never lives in, nor can he ever live in an impure, vile, or base heart. "For great is the Lord and highly to be praised, to be feared above all gods."[196] Leave then, beloved soul, this deceptive and perfidious world, not for fear of Hell as a slave, nor for the hope of reward as a penitent sinner, but as a loving daughter and spouse, out of pure love for your crucified Jesus. Grasp him with great love in the arms of your most tender affections.

Your mother has given you an example. She grieved for not being more or not having more, so that she could leave so much more for the love of Jesus crucified whom she ardently loved with a pure heart and perfect intention.

The Love of Enemies, Reaying Evil with Good

"Love your enemies, and pray for those who persecute you."[197] "Be a peacemaker towards those who hate peace."[198] In the monastery, God comes greatly to those who love him with a most holy love. In one way or another, he lets the soul gain infinite treasures. Know, blessed soul, that this nun was granted many spiritual graces. Jesus had given her signs of benevolence and singular love. She was always thirsty for this grace: love the one with all your heart who does you wrong, much more than the one who does you good.

This servant of Jesus never tired in this prayer of beseeching the Lord, "O my most clement God, if you would reveal to me the most hidden secrets of your divine heart and if you would daily manifest to me the choirs of angels, if you would grant me the power of raising the dead at will, this would not be enough to convince me that you love me with an infinite love. But when I feel that I have obtained the grace of a perfect love; that is, to do good to the one who does me wrong, to speak well of and praise the one whom I know speaks wrong of me and slanders me, only then through this infallible sign, I shall no longer doubt that I am indeed your daughter. Only then will I be conformed to your beloved Son Jesus Christ crucified, who is the only good of my soul; only then will I be conformed to him, O Father, who in dying on the cross prayed to you for his murderers."

Now it seems that this servant of Jesus has obtained this grace. In her soul she does not feel any resentment for any injustice said or done to her. If she had received an injury, serious or otherwise, I will not write of it. God knows of it and so does she. She feels the greatest pleasure in doing and saying things that please her wrongdoers. She is only pained by the damage done to them as a result of their sins. And she prays to God with her whole heart that he may pardon them. She often says a *Pater Noster* and an *Ave Maria* for them in God's holy plan of great spiritual perfection. I wish that you do the same, blessed soul. Follow the sure example of your mother, whom you love. She writes these things for your edification. I hope in the Lord God and in your prudence that the time spent in this is not without fruit, but that it is of great usefulness to your soul. What you can do in one year, never do in two.

Walk, run, fly in the path to God. The just walk, the wise run, those who love fly. If you can run, do not walk; if you can fly, do not run, because time is short. In the path to God, you should always go forward, and never fall back. If one does not add wood to the fire, it will soon go out. The same thing happens to the soul: if one does not add virtue to virtue, love goes out. The soul that began virtuously by saying, *Credo in Deum* [I believe in God], will end up *in carnis resurrectionem* [returning to the flesh]; that is, distracted by a thousand cares and worries in this world. May God, in his eternal infinite goodness, preserve you and every Christian soul from going down a road like this. If, however, you wish to make great progress, then fear God and love those who slander you. Stay awake. Open the eyes of your soul, and keep your mind rooted in God because there are few who ardently desire to attain this angelic perfection, which our most benign Jesus taught with his own sweet mouth. But few arrive at true perfection; that is, in loving their enemies.

I wish, blessed soul, that in your consecration to God you perfectly mirror virtue and holiness to your brothers. And since in the world you exceeded your companions in virtue, honesty, and dignity, and more so since you were a priest; now that you are in a friar, do not let your generous, magnanimous, and strong soul become small. Virtue, according to the philosopher, grows in difficult moments,[199] and so it is extremely difficult to love one's enemies; hence, it is the greatest virtue. In fact, when a person has grown in grace, he no longer has enemies. That person is a friend and loves every person who helps him grow in holiness. How beautiful is this theology! How useful would it be were it understood by all!

The world and hell are friends to man; a man, then, has only one true enemy – himself. No one can any longer impede his salvation – only his inordinate affections can. At peace with himself, man is at peace with everyone else. Blessed will you be, if you arrive at this degree of holiness! Here is hidden the seed of future everlasting life. Here is concealed the secret treasure of peace of mind and soul. He who does not trod along this path, finds no good in this earthly world. Here the soul rejoices with God who wishes peace, *quia Rex pacificus est* [because the King is peaceful]; he wishes to live only with peacemakers in a serene house.

Be on guard and protect yourself from being counted among the number of friars who are foolish, unsettled, combative, argumentative, and suspicious of every little thing. Every flea seems to them a horse; every splinter seems an insuperable wooden beam.[200] Miserable and unhappy are their souls! God's grace will never abide within their souls in this world; in the other world, something will have to be done! Take my counsel. If you seek tranquility, you will find it in everything. Peace will thus take root in your heart, in your conscience, and in your mind. You will find peace by observing the Gospel precepts: love your enemies sincerely, without pretense, and with all your heart.

On Canonical Visitations to Monasteries and Friaries

It is written in the religious Rules, through inspiration of the Holy Spirit, that superiors should visit their subjects, since it is written, "Your providence has preserved my spirit"[201] *Hic jacet lepus* [Herein lies the hare].[202] If you wish to avoid confusion, hold fast to this counsel: if you do not see an apparent serious sin with your own eyes, say nothing! It may seem to ignorant nuns and friars that it is good to communicate to their superiors every rumor and gossip. As a result, they cause division and bitterness for an entire year, or perhaps a lifetime. But I keep my mouth shut. It is not always good to open the eyes of the blind. God himself educated your mother in this. Before entering the monastery, she was ignorant of spiritual things and of the monastic Rules, and she did not understand this important and profound teaching. But when she entered the cloister, she then understood well the counsel of the Holy Spirit.

She has lived for around eighteen years in the monastery as both a subject and superior. Yet she has never said anything particular regarding any of her sisters. If it ever happened that, as a result of the instigation of the devil, and permission of God, for the advantage of your soul that anyone should speak bad of you, do not seek to vindicate yourself; instead, speak well of the holiness of your brothers to the visitator as if they were angels incarnate. Do not seek to discover who spoke badly of you, so that indignation and hate is not born in your heart. These two vices render our prayers and spiritual sacrifices worthless. But one cannot have such an elevated soul unless he truly knows himself and his mind is always focused on God. Only thus can a man be blind to his neighbor's defects. By not seeing the defects and shortcomings of others, one can serenely say that they all seem to be angels on earth. This is how your mother arrived at this gift. She never knew what to say to the visitators; in fact, the novices knew more than her. When something was revealed to her, she marveled as if it came from another world, saying, "I never realized this." Learn, then and see what your mother understood: that a subtle temptation of the devil can deceive even the perfect ones. Since I love you with all my heart, I wish to tell you this. The devil will make the rumors and gossip of friars and nuns appear good. The devil's snare is very subtle, and can even seem invisible to the eyes of spiritual contemplatives. It is like a nasty leech that sucks away the sacrifices of monks and nuns, robbing them of their good works.

This is the worst leprosy with which the prophetess Miriam, the sister of Moses, dirtied herself.[203] Her prophetic spirit did not help her. Since she had criticized Moses, she was afflicted with the most horrible and tormenting plague. If Moses, whom she had criticized, had not interceded for her, her flesh would have been consumed and she would have died within a few days, as is narrated in the Holy Scriptures. Oh ominous example, mirror in which to look, placed by the Holy Spirit in the Old Testament to make gossipers reflect and tremble! People reflect too little on this teaching and understand it less still. But the one who meditates on these things and keeps the leprosy of gossip far has a sure investment in the glory of Heaven. I have compassion on the gossiper and I envy the one who is the object of criticism. "We know that all things work for good for those who love God."[204] Leprosy not only consumes the flesh of the one who suffers from it, but it defiles others by its touch. This is why God commanded Miriam to pitch her tent outside the camp – so that she would not infect others with leprosy. As gossip is damaging to the gossiper, it also harms the one who would listen to it; rather, it harms the second more than the first. In fact, if there were no one to listen to it, there would be no gossip at all. One devil sits on the tongue of the gossiper, and the other by the ear of the one who listens. They both laugh among themselves and mock the fool who gossips and the idiot who listens. I hope you are wise and that you neither gossip, nor listen. If you are able to silence the gossiper, you will obtain two goods: you will expel the demon from your brother's tongue and confuse the other devil who was ready to put the gossip in your ear.

I will conclude here, because I do not wish that you gossip about anyone, nor about anything, neither about good, nor about bad, not of a good thing, nor of a bad thing. Remember this then and follow it, for I do not speak without reason: keep the rein, my beloved, tightly in your hand because, as St. James wrote, "If anyone thinks he is religious and does not bridle his tongue but deceives his heart, his religion is vain."[205]

This is the subtle snare of the devil: he knows that every action of ours which is not founded on charity is not pleasing to God and is not fruitful for man. This is why he tempts people to gossip and spread rumors, which, all things considered, are rather insignificant and ill-founded. However, they are not judged so by less spiritual people, who perceive the words said or deeds done as more serious than they actually are. Thus fraternal love grows cold, and the circle of peace is broken. Many such people first grow cold, and later completely lose their charity. When the devil sees such things, he feels that he is in charge! He no longer frets over our obedience, he does not fear our chastity, he jeers at our poverty. He laughs at our devotional tears, penance, fasting, and all our charitable works of mercy. Only charity renders us pleasing in the eyes of God and opens the gates to Heaven! For these reasons, the devil always shoots his poisonous arrows at this root of fraternal love in order to destroy this virtue. Thus, he tempts [us] to rash judgments, defamation, and slander. This is why during the canonical visitations, he fills souls with suspicions and sows discord in their hearts. He destroys the zeal of honor within the community, because he encourages saying what is best not said.

Alas! How much good, how many gifts of God, how many uncountable graces are lost by souls blinded by their malice! How many sacrifices remain without fruit! How much disquiet of conscience springs from it! Friars and nuns then become so troubled, so incapable of recognizing good. They no longer have love during prayer, they do not trust in God, and their heart is incapable of spiritual joy. All these evils derive from not knowing how to silence the tongue. Be quiet and silent regarding the affairs of others! Be like the psalmist, "I have set a guard against my mouth."[206] I speak to you, my son, because I wish for you to converse in this way. By the grace of God, this is what your most cordial mother did. Hence, she obtained a particular gift of God – that of so much peace that you could never even imagine. I desire that you, too, obtain this gift.

Vigilance and Correct Intention

Keep your soul ever vigilant *ne unquam obdormiat in somno pigritiae, et negligentiae* [so that you never fall into laziness and sloth], and know that "the kingdom of heaven suffers violence, and the violent are taking it by force."[207] These evangelical words were placed in your mother's soul by the Holy Spirit himself, and she continually reflects on them while sleeping or awake. My beloved son, do not let your spiritual life become lukewarm. Many friars and nuns forget their original fervor and work without proper intention or intensity of love. They follow their Rule, their schedules, and life in community. Yet, they are like goats: when one jumps, the others jump without knowing why. Thus, many friars and nuns have fallen asleep spiritually. They continue to follow their customs and habits, which they do not enliven with love, nor do they understand their meaning. They are like donkeys that carry wine, and yet only drink water. Likewise, these friars and nuns make great sacrifices, but they bear little or no fruit.

As matter without form is neither useful nor beautiful, likewise good works performed without clear intention are neither pleasing to God, nor beneficial to the doer. Although a virtuous action is praiseworthy in itself, if it is not accompanied by a proper intention, it is vain and useless – like matter without form. Only a fool performs such acts! You should be prudent and wise. Do not imitate the folly of some! In every work, small or large, elevate your eyes to the mind of God, sanctify your intention, and bear every adversity through his love. Whatever you do – when you make your prayers and spiritual readings, when you sing or chant the Divine Office, when you wash dishes, sweep the house, and perform every work of charity towards the healthy or the sick – do it in love of the Lord. Believe me, when you perform these actions in this manner, you will automatically repeat in your mind, "Lord, through your love!" You will say it even without thinking. This has always been the practice of your mother.

Although it is true that she has been able to perform only little works, because she has been infirm and weak for a long time. Nonetheless, I say these things for your edification; for in truth she has always done more than she had the strength to do. God knows it and knows her conscience. Always have an ardent desire to do penance. Do not do penance in your own way; rather, follow the instructions of your superiors. You will earn much merit before the most Holy Trinity who considers the heart. Take care that your heart is constantly enflamed with charity. For flies will not approach a pot while the water is boiling, but when it becomes lukewarm, then they come and drown in it. In the same way, the devil stays far from a soul burning with divine love. But to the soul that is lukewarm in charity and cold in love, the flies of vanity and useless thoughts attach themselves and there they drown.

Unfortunately, many sleep in the cloister and dream of becoming holy. In the moment of death they will see how false their dreams and hopes really were. Instead, they will find their hands full of the flies of the devil's illusions. Open your eyes, my reverend son, in Christ. Do not play around with the few days of life remaining to you! Stay vigilant and be ardent in love according to the grace that God has given you, so that you may one day say with the Apostle, "His grace in me has not been ineffective,"[208] because "I keep vigil with you, O God."[209] You can be sure that in a short time you will gain much!

Perseverance in the Service of God

Two things in religious life are essential: perseverance and self-knowledge. Without the first, there is no salvation, without the second there is no holiness. I wish for you to be saved and holy since, *sacerdos debet esse perfectus* [the priest should be faultless]. Your mother always desired an amazing miracle and a wonderful revelation. "Without this miracle," she said, "I cannot be saved; without this revelation I cannot be holy." You do the same! Blessed soul, pray with persistence to the Lord that he gives you the grace of performing this miracle: persevere in religious life until death, because "whoever endures to the end will be saved."[210] This miracle is most stupendous!

Three most powerful captains of huge armies of temptations are constantly assaulting the soul to break its resistance. They bring artilleries such that unless a man is comforted by God, he can never achieve this miracle of holy perseverance. These powerful captains direct their strength in a particular way against the intellect. I say they are powerful because by their powerful skill, they have already artfully subjugated practically the entire world. They have preyed on people of every kind, race, and gender, taking them all prisoners.

The wise person can name the three captains in just a few words: the world, the flesh, and the devil! Oh, how dangerous, terrible, and deadly is this war! That almighty God gives his servants the power to raise the dead, give sight to the blind, and heal the sick, is not a great miracle – for it is precisely his divine omnipotence working above our nature. He would not be God, otherwise! But that a fragile creature, about whom it is said, "I was born guilty, a sinner, even as my mother conceived me,"[211] triumphs over the world, overcomes the flesh, and is victorious against the devil with the help only of his Catholic faith, this is a most stupendous miracle!

Let the war not frighten you, my dearest son. Your beloved mother, though a fragile creature herself, with the divine grace and aid of the angels, battled forcefully in the open field and triumphed over the first two captains: the world and the flesh. God sustained her with his grace and gave her victory. Now the world can do what it will; she doesn't care. With dry feet, she has already crossed the Red Sea. By the grace of the Holy Spirit, this enemy, feeling its head broken, will not return anymore; she tied it with an unbreakable golden chain. Your mother tasted the sweetness of divine love – how could she change herself to enjoy the taste of human glories and privileges while everything in the world is bitterness and hellish to her? Her flesh, despite those who would wish otherwise, was made impassible [i.e. not able to suffer]; one could say that it was resuscitated just before death. By the grace of God and the work of the Holy Spirit, she enjoys a young and mortal body of angelic dignity. You should know that in order to overcome this cruel tyrant of the flesh, she allowed her soul to be penetrated with the water of bitter suffering. The iron of its powerful spear pierced her heart. Now that the grace of God is always more efficient in her, she fights against the enemy and wins.

No more, no more! God knows all her deeds and she can say well: "You, my clement Lord, showed me the secrets of your wisdom and power." She saw and worked incredible things for the gift of God. Through her, he converted evil into perfect good in his great honor. He gave her the grace of being able to take the enemies with their own weapons, tie them and present them as willing prisoners before the throne of God, in such a way that now *quorum nomino scripta sunt in libro vitae* [their names are written in the book of life]. The knowable, secret divine wisdom changed the same enemies into most faithful friends. Your mother united a great patience to a faithful hope; with the help of God she courageously embraced the undertaking and obtained victory and, *Deo auxiliante, cui laus, et gloria per infinita saculorum* [To God alone belongs glory and honor forever]. Amen!

Nor does your mother fear the third captain for two reasons: she knows and believes by faith that the devil cannot do anything beyond that which God permits. She chose for her heaven the will of God in Heaven and on earth. So she does not fear the works of the evil one; rather, she desires that he do against her as much as God wills and permits. And she notes that here is born perfect patience with the devil and people because she believes with unwavering faith that neither the one nor the other will ever be able to say or do anything that does not please God and conform itself to his will. And she knows that the infinite Goodness wishes her to be saved and he loves her more than she loves herself. And thus, there is no fear when one is sure and certain of the protection of their heavenly Father. The second reason not to fear the devil is this: it is most certain that God, who through his goodness conceded to her the grace of triumphing over the two more powerful captains, will also give her the wisdom, strength, and vigor to overcome the third captain who is the weakest. The evil spirit cannot do us any evil, unless we ourselves give him our free will.

Rejoice, then! Be happy, my son, in the wounds of our sweet Jesus! Because if a sinful old woman can overcome and conquer in victory this cruel militia *Deo auxiliante* [with the help of God], she has already accomplished two thirds of this miracle. Therefore, what will you who are magnanimous, combative, and manly do in this field of spiritual warfare? In this glorious joust, God, the angels and the saints watch as spectators. From their heavenly castle, they admire the blows of their enamored knights and with delight and pleasure, they keep their gaze fixed on the court of this present life of ours where the legitimate sons of almighty God for love of the crucified Jesus, continually joust with the world and, with the sword in hand, they battle against the flesh and valorously combat against the devil. In this glorious battle, one never knows peace or truce until death.

Quae pars est? [What side are you on?] Do you think it is a little thing to serve God and desire to be saved? He who wants to do well will need to toil greatly. But I believe that you, my beloved son, were born precisely for this; I feel it, I believe it. Before the world was created, you were destined to do this. Your spirit is great, your mind is disposed to this magnanimous undertaking. Do not doubt! In spite of the world, the flesh, and the devil, you will be victorious by the grace of God also with the aid of the prayers of your beloved mother; she knows well that the Lord loves you perfectly. Perform, then, this great miracle: persevere in your religious vocation *usque ad mortem* [until death]! There is no greater miracle than this.

I wish for you to ask God for this wonderful revelation, and that he reveals to you and makes you know: who you are, how much you can do, how much you know, and how much you are worth. Without this revelation, no one will ever become holy. This is a secret that one does not learn from others. It is sealed in the most sacred Heart of Jesus crucified. And he does not reveal it to many, but to few; and he does not reveal it to everyone equally, but according to the degree of holiness to which he calls. Nor do I think that one can arrive at this full knowledge in this present cloudy life, but in the next, yes. Then we shall fully and truly comprehend our lowliness, our frailty, and our foolishness. From here is born that humility of heart, which is not noticed by the eyes of men, but which God considers dear and looks on with satisfaction. Your spiritual mother never desired or sought for any other revelation than the knowledge of God and of herself; and the Dispenser of graces who is infinitely generous, good, and bountiful, has not denied her that one.

A number of years ago, I was praying before the crucifix, when God illuminated me with this truth: that I could not arrive at perfection without knowing another trinity besides the Holy Trinity. Just as to be a Christian it is necessary to believe in and confess the most Holy Trinity – Father, Son, and Holy Spirit, so in like manner, in order to become perfect, it was necessary for me to believe this three-fold truth: that before God I was nothing, foolish, and detestable.[212]

O Most Blessed Trinity, you are neither known, valued, nor believed in by ignorant spiritual persons. "O my God," prayed your mother, "deprive me of life rather than the knowledge of this truth. Reduce my bones to dust, before this knowledge departs from my mind. Only this teaching of eternal wisdom will keep my heart perfectly humble. My crucified Jesus, without this humility, I cannot be pleasing to you, who give life to my soul; I cannot glory in my own power, since my power is nothing; nor can I exalt in my wisdom, because I am but a fool." I cannot presume to be worth anything before you, as I am a wicked creature, disgraceful in the eyes of God. Rather, I am more disgraceful than disgrace itself, because one who commits sin is a slave of sin. And since sin is nothing, in committing sin, as I have often done, I have become the slave of a nothing. Hence, I am less than nothing, since I am as much below this nothing as the servant is below his master. One can reason that sin is nothing from the fact that it annihilates the image of God within us. And from what St. John says *et sine ipso factum est nihil* [and without him, nothing was made]. Therefore, without God, there is only sin. Every other thing comes from God and "is made through him."[213]

When a person feels within himself the power to do good, he may be sure that it is the spirit of the eternal Father who is coming to aid his nothingness. In the same manner, when he sees that he can instruct others in the spiritual life, he recognizes that it is the wisdom of the Son that makes his folly wise. Again, when a person perceives that he loves and is loved, he discovers that it is the Holy Spirit who loves him, and renders his hatefulness lovable. Thus, referring to God every good that he has, a person is freed from his vainglory and rancid pride – the same that expelled the angel from Paradise. Thus, he can sing with the prophet, "Lord, my heart is not proud; nor are my eyes haughty."[214]

Your mother holds this truth as certain. If a spiritual soul does not try to obtain in itself this light, this essential knowledge of itself, it could never sincerely and cordially humble itself before God and before men. Know that this soul[215] is very reverent in its exterior actions, but much more in its heart. It does not show its devotion, because it is a great enemy of all hypocrisy. Nevertheless, not only in private, but in public, it often kisses the pavement of the church on which its sisters have trodden, believing itself unworthy to be able to put its mouth on the footprints of these pure virgins. Consider, blessed soul, that it would prefer to humble itself under the feet of all, were it not prevented by the respect it owes to its charge and its position.[216]

I write this with tears in my eyes, because I feel that only because of your devotion and prayers have I disclosed secrets long closed within my heart. She respects and reveres everyone, from the most worthy through office and rank.[217] Yet she has never been tempted to think of herself as above another. Many times she still reveres the least of the sisters, laughing and joking on the outside, but with all her heart, she considers them spouses of Christ.

Endeavor, therefore, my dear son, to be humble of heart, reverend, kind, pious, and gentle. Look into the most pure Heart of Jesus as into a beautiful mirror. Conform yourself to him, if you wish to have his sweetest friendship and familiarity. From this Heart, from this most sacred side, your mother derived all her interior and exterior beauty. His sweet, loving Heart was her teacher. Here alone was she taught, here she studied. Here you read nothing other than truth, docility, piety, sweetness, cheerfulness of heart, and joy of conscience. Here we find nothing but love and charity: love of God and charity towards men. O Divine Heart! I cannot help naming you, for in you, your mother saw her name written clearly and splendidly in beautiful letters of gold.[218] Beloved soul, enter into that Heart if you desire to become a saint soon! This is the short, sure, and infallible way, which your mother has always followed. Follow it, for conformity begets and preserves love. Turn to God and say, "I wish that you, O Lord, give me this revelation. For without it I can never be perfect. And yet perfection is essential to the dignity and excellence of my priestly office."

Pray to God with your entire heart full, reverend soul and he will certainly give you this revelation. He is so good and generous, so full of every gift and grace, who always, even before asked, "God lavishes his goodness on the just and sinners alike, drawing them to the fullness of his goodness....Therefore this soul, whom you love, will sing the promises of the Lord forever."[219]

Do Not Steal the Honor and Love of God

Be on guard against being a thief! He who steals will be hung on the forks of divine justice. But the soul who wisely steals Christ will be fixed to the forks of the beloved cross of love where it will perfectly serve the Father with its desired Spouse, the crucified Christ. But do not, my beloved son, under any circumstance steal the honor and love due only to God: "only to God honor and glory forever and ever."[220] The Lord laments with the prophet: "If then I am a father, where is the honor due to me? And if I am a master, where is the reverence due to me?"[221]

God does not wish us to consider as ours what is rightly his. Your mother always jealously guarded these two things – love and honor – intact and immaculate for God, the Creator of the universe. She was more afraid of upsetting them than of contracting the plague. She avoided, however, honor and love of man with purity of intention, more than when one avoids a poisonous snake. Many times she begged God with all her heart, "If you see that, because of my evil deeds, I appropriate to myself these two things, deprive me forever of all your graces and gifts, because I do not want them! If I have ever said anything in order to receive a worldly honor, I beg you, who can do everything, to make my words become shame and confusion to me. If I shall ever say something in order to obtain man's love or favor, make my words create hate and malevolence. You, my God, can do anything. If you see me acting as a thief, do not entrust to me your graces and gifts. To you alone are due honor and glory, not to others. If, instead, you see me faithful in these two things, do give me them to me; in that case I shall accept them for the honor of your divine Majesty and for the usefulness of others."

Sometimes your mother, with sincere humility and great fear, prayed to God so that he would give to someone else the graces and gifts that he wished to give to her. In such a way, he would have had greater honor. She sincerely believed that no one else in the world possessed the graces of God more unworthily than her. And if God had listened to her prayer and conceded to others the graces prepared for her, she would have felt a most wonderful consolation, because she sought the honor of God and not her own interest.

I think that the following words of the Gospel are revealed to such souls, "Well done, my good and faithful servant. Since you were faithful in small matters, I will give you great responsibilities. Come, share your Master's joy."[222] To the same people I think the warning of the Apocalypse is aimed, "Remain faithful until death."[223] It is not enough to be faithful for ten or twenty years, it is necessary to remain so unto death, *et dabo tibi coronam vitae* [and I will give you the crown of life]. He is the truly faithful servant who, in dying, not only in living, gives to the Master what he owes him. Be careful, my reverend son, not to become a thief! Before

God it is as nothing to be a doctor, priest, monk, etc. Nor to others is it an advantage to hold a high office. In fact, it is written, [Serve the Lord with fear; with trembling bow down in homage].[224]

From the day she entered the monastery, your mother, out of fear that she would steal God the love due to him, never gave her whole self to any one, nor did she allow others to give their whole selves to her. She is very loveable, therefore she always strove to avoid being loved too much by others. She always avoided occasions to love and be loved. When she became aware that she was being loved in a particular way, it caused her great pain and she prayed to God with most holy tears that he would temper and take away that love from the heart of the other person. At times she presented someone more virtuous than her to these people in her place. And she did all this in order not to steal love from God. It seems that no one is more attentive than her in this.

In short, I tell you with complete sincerity that no one ever received so much pleasure, joy, and consolation in being loved, as she felt displeasure and sorrow when she was the object of such a love. When she saw that these loves were not according to God, she would shed bitter tears. In order to not steal the honor from God, she always hid as much as possible the singular graces and gifts conceded to her from the divine Majesty. She struggled in order not to appear spiritual to her sisters; thus, she would joke, laugh and clown around, "For only to God honor and glory forever and ever."[225] She preferred to be judged as no good rather than as a saint. Now she is in a higher spiritual state, and she no longer concerns herself of anything else. She directs everything towards God, not towards herself. She does not notice honor and love toward her any more than hate and shame. She is happy with everything that is said or done, as if directed toward others and not to her.

My son in Jesus crucified, I am writing you of all the particulars of your mother for your consolation. But be prudent. Imitate her in that which is good. But let God change the condition of your soul as she did. It is necessary to be a "shell" before becoming a "channel". For almost twenty years, your mother was a "shell"; that is, she tried to guard and keep God's grace within her. Then, however, she became a "channel;" that is, she spread and wrote of it to others.

I tell you still that this soul blessed by God was always guarded against stealing honor from God. Sincerely humble, it seemed to her that the graces of the Lord were put in a place that was very wicked. She believed that by having placed so many graces within her, a sinner so poor in virtue and not very spiritual, it was a great shame and dishonor to her celestial Spouse. As a result, she was quiet about them and she hid them with great care. She would sometimes make excuses to skip community prayer, so that the sisters and friars would not notice the grace given to her by God. In order not to make a show of herself, she arranged with the reader during meals not to read the account of the Passion of Christ while the sisters ate. She would say, "The other sisters will not be able to swallow any food while hearing that story of love!" She really said this for herself because she feared that someone might notice that she could not eat or would react in some extraordinary way. Now she rarely goes to the refectory because of this reason.

I tell you this, father and son in Jesus Christ, so that you too will learn to hide the graces of God, until it pleases him to do otherwise. How blessed is the soul who desires no one other than God to witness his holy works! How many difficulties she underwent because of this! How many blames, how many false, rash, and presumptuous judgments your mother endured for what should have been worthy of praise by God and men! Instead, she was reproved and humbled before God and men. But she remained firm and immovable as a strong tower. She was certain, because of her indestructible faith, that her most faithful Spouse, Jesus, at the right time, would have come to her defense and thrown away that shield with which, in order to try her faith and patience, he had kept her covered for so many years.

In many ways, this soul always demonstrated the uprightness of her heart, and sought to please only God without heeding human judgments. In order to safeguard the honor of God, she did not concern herself with her own shame. Be careful, my son, never to steal anything from God. It would be a disgrace to your spiritual mother and an eternal damage for you. Fear, love, honor your God, "because whatever the Lord wishes, he does in Heaven and on earth, in the seas and in all the deeps."[226]

Keep Your Mind Fixed on God

Keep your mind fixed on God as much as divine grace and your weakness permit. This is the most useful and necessary thing that a servant of almighty God can do. Reflecting on God sanctifies the mind, warms the heart, illuminates the intellect, slows passions, keeps venial sins at bay, sweeps away vices, and prepares the soul for prayer. Many people pray daily, but throughout the course of the day, they consider God very little. As a result, they do not feel very devout, but rather dry, not disposed to prayer, and full of distractions. They believe they do not have the grace of prayer, but this is not true. In actuality, they have not properly directed their minds to God, which properly disposes the soul to mental prayer. Those who think often of God arrive at their desired goal very quickly, because they have prepared a place for God. They readily receive graces of tears, compunction, sweetness, and devotion. Wise and spiritual friars and nuns use this holy method in this life and continue to use it throughout eternity in the glory of Heaven. There is no better sign by which to know if one's name is written in the book of life.

Since thinking often of God forces divine goodness to remember us, you can be certain that as often as you remember him, so much more does he think of you. The Holy Spirit himself educated your mother so that this angelic exercise would grow ever more. You should know that she has this grace, and she often invokes the Redeemer in her heart and calls him within. I could never describe to you how many spiritual fruits she has received from this exercise.

I wish to speak to you of three wonderful effects that [thinking of God] generated much good to her. First, it rendered her blind to the defects of others; second, it adorned her soul with cordial devotion; third: it allowed her to speak of God with her heart on fire. This exercise generated fruit for many souls and was very useful to her. "For from the fullness of the heart the mouth speaks."[227] Man speaks from what he has inside; a wine barrel cannot generate anything other than the wine that it has within.

Your mother arrived at keeping her mind fixed on God by two ways. First: by frequently mentally repeating various verses of the Psalms, for example, "Turn away your face from my sins."[228] She repeated these holy words in her mind so often that the routine became such a habit that she uttered them without consciously thinking of the words. This was a practice that she began before entering the monastery. Often she repeated these words even while sleeping. Second: a particular event helped your mother to keep her mind fixed on God; that is, she was greatly afflicted by a tribulation for five years, in which she was forced to call out to God who helped her, day and night: "O God, come to my assistance. Lord, make haste to help me"[229] and "I raise my eyes toward the mountains. From where will my help come? My help comes from the Lord, the maker of Heaven and earth."[230] Her afflicted and anguished soul continually invoked the Lord, "O God, help me! O God, do not abandon me in this extreme trial! Help me, because I lack strength! I cannot take it any longer! Take me with your powerful hand! My God, you fell asleep in the ship of my soul and I am drowning in the storm of this diabolical ocean! Lord Jesus, without you there is no peace!"

Thus, in that dangerously stormy period, I developed the holy habit of not taking my mind off God, and even in peaceful times I faithfully kept it. Similarly, do the same, my son enamored with Jesus, and in a short time you will see the wonders of God. Repeat, then, with the prophet, "I keep the Lord always before me,"[231] and again, "keep the thoughts of my heart before you."[232] In the Scriptures you will find many other verses in which the prophets and saints show us how they always kept their minds anchored in God.

There are many who attain purity of heart in a way that is painful and difficult: through fasts, vigils, scourgings, sleeping on the bare ground, and mortifying their bodies in various other ways. They do all this in order to obtain purity of heart in which one possesses consumed perfection. But this mother of yours believes in the utmost truth that thinking often of God allows one to acquire this gift better, faster, and with less toil.[233] Would a traveler be wise who, being able to easily travel to Rome in one day on an easy and flat road, chose, instead, a more bitter and difficult road taking four days? Choose then, my son, this short, easy, safe, and secret way that will lead you to Heaven without others realizing it! Embrace Christ, and you will make your fortune without anyone seeing!

Now I will conclude in saying that when someone thinks often of God, "God remains in him"[234] and to he who keeps God within himself by grace, nothing is lacking. In your thoughts and intentions, strive to obtain, as much as possible, to have only God as your aim and do not become too attached to created things. For example, when you exercise charity towards your neighbor, it is very good to consider him as your neighbor, but it is much better to consider him a member of Christ's body. This is much more noble, excellent, and meritorious! Think of the difference between these two concepts! Yet still many friars, monks, and nuns lose the prize of their toils over poor created objects. You understand and know much more than I, because you are very endowed in this field, in the difference between formality and noble intentions. When you can have a dukedom, do not take crumbs. Choose God, think of God! *Et meditatio cordis tui sit in conspectu suo semper.* [And may the thoughts of your heart be always turned to him].

Generosity Towards Your Neighbor, Harshness Towards Yourself

I desire, my beloved son, that you be very generous towards your neighbor, but harsh towards yourself. The world does the opposite: worldly people are very generous with themselves and do not deny themselves anything, but they are mean towards their neighbor. If a neighbor were in need of a hundred things, they would not give him even one. O blindness without end! O deplorable misfortune! The Lord of the universe is most generous, prodigious, courteous, infinitely comprehensive. And by contrast, behold the servant who came into the world naked and will leave the world naked, and shows himself most avaricious, mean, merciless, and cruel towards his neighbor and brother. O most high Trinity, I give you infinite thanks. You give power to my impotence, wisdom to my foolishness, and most clement love to my hatefulness. As you give me power to my powerlessness, wisdom to my foolishness, love to my hatefulness, I thank you in the name of all people. In fact, your infinite power, wisdom, and clemency humiliated our arrogance and human pride; they reduced us to what we are; that is, nothing. For in reality, we are nothing and to nothing we will return. This thought gives joy to my heart, and I contemplate your power and wisdom in it. You alone are and shall eternally be what you have always been. In their vanity, avariciousness, and pride, sinful men wish to be masters of the earth and they refuse mercy towards their neighbors! Soon they will return into dust and nothingness. The powerful hand of God will cut the legs out from under the fast horse of their cursed avariciousness. They will fall not to the ground, but into the very depths of Hell.

But this cursed vice has rooted its way into monasteries and friaries, as well. Many people who have left the wealth of the world are tempted to avarice within their religious houses. They skimp giving a little salad or bread to a poor person, or a glass of wine to the thirsty one who asks out of the love of God. How shameful that the servants of God should still be subject to such a detestable vice! What displeasure it gives him, and how much it must pierce his Heart! How can such a generous Lord bear such avaricious servants?

You then, reverend father and my son in the crucified Christ, do the opposite: be most avaricious towards yourself. If you need four things, do not seek even one. Leave to God the care of your body: he will inspire someone to provide for you, and you will never lack anything. This is what your mother did. For her material and spiritual needs, many were inspired to provide for her, and they gave her even more than she needed. I do not believe she ever asked for anything for herself from her superiors; on the contrary, she refused such things when offered, saying, "Mother, I do not need this, please give it to one of my sisters who needs it more than I." I wish that you, my son, be very generous towards others, and that for everything asked of you, you give four in return. God was pleased to draw your mother to the contemplation of his generosity and love in this manner.

Your mother would look up at the sky and contemplate the marvelous beauty created by this most generous, loving Lord: the heavens adorned with the stars, so many glistening planets, the lucidity of the sun, and the flatness of the moon. She would reflect on how many tasty, sweet fruits were born of the earth, how many varieties of flowers with roses and lilies, how much diversity of herbs fragrant with a thousand perfumes and abundantly furnished with medicinal herbs. She admired the multitudes of fishes in the water, the variety of birds in the air, the wild beasts in the forests, and the domestic animals for the use of man. God made all this and more for our usefulness. He gave us rich harvests of grain, wine, oil, and more. If his most generous charity provided all this for our bodies, which in a short time turn to dust, how much more do you think he has prepared for our soul, which is created in his image and likeness? What variety of beatitudes, what incomprehensible joys, what inestimable happiness, what incomprehensible goods he has prepared for us in the eternal city of Jerusalem! "Glorious things are said of you, O city of God!"[235] O blessed city, Jerusalem, you are a vision of peace, dwelling of the blessed, enjoyment of eternal glory!

Why has God created so many great things in Heaven and on earth, in the sea, and in all the elements, if not to manifest to us mortals his immense charity and his infinite mercy? He is all good, generous, and courteous. He fills us not just with the fullness of his riches, but he gives himself to us in the most holy Sacrament. O most gracious God, you who give yourself and everything to us, how is it that the sinner refuses to give to his brother the least thing?

Your mother learned to become generous from these reflections, though the Lord had greatly endowed her with this virtue from her infancy. She enjoys much more in giving than in receiving; she feels this grace growing more and more each day. If you wish to be conformed to God, be very generous. For he loves nothing other than himself and his image and likeness in us. Your mother learned, or actually was taught, this doctrine in the school of divine wisdom. If you do not comprehend it, ask and you will find that every thing in God is loveable, and that outside of him, nothing is good, because only God is good, and no one is loveable except him alone. God is most generous, rich in mercy and love. His mercy is without end. Glory and praise be to him for ever. Amen.

Farewell

Reverend father and beloved son of mine, I wish now to conclude with these salutary instructions and thoughts. I wish that you receive and follow them with the same love with which I have written them. I have wished to console you by narrating to you, hidden within these thoughts, the spiritual life of your beloved mother. It was not very difficult to me. I hope, in my crucified Jesus, that you find it very useful and spiritually consoling.

I did not speak of the three vows of obedience, poverty, and chastity, because to anyone who observes these instructions or thoughts, it is impossible not to be poor, obedient, and chaste. Also, you seem to me very well disposed towards the yoke of obedience, so that I deemed exhortations unnecessary. Just the same, to confirm your good will, I shall add a few words. No sacrifice is more accepting to God than this: give him your will and freedom through holy obedience, for it is written, "Obedience is better than sacrifice."[236]

I shall not speak to you of holy poverty because I know you. You are so desirous to possess Christ, that you would surrender the world one thousand times in order to enjoy him. He is truly blessed who finds this oriental pearl of holy poverty! This jewel of incalculable worth, by the grace of God, was found and bought by your mother for herself and for others. But she alone had to pay the price of many toils, sufferings and tears before God, and with varied tribulations from friars, sisters, secular authorities, priests and laypersons. In truth she can affirm that poverty cost her more than treasures cost all the wealthy. She desired to possess poverty more than the avaricious person desires more money. My dearest son, let your poverty be this: desire nothing other in this life than Jesus crucified! In him you will find the true and highest wealth. O, how poor is he who seeks nothing other than God! How rich is he who has nothing but God!

As to chastity, I did not speak of it and I shall not speak of it, because I know that regarding this virtue you are an example to your brothers. For this reason your mother loves you with the most special love. It seems right to her to have consoled you with these thoughts, specifically because God has adorned your body with this precious gem, and has adorned the fragile vase; that is, your body – with this angelic splendor. For these reasons I have confided to you the secrets of your handmaid so that they may be laid up and preserved in you. *Haec praedicta fac et vives in aeternum. Amen* [Do what I have told you and you will have eternal life. Amen].

I thank you, my Lord and almighty God, because you deigned to lift up the prayers and petitions of this blessed soul. I implore the divine Majesty that he fulfils and follows her desire for goodness.

Oratio

Gratias tibi ago, Domine, Deus meus onnipotens, qui dignatus es exaudire preces et orationes huius animae benedictae; tuam exoro maiestatem ut impleas desiderium suum in bonum et, secundum multitudinem Charitatis tuae, perfice amimam suan, clementissime Pater, in verbis ancillae tuae, et hanc oviculam reporta in brachiis charitatis tuae ad ovile misericordiarum tuarum. Per Christum Dominum nostrum, qui tecum vivit et regnat per infinita saecula. Amen. Laus Deo. Amen.

Jesus, Maria. Paulus testis.

Prayer

I thank you, O Lord, almighty God, who is granted to hear the prayers of this blessed soul. I beg your Majesty to fulfill its desire into good and, according to the multitude of your charity, fulfill its soul, most merciful Father, in the words of your handmaid, and carry back this sheep in your arms of your charity to the sheepfold of your mercies. Through Christ our Lord, who lives and reigns with you throughout the ages. Amen. Praise God. Amen.

Jesus, Mary. Paul as witness.

Purity of Heart

Purita' Del Cuore
(1521)

Purity of Heart was the last work written by St. Camilla Battista just three years before her death in 1524. The anonymous person to whom she addressed this work may have been Father Giovanni da Fano, vicar general of the Observant Franciscans. Scholars have assigned it to about the year 1521.

It consists of 13 chapters, divided and subdivided. It is full of biblical quotations so frequent that they give the work a more erudite character, perhaps taking away from the spontaneity and simplicity in her earlier works. It is the synthesis of a long life of profound contemplation and spirituality; indeed, the work reflects the spiritual life lived for so long by Camilla Battista, who composes it at a very advanced stage of her inner journey.

Purity of Heart
Camerino, 1521.

Introduction

To have learned from the good Master, reverend father,[237] his words: "Ask and you shall receive, knock and it shall be opened to you,"[238] you have tried effectively to ask me and have tried earnestly to get me to write to you something spiritual, composed not in a prayerful style, but with the love of the Holy Spirit. So thinking of your humility on the one hand, and on the other hand of my ignorance, I am compelled to take the words of the innocent Susanna: "I am completely trapped."[239] On the one hand, my father, I can not refuse to say anything, because the strength of your request forces me; on the other hand, I tremble with fear upon having to speak. Nevertheless, O good Jesus, as you say to me those words: "Give to everyone who asks of you,"[240] meaning give yourself to all those who love you, I will take the pen with confidence to do something useful for your servant. You who are the sower of chaste love, pour some burning fire into my heart, so that it will erupt and send out the sacred song of the heavenly union to this holy and thirsty soul. O holy key of David, you who open and no one closes, you close and no one opens, open to your handmaid the immense warmth of your most suave love, so that "everyone shall know that there is no God but you, and then everyone will tell of your wonderful deeds."[241] And sometimes you have deigned to proclaim your praise through the mouth of a woman, even if angelic or human powers are not enough to express how and with what art the Spirit Paraclete, comforter of souls, joins and unites with those who love him.

Three Things Necessary to the Soul that Dedicates Itself to Divine Contemplation

To begin, I am thinking of three things, my father, which I believe are necessary to the soul that is dedicated to those divine embraces of the heavenly bridegroom. The first is purity of mind. The second is the loving crucifixion. The third is the voluntary oblation of ourselves. Of the first I shall say that no soul, while retained in these corporal bonds, will ever see God with the eyes of the mind, nor savor it with the affection of the heart, without this purity of heart and mind, because it is said: "wisdom enters not into a wicked soul".[242] This is like saying: Christ Jesus, who is the wisdom of the Father,[243] in whom are hidden all the treasures of the wisdom of God[244] will never enter into a double soul, or in a wicked mind.

So that you can enjoy this morsel with the holy mouth of your soul, I, your daughter, worthless servant of Christ, tear off with my teeth the rind of this purity of mind, because I hear you say these words: "Tell me, dear daughter, how you mean this purity, so that I may make every effort to buy it." And I, my father, in purity of heart will respond to you not to consider myself uneducated or spiritual, because the Sun of righteousness[245] has taken away my innocence with so many tribulations that he wished to grant me, not for this he has withdrawn to himself his Spirit, nor will he disdain to let you know through this feminine mouth of mine how one should understand that purity of mind.

The Three Purities of Mind Necessary to Savor God

Three are the purities of mind according to my poor judgment: the first towards God, the second towards one's neighbor, the third towards ourselves. It is a great purity towards God to always think well of God, so that in everything you read of God, in everything you hear of him, you look at him with the eyes of a dove and believe him without curiously trying to understand that which you do not understand. Similarly, thinking well of God consists in receiving with gratitude prosperous things as well as adverse things, believing with certainty that they proceed equally from his supreme goodness and mercy, because he says in the Holy Scripture: "Those whom I love I correct and chastise".[246] One achieves thinking well of God when his intention is sanctified in all things. By sanctified intention I mean when everything man does, he achieves it while having God in his heart and for his love. Christ demonstrated this when he said: "I do not seek my own glory."[247] Nor must we seek our own glory, nor our honor or usefulness – even though something good comes out of us – but only God's honor and usefulness towards our neighbor.

O happy soul, that you have within you the happiness of this purity! I am sure that you hear the heavenly bridegroom often say to you these words: "How beautiful you are, how pleasing, my love, my delight"[248] in these delights of your purity! "Your eyes are doves behind your veil"[249] in this your purity, which is not shown to men of this world, but to angels. "Let me hear your voice, my love, my dove, my beautiful one; your voice is sweet";[250] that is, your love is sweet and lovable to me and "your face is comely,"[251] namely, your pure intention is too beautiful.

Strive to have this purity, my father, so that your soul, most beautiful of all the others, always dares to sing these continual songs of love to his beloved and say to him: "May my beloved come into his garden";[252] that is, into the soul, into my conscience, and into my purity and his, by the infusion of grace, the Holy Spirit who works "in the flowerbed of spices";[253] that is, in the ardor of contemplation, and "may he seize the lilies of purity";[254] that is, may he collect in this field the works of your simplicity. "My beloved come to me and do not delay, because I kept for you every new and old fruit";[255] that is, I offered you all the works of virtue, I have done all of them for your love and not to please the world. Then that peaceful wise King, Christ our God, will embrace the Queen of Sheba; that is, your beloved soul, with his chaste embraces, as the Scripture said that King Solomon gave the Queen all that she knew how to ask of him.[256]

O merciful Jesus, what does the soul in love with you ask of you, if not you, sweet delight and its Spouse? And what does the soul ask, which languishes because of love, if not your holy kisses and holy embraces, your honor and the salvation of your souls? But if it searches for something else, how can it say that it loves you, O benevolent Jesus? That mind lies if it says that it has purity of heart, while realizing that it is very far from your love. So you, most cautious one, beware of the leaven of the malice of the Pharisees,[257] by preserving yourself pristine from the superstition of the religious [friars and nuns] who deceive their own souls and do not seek anything other than their own comfort and interests and "not those of Jesus Christ,"[258] Rather follow without delay in the footsteps of my dearest Son, which is a mirror of those who yearn for the perfection of spiritual life, because in this way you will fulfill your purpose.

Of The Second Purity of Mind Necessary Towards One's Neighbor

The second purity is towards our neighbor, which we are commanded: "Love your neighbor as yourself."[259] Oh, if we loved our neighbor as ourselves, oh, what purity of mind, oh, what purity of heart would reign in us! And what does purity of the mind toward our neighbor consist of? In this: that we never judge him, but always honor him and consider him devoted and honest, because true purity towards our neighbor is in loving him with God and through God and not speaking ill of him nor harming him either with the mouth or with the heart. This is the true observance of the holy commandment.

Oh, what beautiful purity, O, how beautiful is this innocence! O sweet and gentle way, which you have such a sweet openness to God! The will of such a mind can never be stopped by anything; in fact, "the earth is his footstool,"[260] because through his virtues all earthly and perishable things are trampled under foot. O mind [filled] with such chastity and simplicity: without doubt the throne of the Kingdom of heaven is yours, where you dwell with your loved one and you are in front of that immortal King as a bride adorned with a beautiful crown by her husband, wearing on her head the crown of purity if [it were] of precious stones. You are the one in this mortal life who imitates nature and the purity of the angels. This is the purity of the one which that simple, holy, and righteous Job boasted, saying: "I harmed no one and justly I lived among men."[261]

My Lord, who can rightly ask help against me, since you know the purity of my conscience? Do you not know, Lord, that I was important and rich among all the orientals, but I never harmed any person? Do you see, my father, in God's eyes how much courage this holy purity towards one's neighbor gives man? Who still doubts that in the moment of death because of this purity, his fear would not be taken away from him? Believe me that, in that extreme moment, those souls who possess it will hear from the bridegroom some sweet and affectionate words of his love. Then the bridegroom shall say: "Come from Lebanon, fairest among women, come from Lebanon, wife, come."[262] And therefore in the Canticle, she is called three times to indicate these three purities. Thus it will be said to the pure and simple soul: "Come, sweet and lovely as Jerusalem, city of the great king, because the fragrance of your garments is more agreeable than all spices";[263] that is, the fragrance of your works to the neighbor gives divine fragrance to my divinity. "Your breasts are like twin fawns";[264] that is, like two twin sons are the breasts of your purity to me and to others, because one without the other is not conducive to salvation.

Take, my father, this purity for your sweet spouse and at every hour and every moment kiss her [the purity], hug her, make resound those inner voices toward your heavenly fellow citizens and tell them the cause of your great love. Appropriate for yourself the words of Wisdom: "I loved her and sought after her from my youth,"[265] I sought her as a wife and I fell in love with her and her beauty. It is she who shows discipline, which is the full knowledge of God, she shows sobriety, prudence and justice of which in this life there is nothing more useful. O dear father, do not be surprised if I am faint for love[266] because even the Lord of all loved her.[267]

The Third Purity of Mind Necessary Towrds Ourselves

The third purity is towards ourselves, which never presumes to itself any good. Saint Paul had this purity when he said: "We are not able...";[268] that is, we can not think of a good thought as proceeding from us, but our sufficiency comes from God. They are few words, but contain in them great substance, but are understood little today. Believe me, father, he who listens to them sings that verse of the prophet: "I will pay my vows to the Lord in the house of the Lord, in your courts, O Jerusalem";[269] that is, I attribute my good works to you, O Lord, and I will not cease to do good in public or in secret, until my light and the works you make me do render glory to your Majesty, not to mine. So the purity towards ourselves consists in having the lowest[270] recognition of ourselves; I'm not saying that it consists in bad words or blame that man says about himself with his lips, but in the opinion that he has in his heart of recognizing himself as truly the lowest, because if God did not guard over us, we would fall into all sorts of very grave sins. For this reason the holy one, Job, said: "Deliver me, O Lord, and set me beside you, and let any man's hand fight against me,"[271] as long as you, Lord, watch over me.

Oh, how useful is this purity, because it always makes prudent those who have it. The grace of God will go forever before this purity, as thunder and lightning come before the hail. O sweet maker of this purity! O great virtue! Blessed are those who always possess it, and have no false esteem of themselves, so that they shall enjoy and savor the sweetnesses poured out of his goodness into the soul that has this purity. Also to this purity belongs with pure affection of heart knowledge of just how powerless we are to withstand the adversities of the world, as the Prophet recognized: "You are, Lord, my patience and hope."[272] Namely Lord, where do I have the virtues to withstand challenging things with patience? You, you, Lord, are my patience, and whoever does not have this patience walks in darkness; but the soul full of this purity "shall spring up in his days justice and abundance of peace."[273] Oh, what gusto! Oh, what peace! Oh, what tranquility of mind! "That peace that surpasses all understanding" [274] an indescribable joy that often will raise up the eyes to the mountains.[275] And what mountains? Mountains of the mercy of God, from which will come to him the help to endure hardships, and he will confess to almighty God his nothingness and impotence. Oh, how pleasing to God is this humble confession that comes from the purity of heart!

No wonder the bridegroom said in the Canticle: "You are all beautiful, my love, my pretty because in you there is no stain,"[276] stain of false esteem of self. "How beautiful are your footsteps."[277] The footsteps that walk with angelic purity should not be beautiful? "O prince's daughter"[278] holy friendly soul of the King of kings, in which is joyous purity, the dove of the Holy Spirit who nests in the crevices of stone.[279] What are these crevices, what is this rock? "That rock was Christ";[280] the cracks of the stone in which this dove nests are the wounds of Christ. "In the cave";[281] that is, in the wound of the sacred side [of Christ], there, there throw your heart like water and say with the prophet: "My heart melts like wax."[282] O holy purity, how lovely is your condition, your yoke, how easy and light to he who loves you![283] "Your name spoken is a spreading perfume, that is why the maidens love you,"[284] the holy souls, the pure virgins longed for without measure. But we, weak and infirm, "will follow you eagerly to the fragrance of your perfumes";[285] that is, we will follow your fragrance, but the perfect soul will rest in you as in his bed.

You have here, my father, the three purities, which I have named thus, because they do not have in themselves any mixture of falsehood. Take pains to place them "in the parched land,"[286] in the land of your heart, that longs so much for the divine love, and they will be for you as an honored mother, because soon you shall say: "Yet all good things came together to me in her company."[287]

The Loving Crucifixion Necessary to Savor God and the Three Kinds of Crucifixions

But let us now turn to the loving crucifixion. "He who wishes to come after me must deny himself."[288] O sweet Jesus, with what harsh words you wish that I take up the cross! So therefore, ineffable goodness, do you want to put me on the cross? Do you not know how I am weak in suffering? But poor me! If you, who are refulgence of eternal light,[289] true God and true man "the most handsome of the sons of men,"[290] so delicate, were placed on the cross, should I, who am but dust and ashes, remain free from this cross? You who did not commit sin[291] have been crucified for me, and I will refuse being crucified for you? Give me, Lord, this greatness of soul and gratitude so that I wish with all my heart to suffer for you, to be crucified for you, so that nothing gives a more fragrant perfume to your divinity than the lily of this desire. But let no one doubt that after that holy purity this crucifixion should come for her, because the soul adorned with this purity constantly burns in the love of this crucifixion. She never speaks to her Spouse without wanting to be united with him and do for him as much as she knows that he has done for her.

We must then consider three types of crucifixion: the first comes from God, the second from man, the third from the devil. At the first cross you, father, availed yourself when you bravely embraced the advice of the Lord to be locked in the prison of holy religion [consecrated religious life]: all true lovers of God must be crucified to this first cross, because it is necessary to first suffer and then with the crown of immortal triumph enter "in the joy of his Lord."[292]

And if you shall verify, you will find that in this crucifixion are five things: the cross, the naked man, the nails, the hammer and the executioner. To these five correspond five other things: to the cross corresponds religious life and the way of life in this cloister; to the naked man, the spiritual soul stripped of love of visible things; to the nails, the obedience with which we are attached to the cross of religion, and this is a nail; the other two are poverty and chastity, without which we could not stay attached to religious life. The hammer is the love of God, that hammers the three nails and makes them enter into the will, because no one could ever receive in himself those three nails, if the hammer of the love of God does not spur them on. Finally, the executioner, who is God, or man or the devil. We come now to the three individual crucifixions.

The First Crucifixion Coming from God

The first crucifixion is when God deprives the soul of the flame of his love and leaves it dry, taking away his lovely presence that [the soul] was used to contemplating. Of this the bride complained in the Canticle, saying: "I searched for him and did not find him";[293] I have searched for him with crying affection of my heart and he did not answer. And as a woman who lost her husband will call her relatives and friends and with them mourn bitterly of her widowhood, just the same the soul thusly crucified calls the saints of God and the help of the Angels, saying, "I beseech you, daughters of Jerusalem."[294] I beg you, holy souls, who are in heavenly Jerusalem, I mean in the vision of peace, find my beloved and let him know that I languish for his love; that is, help me with your prayers, because I am languishing in this crucifixion. This pain has become intolerable, and I could not explain to you the pain that I suffer. O bitter crucifixion, who can ever express your torment? But here is the answer to this soul: "What is your beloved, O fairest among women?"[295] That is, O sweet and beautiful soul among all the others, not only among the devout souls, but also among the choirs of Angels, for your affection and your love are so ardent, that they seem more angelic than human, who is this your beloved?

"All you who pass by the way,"[296] O you seekers of God who pass through this valley of tears along the pathway of divine love who, because of his goodness, are worthy to savor, observe a little and see with the eyes of your prudence if there is any sorrow in the world compared to mine. I was a woman; that is, a sinful soul, "my love was my father and my mother,"[297] because the devil and the concupiscence of the flesh had generated me towards sin. But my delight, I am trying with all my heart, passing through my quarters with his grace he had mercy on me and covered me with the vestment of grace and honored me as his wife[298], placing the crown of his love on my head. "His left hand is under my head."[299] that is, he placed his left hand under my head, placing in my memory the pains of Hell, and with his right hand he embraced me with the sweetness of his love so that I would have no reason to go and see foreign nations[300]; "He anointed me with oil of gladness,"[301] giving me the sweetness of his mercy; "He adorned me with gold, and honored me with silver of purity";[302] that is, he dressed me with gold filling me with feelings of love and he honored me with the silver of purity, illuminating my mind and intellect of pure discretion. "And I received from his mouth milk and honey";[303] that is, in my contemplation, I sipped milk and honey; that is, the brightness and the sweetness of his virtues that he inspired in my heart, and from him I was provided with such gifts.[304]

But behold now, in a moment, I am sunk in my helplessness and misery, deprived of my joys.[305] O you who pass by the way of life and discipline, hear my cry: "Hear, heavens, what I say"[306] and "you earth be attentive with your ears";[307] you O heavens, and you perfect souls, and you earth, I mean souls that are full of sensual and earthly appetites, hear the laments that are mine, so that you also may know [how you should] get away from evil and get close to the goodness, which is grace. "To you, O daughters of Jerusalem, my mouth is open,"[308] that is, I address my words to you, souls in love with God; with you it is sweet to speak of love, because an icy heart could not understand me. My beloved Spouse, blessed Jesus, whom I loved and savored, I still also embraced with pure devotion, this is my beloved "who is white and radiant;[309] His head is fine gold, his eyes divine, his cheeks like beds of spices, his lips dripping with myrrh, his throat is very sweet, his hands full of hyacinths";[310] "his words are words of eternal life."[311]

Finally, my beloved is all love, all desirable, chosen from among the thousands.[312] Such a beloved I lost and for this reason my soul is troubled and my innermost being is agitated. I no longer have my heart or spirit; my whole soul is poured out in tears because I no longer find the one who loves my soul.[313] O spiritual guides of souls, weep with me "because as big as the ocean is my affliction."[314] O great loss, O indescribable woe! But you, O merciful Jesus, look how vile is my soul: this life of mine without you is unbearable for me as a war, because you are my peace, you are my heaven, you are my ineffable love, from which I now find myself alienated, for you have cast me behind your back and for this I can find no rest.

O unhappy soul, who will heal you from such a sickness? Oh, what a Spouse you have lost! However, I do not marvel that your joy has changed into tears because your comforter has distanced himself from you. O my father, believe those who have been tried [and know] that there is no greater tribulation than when the soul suffers the tribulation of the removal of grace. But among many similar torments there are three that seem unbearable and for which the person could not be saved if God had not trained them, because after the subtraction of grace and love, the soul suffers in three things: in memory, intellect and will.

In memory it suffers because it recalls the benefits received from God: the tranquility and peace that Israel had; that is, the soul that sees God and with compunction said: "The Lord rejected his altar";[315] God has kicked out my own soul; he cursed that which he had blessed "and I forgot all good."[316]

Intellect then suffers because she seems to consider a negative all that God does in her, not knowing how to discern right from wrong because of the withdrawal of the light of the intellect. In such a way, sometimes she even doubts Holy Scripture, seeming to her that what she reads is contrary to the truth, to the point of asking herself where the words of Christ Jesus are: "whoever drinks from this water;"[317] that is, who drinks of this water that I shall give will never have thirst; and that other, "Whoever follows me will never walk in darkness";[318] and the other still, "Everything you ask in prayer, believe that you have received it."[319] Now, about me, Lord, are these things vain? Did I not drink to myself this water of your kindness? And still here I am thirsty and tormented by dryness of spirit. Did I not follow in your way and behold, my soul is in great darkness? Have I not prayed, did I not shed many tears before your face? What profits me if your light "is clear and does not illumine me to walk in your way? Your inheritance has passed to strangers;"[320] that is, the soul that you had possessed from inheritance is totally foreign to you. And what else do you believe the prophet suffered when he said: "Give me understanding and I will live?"[321] So great a prophet, feeling deprived of the light of grace, asked for intellect to live, because without that light he considered himself dead.

The third passion and torment is in the will. When the will becomes lukewarm and cold, virtues are accomplished with great difficulty, one walks in the way of God with sadness and melancholy, as if it were very tiring, and he goes looking for consolations outside, feeling a great inclination to do evil because of penury and lack of good will and, even without wishing, he arrives at many imperfections. Oh, how easily he jumps into a rage and is disturbed by a little word as if it were a bolt of lightning! O good Jesus, how you changed the food and meal to this soul! Who could ever think of the strength of this tormented [one] and consider with fear the weight of that [passion]? "Forgive, O Lord, forgive and let your servants beg you!"[322]

But the soul should not despair in this, because the good Lord said that he will give paradise to the one who drinks of this crucifixion.[323] You can well believe that it is a great torment that makes a soul almost crazy and makes it almost fall into despair, so that the words of Job burst forth: "May the day of my birth perish... Why did you set me against you, and I became burdensome to myself?"[324] Have I not stood guard from offending you? Have I not devoted myself to your love? Why has your anger now reached me?

The Second Crucifixion Coming from Man

It happens sometimes, as happened to Job, that his own family and friends heap pain on top of pain in the form of consolation.[325] But he who knows and sees all things disapproves of the "accusers" of Job and [truly] comforts him, because the misfortunes of this spiritual warfare are not written in the book of divine justice, since the soul is practically deprived of reason out of its great dryness and weakness of spirit. And as a dead man does not savor anything that is good in itself – neither blessed words, nor readings from Sacred Scripture – just the same the soul, lacking in substantive and nourishing virtues that God gave it, remains as if it were dead and in such a state that the words of the prophet have meaning: "I wail with anguish of heart,"[326] and those of Job: "My soul is weary of my very life,"[327] and those of the other Psalm: "I have sunk into the deep mud and there is no foothold,"[328] and that one again: "the Lord put his hand on every delight of my soul;"[329] that is, the Lord laid hands on all the things that delighted me and oppressed me in the land of misery and calamity. "The Lord has taken away all my mighty men; in the midst of me has taken away all my splendor is spread on the floor of my bile ... and here I despised all those who honor me";[330] that is, the Lord has removed all the spiritual enlightenment; my affection that used to pour out all in him has turned to earthly things. The angels that were watching over this purity of mine have turned away from me.[331]

O you who pass by the way of purity, see if there is any sorrow like mine. And it happens sometimes that the Lord's hand lowers itself to the depths, adding to this forlorn soul the spirit of blasphemy, that without the consent of the will, makes it say awful things against the Majesty of God: and this spirit drives away all virtues as a moth chews away at clothes. And not just this, as well as the torment of the spirit at times is added that of the body. And when man is tormented in body and spirit, then he thinks what a great martyrdom he has, so he can sing that verse: "day of calamity and misery ... awesome and very bitter day";[332] it is well a day of calamity and misery, because it is day and not night, because in any case is sent by God to punish and not to kill.

Nor does God sometimes fail to send men a valiant Captain, who afflicts them in [temporal] goods and in fame, as he did to Job when he said to the devil: Behold, all his possessions I put in your power, just do not harm to his soul.[333] Now if a man really seeks God, he should not care of any damage [or loss received] to temporal wealth; on the contrary, he should rejoice in knowing that all things proceed from God, and the one who takes away material things in this life is actually a minister of God, and as such must be loved, especially because through material sufferings, [this minister] allows him to gain eternal life. They are certainly bitter pills to swallow; even the perfect ones [i.e. saints], if the grace of God does not help them, bend under such a weight and recoil from the yoke of patience. But the soul alight from the fire of love does not rest in anything other than God so that this fire cannot be extinguished by the fire of tribulations, since love is stern as death,[334] so he who loves seeks out his beloved equally in adversity as in prosperity, in consolations and in afflictions.

But the bride in the Canticle [Song of Songs] describes another kind of torment, that is sometimes given to us by the prelates and pastors of our souls, when she says: "As I searched for my beloved, the watchmen of the city found me and beat me; the custodians of the walls took away my mantle";[335] the guards of the city are the prelates to whom belong the care of souls, who are the beautiful city. So says the pure and simple soul: while I was looking for my beloved Redeemer, my [spiritual] fathers, from whom I had hoped for help and consolation, beat me with harsh words and wounded me with worse deeds and under a pretext of good, they took from me a [natural?] father who was my refuge in my tribulations. These prying prelates are guardians of the ceremonial walls of religion but not the walls of the good and holy life: woe to those prelates and pastors who dissipate the flock of the Lord![336]

But what God allows to happen with his great and ineffable providence is not for us little men to judge, and we should not stop honoring these prelates because of this; rather, we must frequently pray for them and say with the prophet: "May the sword of sorrow and compassion come into their hearts and may their bows be broken";[337] that is may their hardness and dignity break. "Yet I will dress in sackcloth and my prayer for their salvation will come back in my heart;"[338] that is, when they trouble me, I will dress in sackcloth and ashes of humility and patience, and my prayer, which when done for them, will return to my benefit.[339]

But let it be: he who can understand these things [already] knows them; it is enough to know that sometimes such unpleasant things happen and for this he who was master of errors then becomes disciple of truth and compassion toward others. But listen, my father, to what is acquired through that patience, "For thus says the Lord, I will make you a pillar in the temple of your God and you will no longer go out ... and I will give you the morning star."[340] Because you have been patient for my sake, I will make you as a column in my house, and give you a unique light and a marvelous understanding of my ways. "O beautiful and graceful bride ... Your lips drip honey from the comb";[341] that is, beautiful Spouse, who despite [the fact that] your prelates were hard and unbearable to you, you had so much sweetness and prayed for their salvation, so the good example that you gave your neighbor with this constancy and patience has come from the nostrils of my divinity. "Your soul is a locked up garden, my sister, noble spouse; you are an enclosed spring, a sealed fountain";[342] that is, if your soul had not been closed up in me, you would go looking for other consolations and perhaps you would have broken your neck. But since you have been steadfast in suffering the torments that the prelates have given you, so your actions are full of the sweet fruits of heaven.

The Third Crucifixion Coming from the Devil

The final crucifixion comes from the devil when he turns the soul to vices, and truly *libera nos, Domine* [Deliver us, Lord][343] from this crucifixion, because this one causes many stars to fall from the sky of their purity; the sun and the moon of love darkens; that is, good behavior does not give light to his neighbor. Weep Jerusalem, faithful soul, in this crucifixion, because other times have you been a holy city, and now you have become a city of vices. "You were a noble Lady of nations full of people";[344] that is, you were a noble Lady of your feelings, full of good and holy works, and now you have become a city of sin.

Oh, what cruel affliction is inflicted by vices, excited by the envy of the devil that drives pride against God, envy against his neighbor, and lust against ourselves. Blinded by pride is the intellect, while in a certain way we flaunt our own good works in front of God, as if they did not proceed from him; and we think we have left the vanity of the world, that we had disparaged worldly honors and wealth, that we could have harmed [someone] and we did not, that we could have sustained injuries and insults for his sake, and so on.

Oh, what hidden instigation of the devil is this: "They have set a trap for my feet, they have dug a pit before me,"[345] as the prophet said: they laid a snare and dug a pit before my feet for my esteem [of self]. But the prudent soul takes up the shield of his lowliness and misery and goes to meet him with the light of humility, recognizing himself most vile, indeed as nothing, and in this way is freed from temptation and sin. Envy then is what really closes in hell the soul still united to the body; it destroys the beauty of religion which is union and charity, and, as a bad show, devours the peace of those who live in holiness.

O cruel beast, bloody from the blood of others, who could ever lower your anger and slow your momentum? O good Master of purity, compassionate Jesus, take away from me this cup, if possible, as well as all those who seek "the face of the God of Jacob."[346] Do you know then that the soul must respond to similar evil suggestions? O most evil devil, I have already stripped myself of my [worldly] tunic, how shall I vest?[347] That is, I despised the honor and magnificence of the world, now shall I envy those who have the holy honor of religion [in the monastery or friary]? I have washed my feet, I have taken myself from the heart of my father, mother, relatives and friends for the love of God; shall I perhaps return smeared with envy of my dear sisters, who are here with me in religion [the monastery]? To your scorn, [i.e. the devil's] not only do I not wish to envy them, but I want to be pleased with their honor as if it were mine.

Regarding the vice of lust, it is better to remain silent now than talk about it. But if the Apostle, caught up to the third heaven, in whose heart resounded always Christ Jesus, complains of this stimulus,[348] what shall become of us miserable ones? He who touches such a crucifixion can rightly shout: *Deus meus! Deus meus*! "My God, my God, why hast thou forsaken me?"[349] The man almost sends out his spirit and, as he dies, dies to the world, and bowing his head of pride, hands over his spirit to God.[350] O holy death! Blessed is he who dies such a death and casts out the harshness of his head in humility. "May my soul die this death";[351] that is, the death of the just, because "precious in the sight of the Lord is the death of his saints."[352] Oh, how precious this death, oh, how pleasing to God!

How the Soul Purified from its Vices must Acquire the Virtue of Humility in Order to Savor Divine Sweetness

But you should know, father, that even though it's in the crucifixion of these vices and sins, the soul is made pleasing to the divine presence; however, if the virtue of humility does not penetrate the heart more deeply, the heavenly bridegroom, while the said crucifixion lasts, as one who is scorned does not speak to his beloved spouse; that is, to the soul. Indeed he shows a certain contempt, for which the spouse remains so afflicted that, for excessive love, says to herself: "At least he should speak and say all the reproaches and insults that I deserve; at least then I would have the consolation of hearing that holy and blessed voice of his beloved mouth, because even though he threatened me, his voice would be to me the sweetest melody. But I remain troubled because I do not hear him say either good or bad words."

When you're at this point, O soul, then rejoice, because your beloved is not angry, but says nothing in order that you humble yourself more and you light up with perfect love. This is what the bride in the Canticle said: "This is my beloved standing behind the wall, looking through the gate;"[353] that is, the bridegroom of the soul is watching this crucifixion and secretly waits for your victory against vices based on your humility. And so, therefore, have in mind the words of Revelation: "the victor will not be harmed by the second death, and I will give him hidden manna;"[354] that is, he who shall conquer this pride and make extinct these vices will not be offended by the treacherous death of Hell; I shall give the sweetest manna unknown to those who do not [currently] taste it, and a little white stone in which is carved my name, so that no one can understand, but only the one who receives it. Do not believe that a living person can imagine this intimate and gentle knowledge, if before he was not allowed to savor it.

"Forget the disgrace of your widowhood, for your Lord is your Creator."[355] God said through the mouth of Isaiah. You, soul, exercised in such a battle, forget the shame of your widowhood when you were devoid of the grace of the bridegroom and you were without merit, because from now on he who made you will hold you in his own way; he will never let you be led by the infernal enemy in those disordered appetites in which he left you for a short time, but now and forever he will embrace you and he will pull you to himself, as is the meaning of those words: "for a moment I abandoned you, but will welcome you with great mercies: the moment of my wrath I hid my face to you, but with everlasting mercy I had mercy on you."[356] That gracious Spouse allows us to have difficulty in this life just for a moment; but then he embraces and welcomes us into a close friendship that lasts forever; but he first has us walk the path of virtue founded upon a perfect humility and he has his angels guard over us, as is revealed by these words: "Behold, I shall place stones as the foundation";[357] that is the virtues, and "I will rebuild you in sapphires and rubies and I will set you in carved stones, you will be established in justice and in an abundance of peace; because I liken you to a mare of Pharaoh's chariot horses."[358] I will give you the foundation of humility, your fortifications will be the angels; I will put in order your feelings which are the doors to your soul, so that no one can remove them from obedience of the humbled and sanctified soul, and you will have in you all righteousness and such an uprightness of mind that the whole world will not be able to disturb you, because when you were laboring so much in resisting against vices for my love, I almost equalized your strength and purity to the virtue of the Angels, who are my knights. "Winter has passed, the rain are gone and are over. Arise, my love, and come"[359] and the sacred repose of virtue enters.

You realize now, father, as God causes all things to lead to the salvation of his elect[360] and therefore "praise, Jerusalem, the Lord,"[361] because he has freed you from death of sin and freed you from the fears and [false] fruits, from which you derived no benefit. Do not let yourself fall again into sin: "Put on the garments of splendor";[362] that is, recognize the priceless grace that he did for you and dress your soul with it so that you are always in this grace, and never leave her [grace], because your Spouse will always be with you and "will rest forever in your tent."[363]

Renewal, Illumination and Peace Enjoyed by the Soul Purified from Vices and Clothed in Virtues

After this loving crucifixion, you will be able to say: "then I saw a new heaven and a new earth."[364] Oh, what marvelous new [things] that take place both in the body as the soul when these vices are crucified, and while having passed through so many bitter [events] patiently and victoriously, one truly sees risen a new heaven and a new earth. By heaven I mean the soul and by the earth I mean the body, like two things that are renewed in humans when they are offered to God with purity of heart. And this offering [oblation] is made as mentioned above: in the memory, the intellect and the will, because in these three powers, the soul is crucified and dies.

Oh, wonderful Master, how orderly your works proceed to those who wish to search them out with holy speculation! The more this Master loves us, the more often he afflicts us. He intends it to [he] who can. He always tries to make earthly things become more bitter every day, so he alone is sweet. In a way, he kills the soul every day and in a way he revives it, so that he almost leads it to Hell and in an instant he pulls it out; and when it seems that it hurts most, precisely then he heals it, so that having passed through this crucifixion and death of which we have spoken, the soul is resuscitated almost immortal and untried; and [then] it behaves in this mortal life not in a worldly way, but as in Heaven; not as a human creature but angelic.

And whence does this come? From the strength that the Holy Spirit gave [the soul] in memory, from the light that it gave in the intellect, from the love that it gave in the will. Since it was first troubled by the memory so that it could not remember things other than those of the world; in the intellect because it did not know things other than those of the world and it was blind of the things of God; in the will because it did not love things other than those that could be felt with the senses and it was icy towards the things of God; for this [strength, light, love] I began to sing the sweetest Hallelujah, which is sung by the angels in Heaven and say: "The Lord is truly risen, alleluia."[365] What joy, joy! for the Lord, who died in me for my sins, was raised.

This is also represented by the gesture of Jacob who woke up in the morning and picked up a stone.[366] Jacob represents the simple and pious soul who, having awoken from the sleep of sin, in the day of grace picks up the stone of divine love which in his torment he had behind his head, and upon this rock spreads the oil of gladness[367] and rejoicing of the heart, which is an acceptable and enormous sacrifice, when the jubilant soul says to itself: "Behold, the Lord was with me and I did not know him."[368] Noah acted with God in the same way after the flood water;[369] that is, in the same way all the friends of God, after having escaped from danger, offer sacrifices and oblations to the Lord that are figures of the oblation that the soul makes of itself to God after the liberation from above said tribulation, submitting itself completely to the divine will, which seeks nothing more from us than our sanctification in three things already said; that is, memory, intellect and will.

How the Three Powers are Sanctified, and Firstly the Memory

The memory is sanctified when one completely engages in three things: firstly, he always remembers the Passion of Christ; secondly he has constant pain and regret for his sins; and thirdly, he always remembers the benefits received from God. The memory of the Passion of Christ is like an ark of heavenly treasures,[370] a door that gives access to enter and enjoy glorious Jesus who is the perfect Master of all spiritual arts: "an inexhaustible source of living water,"[371] a deep well of the secrets of God. Oh, blessed is he who has [this memory], probably because it is a sign of predestination, through which all are written in the book of life.[372] O sweet memory, you who make flow sweet tears of love with which because of your sweetness, you move the interior and the roots of the heart and you bring countless ornaments to the soul! He who does not believe in [this memory] should prepare himself to test it a little and by experience will find that this memory exceeds all the mental works that man can do in this life. Therefore, whoever wants to be free from all impurities and have a sign of future glory and beatitude, inasmuch as one can have in this life, should strive to have this sweet memory of the Passion of Christ, as the apostle Paul had, who carried continuously the stigmata of the Passion in his body.[373] So do not marvel that he dared to say: I am sure that neither death nor life, nor danger in the world will separate me from the love of my Lord;[374] and he dared to say that the crown of righteousness was prepared for him.[375]

The memory of sins is also very pleasing to God, as long as you do in the way indicated by the prophet: "I shall go on through all my years despite the bitterness of my soul";[376] that is, remembering their sins with very bitter pain. For here is born true contrition, which returns original innocence to the soul, making it acceptable and loving to God, so much that it remains always in grace, as a fruitful olive tree.[377] In these oblations the soul begins to feel the trumpet of most ardent charity, thinking of the abyss of so much goodness that it finds in God. As with so little effort it feels it has returned in grace to the Lord whom it had so offended, it starts to play the organ of seraphic affections, and with eyes downcast out of contrition it worships God with true adoration, deeming itself nothing. And bowing to the one who is all and is above all, expanding in the memory of the great blessings unworthily received from God, it ruminates and chews on the affliction of the heart, on the providence of the heavenly Spouse in its life, it considers the prudence and effectiveness in healing the wounds of its iniquity, and in such a consideration it completely dissolves and liquifies and in the secret of the heart sends to Heaven voices that rise up from the marrow of the loving heart, making a certain silence full of voices of loving prayer, saying continually: "O Spouse of which I am unworthy, O Father not deserved by such a miserable soul, who will give me strength and power to die for you? O highest and lovable goodness of mine, O everlasting life, O peace who overcomes every feeling, O inexplicable sweetness, indescribable love (and many other items of similar content that the spirit continually gives to her). O love, O happy memory that you are fully dedicated in remembering the sweetness and wonderful goodness of your God and your miseries and sorrows as did the poor man, the seraphic St. Francis."

I dare say that even though you are still in this mortal body, nonetheless you already have rewards of immortality, because, whether at home or away, either in bed or in a room, or sitting or standing, or silent or speaking, you always have God in your constant company who, though a thousand fall at your side, ten thousand at your right hand, he defends you from the arrow that flies by day; that is from the smoke of vainglory, which is dangerous in the necessary works of the flesh, which is a night.[378]

Illumination of Our Intellect and His Works

After this oblation of the memory, right away the intellect is illuminated by the rays of divine knowledge of heavenly secrets and intimate understanding of the theological reasons; and the more the soul is enlightened, the more it recognizes itself obscure and impotent and, discovering in itself its ineptitude and misery, it seems that every other person is superior to itself.

The soul then makes three other offerings of its intellect, because when the intellect illumines it to know the theological acumen, it is surprised with fear and trembling in reflecting on the King of kings in his majesty and in considering him wounded and immortal, who, though not needing anyone, provides everyone with such largesse. And it is frightening [to think] that such a Lord that he is, and he alone can know himself, lowered himself out of such boundless love for his creature, to the point of exposing himself to so many sufferings and even death for his miserable sheep. And he practically forgot about himself and, having taken the form of a servant, almost forgot his divine form by putting it aside to show himself effectively a man who was wounded and mortal like us.[379]

In such thoughts, the soul exclaims to itself, "O love who has no equal, O inebriated love, how much highness lowers itself, how much wisdom becomes foolish! O eternal Father, who are you and who am I? Are you not the source of all perfection, the highest good of every creature, and I am a nothing? Are you not all love and charity, and I am all hate? Are you not an inextinguishable light and I am a darkness? Are you not the highest charity and peace that surpasses all sweetness, and am I war, unrest and disorder?"

O goodness, O mercy, O sweetness of my heart, the joy of my soul: "my reward is too great."[380] Why did you love me so much? What did you find in me? Why did that gracious loving Heart of yours dedicate itself so tenderly in loving me? O unworthy soul, is it licit to say or think such a thing? Did not my beloved Spouse sing this song: "you wounded my heart, my sister, my bride?"[381]

How have I hurt you, my God? Do you say to me, my dear Lord, these sweet words of yours? Am I that sweet flower of yours that you say you had known before you created the world? "My sweet perfume spreads like nard."[382] O my dear Lord, you liked so much the fragrance of these crucifixions of mine, that they made you fall in love with me; I made little effort, everything proceeded from your kindness and goodness! O wonderful thing. This is the illumination that the prophet desired when he said, "send forth your light and truth";[383] send me, Lord, your light, so that you take me away from the darkness of self-love, and lead me to the mountain of knowledge of your beauty and my deformity, and in your tents; that is, in your charity which is the special seat of God, because "where charity and love abound, there is God"[384] and without love no man shall see God either in this life through grace nor in the other through glory. This is one of the theological and irrefutable virtues that the soul learns in the book of life, with the eye of the intellect, because blessed is the man whom God teaches in his law.[385]

This is the love of God and neighbor: for God "the fulfillment of the law is love,"[386] so that those who can not read and can not study so much have to do nothing other than love well, and when they have done this, it includes all the divine law. After that, the soul is enlightened of the knowledge of its own nothingness and misery; this is the greatest enlightenment that one can have, because it proceeds from the thunder and the lightning of seraphic love, and behind it always comes the fiery lightning of divine love that burns and consumes every defect. Oh, what philosophy is in knowing oneself and knowing God, as much as possible for human nature.

O Francis, patriarch of the poor, this is your philosophy [i.e. his Rule of Life] to which many make professions in words, but not in your presence and in their feelings and intellect. Who are you and who am I? And since we are on this subject, [the soul] is stupefied with admiration and ecstasy and at the same time receives a huge light and ineffable savor, with which light, even if everyone exalts it, could not budge from the clear knowledge of its own nothingness, and the more it heard itself being praised, the more it would abhor the madness of those who praised it, and it would not cease saying with Job: "What is man, that you make so much of him? And why did you ask him in your heart?"[387] What is man, if not rotting inside and out, incitement to sin, as a leaven of vice, as a deadly and infectious poison that corrupts the whole mass of souls, which is mirrored in him? Finally, who am I, if not a lost sheep among the thorns of sin?[388] And what is the love that I bring you, my sweet Lord, if not annoying hatred? What are my praises, if not blasphemy? What are these works of mine, which seem to be virtues before men, other than a polluted rag?[389] O God, before whom the stars of the morning are not clean, that "you found flaws even in the angels,"[390] before whom no living man will be justified by his virtue: throw me away from you, Lord, because it is too unworthy a thing to be with you!

O my father, he who does not really humble himself interiorly, labors in vain to humble himself outwardly. "The deep is calling on the deep;"[391] in fact, he who totally immerses himself in the knowledge of divine greatness and knowledge of their own misery, deeming himself less than the dust of the earth and not only of this but also of their own deeper abyss, says to God: "Lord, I deserve a thousand hells, cast me away from you because I am a sinful man," as St. Peter said[392] for having known this truth in your light; for the confusion I feel in me I can no longer tolerate the presence of your great sweetness. "Flee, flee, my beloved, like a deer and a deer in the mountains of Bethel."[393] Send your presence away from me as far the east is from the west. Go up, now, to the mountains of Bethel;[394] that is, visit, Lord, and possess the high mountains of the holy and immaculate souls, and do not send your rays upon this mud.

"O sun, that never fades,"[395] such splendor is not deserved by this dark soul, as my eyes can not bear so much light. So do not stay with us, Lord, but fly to your royal room where there are cherubim and seraphim and holy and worthy souls. This is the worthy oblation and the acceptable sacrifice, the victim of peace burned by the cherubic fire, of whose fragrance the blessed Trinity fills itself, then to the mind burned in this way send the cherubic spirit that lights it up and offers it to God in sacrifice of the most sweet fragrance.[396]

Finally, the intellect is enlightened by always thinking good of his neighbor and considering all that he sees [in his neighbor] as a good intention, so that it does not happen to him a great drawback that always occurs in men. Because it happens to many that, upon seeing some virtue in his neighbor, they say that he only pretends to have it; and if they see that someone generous in giving alms, they say that he does it for ambition; and if anyone talks about the things of God and sings of God's praises with gusto, they say that he is a hypocrite and that he likes [hearing] himself speak. But those who are enlightened by those divine rays do just the opposite, and the more someone tries to hide their virtue, they recognize it admirably; and if any man were so clever in simulating a virtue that was really concealing a vice, these illuminated ones have a remarkable sagacity in discerning true virtue from vice; and God also opens their eyes so that they can fall in love with the virtues of others and have compassion for their defects and remedy them as much as possible. For this it happens many times that the virtues of others are valued much higher than one's owns and vices are judged to be very minor. If he sees a generous person, he says that not he is not only such, but that he is a saint of heaven. If another speaks sweetly of God, he says he is another St. Paul. Similarly he says that the defects of others are fragility, and excuses them as much as he can.

Oh great merit one finds in this love of neighbor; because he considers all [the other's] virtues without any watering down and he likewise is able to consider [the other's] vices to be virtues. From this it follows that he considers religious houses of friars and nuns to be like Heaven in the likeness of the celestial city, where this [earthly] sun does not shine, but the love of God and of the immaculate Lamb "is radiated."[397] So in these monasteries, their light is love, which is God,[398] and in that light one can not see where any darkness of envy or hatred. Whoever has this charity is so pleasing to God that he can not refrain from offering the beautiful words from the Canticle: How beautiful you are, my love, in your delights][399] how beautiful you are, God says to the soul, in these sweet delights of love; "Your stature is like a palm tree, the hair of your head like purple of the king."[400] But the soul that feels exalted in mind, when it is founded upon the solid rock of Christ's humility and its own misery, responds with a certain joy of humility, with a certain melody of its own nothingness and says: "Flee, flee, my beloved, to the mountains of Bethel";[401] My Lord, I do not deserve you to be with me, nor that you give me this sweetness. Give it, Lord, to your mountains; that is, to your holy Angels, because since I am so vile, I should not have the King of glory in this misery. It will be enough [for me], my Lord, to have you in Heaven; I do not want you, Lord, in this valley of tears, in this sickness and great misery, but with the glory of the saints. Your visitation will not suit me in these miseries and misfortunes, so when I think of you, it makes me cringe: "In your light, I saw your light";[402] Lord, I have seen the light of your divinity in your lowliness and your lowliness injured my heart.

O humility, guardian of all virtues, mirror of those who walk in the yoke of the holy faith, with which the more you drive out God from you, the more you drive him closer; the more you flee from the fire of divine love, the more you close yourself in the furnace of charity; the more you fear entering into the source of living water, the more you enter with closed eyes in the sea of fiery seraphim. To he who makes a sacrifice of his own intellect, God responds: "I have chosen and sanctified this house";[403] that is, I have chosen and sanctified this sacrifice of yours for myself, so there my name shall remain forever, and my eyes and my heart shall forever be in your mind. But you, father, take this difficult pathway, because in our day "the streets of Zion mourn";[404] that is, the streets of heaven are crying out. And why do they weep? They weep because they do not find the one who comes to the solemnity of this seraphic love in which the eternal feasts of heaven celebrate.

How the Intellect is Illuminated and Enflamed by Seraphic Love

After this cherubic illumination of the intellect, the seraphic fire of that same intellect gradually follows, because the cherubim and seraphim are so conjoined in love that they cannot be separated. So it is no wonder that the fire of good will follows the illumination of the intellect. That fire lights up the souls with love of God, with the desire of the salvation of one's neighbor and with hate towards one's appetites. This is the fire with which one burns up his voluntary sacrifice, the sacrifice of the marrow of the heart, the peaceful and reasonable oblation of the inner man, which is so pleasing to God, who moves from being angry to being sweet.

This sacrifice was the meaning of the oblation of Elijah, above whom the fire fell from Heaven and consumed the holocaust, wood, stones and even the water that was in the trench;[405] in the same way the fire of seraphic love melts love and tears in the soul and body words and thoughts, inside and out, so that on all sides sighs are heard coming from the heart. It was thus that Elisha lay over the dead child,[406] whose name in Hebrew means what we would say in Latin: *Deus meus salvator* [God my Savior], who extended and lowered himself above the child, like God lowers himself above our souls, which for God is much lower than the father of a child born today. He lays his eyes and his hands on those of the child, he puts everything on him and breathes into his mouth seven times; in the same way, God puts his most holy mouth over ours, he does it with the merits of his Passion and connects it with our living merits, since blowing seven times in the mouth he gives the seven gifts of the Holy Spirit. In this way the child; that is our soul, warms with seraphic love and leaps up resurrected from the death of sin.

O ineffable condescension, O inscrutable union! This is that union of divine marriage that divine nature contracted with human nature. Come, O lovers, to the wedding the immaculate "eat, friends, and let us become inebriated O dear ones";[407] eat friends of the noble Spouse and drink of the wine of love. You beginners[408] try a little of this wine, but you perfect ones[409] drink it fully, become inebriated at the wedding of the King most high!

"O daughters of Zion,"[410] O contemplative souls who desire to taste and see how sweet and beautiful is this bridegroom, now with your minds go out of this valley of misery and tears and contemplate this peaceful Solomon, Christ Jesus, crowned with the diadem that his mother placed on his head,[411] the love that brought him and she brings us. "Arise north wind and come south wind, blow upon my garden, that your ointments may spread. Let him kiss me with the kisses of his mouth, because your breasts are better than wine and your name is a spreading perfume."[412] What diadem is this if not the crown of thorns and the cross that his mother of love placed over the holy shoulders of my sweet Christ, that is, the love that he brings to his bride, the holy Church? What is this north wind if not the cold wind of tribulations, and what is this south wind if not the hot wind of prosperity, to which you went with your eyes closed, driven by humility, to burn in those seraphic ardors?

But endure it in peace, be patient and do not look forward prematurely to your hour of glory, because when the death of this wretched life will be transformed into victory,[413] and in your soul will appear the glory of Jesus Christ, your Spouse, then you will be sanctified in everything. But while that hour is approaching, offer yourself to God never doing your own will, but only that of the heavenly Spouse, and your only pleasure will be to realize you have done his will, not yours, because this is the infallible sign of perfect friendship and union: having *Unum velle et unum nolle* [the same desire and not desire].[414]

And since Christ came only to save the lost, it is well that he who is so united to him should be solicitous for the salvation of others. This is what is meant by the Canticle in the words: "Come my beloved, let us go out in the field of salvation, come with me to cultivate the vines, come and we will dwell in the villages, and there I will give you my breasts";[415] that is, we go out, my beloved, to save souls, come, help me to win them, because without you we can do nothing.[416] We have compassion and zeal for the sins of others; I will give you my breasts so that you can suckle them; that is, I will offer you the milk of my good memories and examples of me given to others, white and without stain of one's own concupiscence, and I will offer my life for his salvation and I will consider the sins of others as my own, as the apostle Paul when he said: "Who is led into sin and I do not burn, who is weak is and I do not feel weak?".[417]

O true zeal, O fiery Heart of the true love of God! This zeal is born from the holy and divine kiss and says: "the zeal for your house consumes me";[418] that is, the zeal for your house that is the soul of every neighbor of mine in whom God lives more worthily than in his temple. Oh, what a good church is every Christian soul, whose altar is the heart and the priest is Christ! If we consider how out of love for her [the soul/church] he was wounded, despised, crowned with thorns and died on the cross, we will be able to understand very well how this church was dear to him, and for that consideration we come to fall in love with her [the soul/church] and we become willing and hurry to [the soul's] salvation as our own.

O sower of all chaste love, I give this poor soul which by your grace melted for love of its neighbor, for whose salvation you were thirsty on the wood of the holy cross.[419] Now I know your goodness and understand that the sweetest affection that we can give you is the desire of the salvation of one's neighbor, so be pleased to receive this poor soul of mine, which is like wax placed in fire and is consumed and melts for the zeal the salvation of neighbor.

O blessed soul, that for this zeal for God you were made a honeycomb and a sweet wine! This is the great sign of the woman clothed with the sun who appeared in the sky,[420] that is of divine love, and beneath her feet was the moon, which is the clarity and sweetness of the words and works towards one's neighbor. She had on her head a crown of twelve stars, and this crown is the constant attention of the soul towards the twelve articles of faith that are her crown. This woman has children of her body, that are the works she birthed with true charity and groans filled with sweet affections, with which every day hatred of herself grows more and more, remembering the word of the heavenly Spouse "anyone who hates their life in this world, keeps in eternal life."[421]

Oh, what good hatred is this! It is just like the stone that did not fit in any place, so it was thrown away; but then it was discovered that it was suitable for the cornerstone and it joined one wall to the other;[422] thus is similar this hatred that unites the soul with God, as sweet Jesus prayed to his Father, saying: "I beg you, Father, just as you are in me and I in you, may these chosen and beloved ones be the same in us."[423]

O loving God, whose sweetness is not understood by those who are always in the mud of their negligence, who think they have a spiritual life because they have spiritual habits, but it is not so. This [correct] hatred is the foundation of true perfection and from it comes the virtue of patience in the just man's soul, which is a work of perfection, because without patience, one cannot ascend to the summit of perfection, and in order to sow this hatred and patience in this world the eternal word came down voluntarily from the bosom of the Father[424] and embraced in himself this hatred and this patience and took them unto death. This is what the bride meant in Canticles, when she cries: "Draw me after you."[425] I understand too well, my Lord, that by myself I can not have hatred in myself, as you had for yourself, inasmuch as [you were] a man, but by your grace draw me to this end, because I remember that to the one who called you good, you answered by saying that "no one is good except for him alone."[426] O good Jesus, there is no doubt that the more a man loves you, the more he hates himself. This is the rule of love, this rule leads the soul to those desires that are considered crazy by the world when the soul cries out with true and cordial affection: my sweet God, why do you not punish me, why do you bear my iniquities? Send me to Hell that I deserve, provided that I could still love you there. O Father of eternal life, comforter of the soul, do not wish to love something so worthy of hate that I am, do not have mercy on the one who deserves it little.

This is the royal and safe road that leads the soul to perfect union of gracious God; and the clearest evidence to know whether a man really hates himself is when one is patient in tribulations, because, as the Apostle says, patience is a perfect work.[427] Here, now with the help of God I made the voluntary oblation; may the Lord God give everything to those who want to properly celebrate this offering; and may his sacrifice be greatly increased, and may the fire of divine love descend and devour the sacrifice and the victim, such as material fire that came down from Heaven and consumed the burnt offering of Solomon,[428] and may the divine Majesty fill the mind so that nothing else will find a place in it.

And you, father, who did not become irritated in being taught by an old woman without education and without culture, please now modify my womanly verbosity, correct the false statements and take away every error that is found. Because I simply obeyed your request, so now I humbly beg you to bless me. Amen.

Endnotes

1 The Italian word, *malpatire*, was not common in old Italian. By adding a suffix *mal* "bad" to *patire* "suffer," Camilla created a word meaning "to suffer intensely or greatly." It is translated "to suffer badly" throughout.
2 Hereafter, the word "monastery" will be used to describe the religious house of the Poor Clares instead of "convent." In the Italian language, *convento* is used for either men's friaries or women's convents, as long as it is *not* cloistered, while *monastero* is used for the religious houses of either men or women as long as it *is* cloistered.
3 Cf. 1 Corinthians 2:2
4 General Audience, January 5, 2011
5 Homily of Pope Benedict XVI, June 3, 2007
6 John 18:36
7 1 Kings 8:27
8 Philippians 2:6-8
9 Romans 5:7-8
10 Cf. "Letter to the Entire Order, 51" of St. Francis of Assisi
11 Cf. Second Letter of St. Clare to St. Agnes of Prague, 20
12 Cf. Instructions to the Disciple
13 John 19:30
14 Cf. Paragraph 1435; 2015, Catechism of the Catholic Church (1997 edition).
15 Matthew 16:24
16 Cf. Luke 9:23
17 Colossians 1:24
18 Luke 23:34
19 Quoted from "Mental Sorrows."
20 Christ is speaking in lines 1-4 and 9-12; Camilla speaks in lines 5-8.
21 i.e. that of the Trinity.
22 *Or surge et comede, pater reverende* (Cf. 1 Kings 19:5)
23 She is referring to Fr. Domenico of Leonessa, to whom she will also address her *Spiritual Life*, the autobiographical letter that St. Camilla Battista wrote during the same period. The 'fruits' refer to a sermon preached by him a few years earlier, during which he counseled his listeners to shed a little tear for love of Jesus Crucified.
24 *fructus et opera manuum tuarum* (Cf. Ps 128:2)
25 Camilla Battista is writing under divine inspiration, and the booklet takes the form of a letter written by Jesus to her. In it, he refers to her as "sister", as does the groom in Song of songs towards his beloved.
26 The Italian expression used is "patir male," which we have translated as "suffer badly." It is a strong expression and occurs throughout St. Camilla's writings; it is the one

of the three "lilies" described at length in "Spiritual Life." It alludes to her innermost desire to be where her beloved was – to share Christ's suffering on the cross in penitential and co-redemptive sacrifice. Saint Catherine of Bologna, also a Poor Clare, expressed similar desires in her writings, with which St. Camilla was surely familiar and likely inspired.

27 Christ sometimes speaks in the first person plural, a reference to his connection with the Trinity.

28 Cf. Matthew 26:42

29 Cf. Matthew 26:39

30 This seems to put St. Camilla in the place of Christ as a co-participator in Christ's suffering and plan of salvation for others, and is likely why she inserted the doubt "it seems that he says."

31 Cf. Rule of Saint Francis of 1221 (*non bullata*).

32 Cf. John 18:4-5

33 Cf. Isaiah 53:3

34 The nudity of Christ is a theme that recurs frequently in Franciscan literature; St. Clare refers to it in her Testament.

35 Here St. Camilla is speaking to herself.

36 Cf. John 16:12

37 Cf. John: 15:5

38 Cf. St. Paul who wrote: "What do you possess that you have not received?" (1 Cor 4:7).

39 St. Camilla Battista introduces the absurd paradox of being happy to go to Hell, which consists in the absence of God who is love. Because she is interested only in "the honor of God", she is absolutely and resolutely disposed to everything to the extreme of going to Hell.

40 These are local proverbs from her native region of Camerino.

41 Cf. Psalm 22:1; John 10; also VI Admonition of St. Francis.

42 Jesus is now the speaker.

43 Psalm 21:1

44 This is a reference to her great spiritual trial from October, 1488 until 1491, which Camilla Battista describes in her *Spiritual Life*.

45 Cf. Revelation 2:10

46 This work was written when she was in the monastery of Urbino in 1482-83; so she had this revelation around 1477-78 when she was in her father's castle in Camerino.

47 Cf. Song 2:16

48 The following phrase was written at the end of the manuscript written by hand in Latin by Anthony of Segovia: "I, Anthony the Spaniard, unworthy monk, transcribed the present book from the original writing in her hand by the above said Blessed Sr. Battista da Varano, to whom God mercifully united me spiritually in charity."

49 *Bonum mihi lex oris tui super millia auri et argenti* (Psalm 119:72)

50 *Beatus homo quem tu erudieris, Domine, et de lege tua docueris eum.* (Psalm 93:12)

51 In the beginning of the manuscript, this introduction addressed to Blessed Pietro of Mogliano, Camilla's spiritual father appears. It was not part of the original work, but was added later to clarify who was the author.

52 In chapter XVII of her Autobiography, she wrote that Jesus himself commanded her to write his mental sorrows.

53 This second introduction addressed to Blessed Pietro of Mogliano has appeared in

some manuscripts. In the Italian edition of her writings, it appears at the end of the work; we inserted it at the beginning, as it explains her intentions in the writing.

54 According to tropical astrology, that would be July 22 - August 22.

55 *quia est in domo propria*

56 *quia tunc erat sol suorum dolorum in leone, id est in culmine et vigore fortissimo atque potenti, tamquarn in domo propria* St. Camilla quotes in Latin from a work from Ubertino da Casale, *Arbor vitae crucifixae Iesu*, "The Tree of Life of the Crucified Jesus." She considers that Jesus's human life was full of sufferings, but the pinnacle of his mental sufferings happened during the agony in Gethsemane.

57 St. Camilla here and elsewhere expresses cultural attitudes towards women who were considered inferior in her era; yet, she does add that gender is irrelevant for those who seek God in truth.

58 Quote from the Book of Lamentations 2:13, which the Saint refers to in her *Autobiography* to express the sufferings she felt.

59 Cf. Psalm 119:80

60 In this original introduction, St. Camilla maintains that a nun from Urbino was the original author, but it was really her.

61 This "chamber" refers to the nuptial bed that would be the cross.

62 More painful than any other suffering for the damned is the certainty that they will remain forever separated from God.

63 Cf. Mark 16:1-6; Luke 24:1-6

64 Cf. Matthew 26:38

65 Cf. Exodus 19:5-6

66 In her Autobiography, she compares her father to Pharoah who tried to impede her entrance in the monastery.

67 Cf. Ps 36:10

68 *Alia sunt iudicia Dei, alia sunt iudicia hominum*

69 The feet of Jesus were an object of particular veneration by St. Camilla, as she mentions in "Spiritual Life".

70 *nunc et semper in saecula saeculorum*

71 *Bonorum laborum gloriosus est fructus* (Wisdom 3:15)

72 *Iesu bone, propter verba oris tui ego custodivi vias duras* (Psalm 17:4)

73 *Modicum laboravi et inveni mihi multam requiem* (Sirach 51:27)

74 Cf. Isaiah: 5:6 and Isaiah 7:23

75 John: 10:11

76 Psalm: 27:9

77 She compares herself to a ship that escaped from the storm but goes down in the port. Although she overcame the snares of the world, she now fears losing her life as a consecrated nun.

78 Luke 18: 9-14

79 Cf. Luke 15: 11-21

80 From 1488-1490, St. Camilla suffered an intense period of spiritual desolation and darkness. These words allow the prayer to be dated to 1490.

81 The Italian expression used by St. Camilla, *la più vile*, does not have to mean sinful, but could be translated also as "lowliest" or "most humble."

82 Luke 1:28

83 *Generationem eius quis enarrabit?* (Isaiah 53:8)

84 Psalms 69:22

85 Luke 2:35

86 This is a frequent Franciscan theme appearing in the writings of both St. Francis and Clare. Cf. the Later Rule of St. Francis, Chapter 6, and the Rule of Clare, Chapter 7.
87 Cf. Luke 2:48-49
88 Luke 2:14
89 Luke 23:21
90 Luke 2:10
91 Matthew 27:29
92 Acts 1:11
93 Luke 24:36
94 The year was 1491.
95 Cf. John 19:34
96 This is from Lamentations 1:12. Camilla repeats it eight times throughout the letter.
97 Camilla wrote the letter in 1491. Father Domenico of Leonessa preached at Camerino in 1466 or 1468. The years gone by are 25, subtracted from 33 makes Camilla 8 years old.
98 Cf. Luke 23:7-11
99 The Italian expression used was "*una lacrimuccia sola sola.*"
100 *mecum lauda Deum et gratias referamus Creatori nostro, a quo hoc atque cuncta procedunt.* N.B. This is a reference from the Rule of St. Francis, Chapter XVII.
101 This would be around 2:00am.
102 It appears that the ascetic practices and penances she imposed on herself were the way she attempted to reach Christ while still a young girl. But after entering the convent, her relationship with Christ matured and she renounced physical mortifications, choosing instead to meditate on Christ, as also stated in some of her other works.
103 *Ego dormio et cor meum vigilat* (Song 5:2)
104 She seems to mean that her damnation would have been a result of her worldliness, not from merely remaining as a layperson.
105 Camilla, who was experiencing peace during meditation and prayer, hopes to receive some clarity from this friar whom she believed was more an angel than human.
106 Given the power of Camilla's father, and his plans for her, spiritual direction from a friar of the Strict Observance and such a vocation could have caused problems.
107 She is likely referring to shows or dances, or other secular entertainments within the court.
108 Camilla takes up a concept already written in Mental Sorrows, as she compares herself to the Hebrew people who were freed from slavery in Egypt and had to offer sacrifices to God in the desert.
109 This expression used here and elsewhere towards herself refers to a frequent Old Testament comparison of the betrayal of the covenant, or sin against the love of God, as adultery or prostitution.
110 This is a local proverb, not biblical.
111 The friar probably spoke to her in Latin, as he was quoting Jesus's words from John 5:14.
112 The Poor Clare convent in Urbino was associated with the Strict Observance; i.e. an austere, ascetic, and penitential reform movement within the Franciscan Order. Further, the nuns there followed the Rule of St. Clare.
113 *Quid ultra potuit facere Deus et non fecit* N.B. The Latin is a paraphrase of the Good

Friday liturgy when Christ speaks to his persecutors.
114 *In corde meo abscondi eloquia tua ut non peccem tibi* (Psalm 119:11)
115 *Anima mea liquefacta est ut dilectus locutus est* (Song 5:6)
116 *Quam dulcia faucibus meis eloquia tua, super mel ori meo* (Psalm 119:103)
117 *Ignitum eloquium tuum vehementer et anima mea peccatrix dilexit illud* (Psalm 119:140)
118 *In quacumque die conversus fuerit peccator non recordabar amplius iniquitatum eius* (Ezekiel 18:22)
119 *quod initium sapientiae, hoc est quod principium saporis divinae, dulcedinis, est timor Domini* (Psalm 111:10)
120 Lamentations 1:2
121 Job 19:19
122 Jeremiah 8:23
123 Lamentations 5:16
124 Psalm 119:136
125 Lamentations 1:12
126 *Quantum fuit in deliciis et gloria, tantum date ei tormnentum et luctum* (Revelation 18:7)
127 *ille qui est flos campi et lilium convallium et* (Song 2:1)
128 *inter lilia poscitur* (Song 2:16)
129 Next to Camilla's relics today are three lilies at her side.
130 Here, "to enter religion" sounds like she means to entering Religious life; i.e. a monastery, but it could also mean simply to be with Jesus, sharing his life completely.
131 This harsh judgement of Camilla Battista arises from her state of mind: she is immersed in the mental sorrows of Christ crucified and is in love with her crucified "Spouse." The world, on the other hand, is "hell" for her because her experience of it refuses Christ and would leave her immersed in the ephemeral pleasures, egoism, and violence. Cf. 1 John 5:19.
132 This expression "*mal patire*" used here and elsewhere is to suffer like Jesus; that is, without any consolation either from God or from men.
133 Details of this illness are unknown.
134 *quoniam ab ipso patentia mea* (Psalm 62:6)
135 Father Giorgio Albanese, whose name Camilla mistakes, was a soldier who converted after hearing a sermon preached by Saint James of the Marches in Camerino in 1445. He become a friar and led a holy life. He died in the friary of Morrovalle in 1495.
136 *Gustate et videte* (Psalm 34:9)
137 *Coeli enarrant gloriam Dei et opera manuum eius annuntiat firmamentum* (Psalm 19:2)
138 Song 1:3
139 Song 1:1
140 Song 4:10
141 Song 1:1
142 Lamentation 1:12
143 *Illa anima infelix quae erat sponsa et secretaria summi Dei et in croceis iacebat amplexata est stercora fetentissimi diaboli* (Lamentation 4:5)
144 *quia omnia tempus habent* (Ecclesiastes 3:1)
145 Camilla once again compares her story of the exit from the secular world and

entrance into the convent to the story of the Hebrews being freed from the Egyptian Pharoah (cf Exodus 12 and 14).

146 Exodus 15:21

147 *in materiali deserto invenitur cantus avium, florum pulchritudo, secreta cubilia animalium* N.B. Ubertino of Casale (1259–1329) was a Franciscan friar and one of the leaders of the Spiritual branch of the Franciscan Order (together with Michael of Cesena, preceded by Peter Olivi).

148 Exodus 3:1

149 Song 1:13

150 This is a unique experience and it does not appear that Camilla has borrowed this image from other mystical writers of her era.

151 Lamentation 1:12

152 The nuptial bed, or wedding chamber, of her Spouse is his suffering.

153 Song 2:12

154 Camilla compares Jesus to King Ahasuerus who loved the Jewess Esther so much that he took her as his spouse and filled her with every gift and favor, as is recounted in the book of Esther.

155 Details are not known, but the "scandal" was likely due to the consequences of someone of her high station in life joining such an austere and penitential movement.

156 It appears that Fr. Domenico was against some aspect of the convent in Camerino, or had been in the past, and Camilla is scolding him; however these lines allow the reader to get a glimpse into her personality. Further, she believed that their convent served a great good for Camerino, and he needed to be aware of it.

157 The verse was by Jacopone of Todi (1230-1306), a Franciscan friar from Umbria, Italy who wrote well-known *Laudi* (songs in praise of the Lord) in Italian.

158 That would be between 5:00 and 7:00pm.

159 Lamentation 1:12

160 She is referring either to Paul (cf. 1 Cor 10:2) or John the Baptist (Matthew 3:11).

161 Clare wrote her Rule approved by Pope Innocent IV on August 9, 1253, two days before her death. In 1263, Pope Urban IV wrote a new Rule for the Poor Clares that slowly substituted Clare's Rule in Poor Clare convents. However, in the 15th century, with the enthusiasm generated by the Observants, many Poor Clare monasteries began to reclaim the original Rule of St. Clare, including the monastery in Urbino. This next tribulation in Camerino suffered by Camilla is likely because her father wished to endow the Camerino Poor Clare convent with fixed income, forbidden by the Rule of Clare, but not the other Rules.

162 i.e. September 17

163 This was an interior vision, not a physical one.

164 Lamentation 1:12

165 Psalm 119:129

166 i.e. morning lauds

167 The term used by Camilla was "desgraziare" and could be translated as "disgrace or disgraced" or even "blame" or "curse."

168 Battista asserts in her *Novena to the Virgin* that "the Holy Trinity exalted [the Madonna] above all the choirs of angels," and "she is more able to contain divine love and the Holy Trinity that all the nine choirs of angels and saints that ever were and ever will be."

169 Job 30: 31

170 Literally, accompanied by organ music, as during a wedding march.
171 Philippians 1:23
172 Psalm 142:8
173 According to classical and medieval hierarchies of angels, Seraphim were of the highest order and they flew above God's throne; second were the Cherubim. Seraphim were angels of fire and love, while Cherubim were believed to be angels of strength, light, and intellect.
174 *Ecce panis angelorum...vere panis filiorum* N.B. Camilla Battista cites the Latin from the Liturgy of Corpus Christi.
175 In her era, the faithful received Eucharist usually once a year on Easter. The Rule of St. Clare prescribed the nuns to receive Eucharist seven times a year. A confessor could allow the penitent to receive it more times, as was conceded to Sister Baptist, but only for a fixed period.
176 i.e. from 1485-1488.
177 She does not mean that the other feasts and solemnities should be disregarded; only that she received a particular call to make every day a Good Friday.
178 Song 8:5
179 Sirach 23:20
180 Revelation 3:16
181 Psalm 137:2
182 Cf. Judges, chapter 16 for a comparison to Sampson.
183 *insuper percusserunt, vulneraverunt et semiviva relieta, abierunt* (Luke 10: 30)
184 Lamentation 1:12
185 *quae pervenit in altitudinem maris divini amoris et spiritualis dulcedinis, nunc autem tempestas valida demersit eam in profundum abissi et inferi.* We are not sure what this is referencing.
186 Ecclesiastes 1:7
187 Ibid.
188 1 Corinthians 3:6
189 *Ego virum non cognosco* (Luke 1:34)
190 St. Camilla is speaking in third person, but referring to herself.
191 Galatians 6:14
192 *Venerunt mihi omnia bona pariter cum illa* (Wisdom 7:11)
193 This is a local proverb.
194 *lux orto est iusto et rectis corde laetitia* (Psalms 97:11)
195 *Beati mundo corde, quoniam ipsi Deum videbunt* (Matthew 5:8)
196 *Quia magnus et excelsus est super omnes deos* (Psalm 96:4)
197 Matthew 5:44
198 *Ut sis pacificus cum hiis qui oderunt pacem* (Psalm 119:7)
199 She is quoting a classical philosopher, unknown to us.
200 Cf. Matthew 7:3
201 *visitatio tua custodivit spiritum meum* (Job 10:12)
202 A classical expression meaning, "herein lies the difficulty."
203 Cf: Numbers 12: 9-16
204 *Qua diligentibus Deum, omnia cooperantur in bonum* (Romans 8:28)
205 *Religiosus non refraenans linguam suam hujus vana est religio* (James 1:26)
206 *Silui a bonis* Cf. Psalm 38:2
207 *regnum coelorum vim patitur, et violenti rapiunt illud* (Matthew 11:12)

208 *Gratia eius in me vacua non fuit, quia ad te de luce vigilo* (1 Corinthians 15:10)
209 Psalm 16:7
210 *qui perseveravarit usque in finem hic salvus erit* (Matthew 10:22)
211 *in peccato concepit me mater mea* (Psalm 51:7)
212 This is her response for herself to the question the friar should propose to God in the preceding paragraph: "who you are, how much you can do, how much you know, and how much you are worth."
213 *et omnia per ipsum facta sunt* (Cf. John 1:3)
214 *Domine non est exaltatum cor meum, neque elati sunt oculi mei* (Psalm 130:1)
215 She is speaking of herself.
216 Since Camilla was often Abbess.
217 She is again speaking of herself in third person.
218 She described this vision in "Spiritual Life."
219 *Ideo misericordias Domini in acternum cantabit anima illa, quam tu diligis* (Cf. Psalm 89:2)
220 *soli Deo honor et gloria* (1 Timothy 1:17)
221 *si ego Dominus, ubi est timor meus? Si ego Pater ubi est amor meus?* (Malachi 1:6)
222 *Euge, serve bone, quia in pauca fuisti fidelis, supra multa te constituam, intra in gaudium Domini tui* (Matthew 25:21)
223 *Esto fidelis usque ad mortem* (Revelation 2:10)
224 *Servite Domino in timore et exultate ei cum tremore* (Psalm 2:11)
225 *quia soli Deo honor et gloria saecula saecolorum* (1 Timothy 1:17)
226 *quia quaecumque voluit, fecit in coelo et in terra, in mari et in omnibus abyssis* (Psalm 135:6)
227 *Ex abundantia cordis os loquitur* (Matthew 12:34)
228 *Averte faciem tuam a peccatis meis* (Psalm 51:11)
229 *Deus in adiutorium meum intende, Domine. ad adiuvandum me festina. Ad te levavi oculos meos in montes, unde veniet auxilium mihi. Auxilium meum a Domino* (Psalm 70:1)
230 Psalm 121:1-2
231 Psalm 16:8
232 Psalm 19:15
233 In "Spiritual Life" she makes the claim that by meditating on Christ's Passion, one reaches God faster.
234 *Deus manet in eo* (1 John 4:15)
235 *Gloriosa dicta sunt de te, civitas Dei* (Psalm 87:3)
236 *oboedientiam volo plus quam sacrificium* (1 Samuel 15:22)
237 This is likely addressed to Father John of Fano.
238 *petite et accipietis, pulsate et aperietur vobis* (Matthew 7:7; Luke 11:9)
239 *Angustiae sunt mihi undique* (Daniel 13:22)
240 Cf. Luke 6:30
241 Cf. Psalm 145:5
242 *in malevolam animam non introibit sapientia* (Wisdom 1:4)
243 Cf. 1 Corinthians 1:24, 30
244 Cf. Colossians 2:3
245 Malachi 3:20
246 *Ego quos amo corrigo et castigo* (Revelations 3:19)
247 *Ego gloriam meam [non] quaero* (John 8:50)
248 *O quam pulchra es et decora, soror mea sponsa* (Song 7:6)

249 *Oculi tui columbarum absque eo quod intrinsecus latet* (Song 4:1)
250 *Sonet vox tua in auribus meis, amica mea, columba mea, formosa mea! Nam vox tua dulcis* (Song 2:14, 10)
251 *facies tua decora* (Song 2:14)
252 *Descendat dilectus meus in hortum suum* (Song 5:1)
253 *ad areolam aromatum* (Song 6:1)
254 *lilia puritatis colligat* (Ibid.)
255 *O dilecte mi veni et ne tardes, quia omnia poma vetera et nova servavi tibi* (Song 7:11,13)
256 cf. 1 Kings 10: 13
257 Cf. Mark 8:15
258 *non quae Iesu Christi* (Philippians 2:21)
259 *Diliges proximum tuum sicut teipsum* (Matthew 19:19)
260 Isaiah 66:1
261 *Nulli nocui et iuste vixi cum hominibus* (Job 27:6)
262 *Veni de Libano, O pulcherrima mulierum, veni de Libano, sponsa, veni* (Song 5:9, 17; 4:8)
263 *Veni, O suavis et decora sicut Ierusalem. Civitas Regis magni, quia odor vestimentorum tuorum est super omnia aromata delectabilia* (Cf. Song 5:16)
264 *Duo ubera tua sicut duo hinnuli capreae gemelli* (Song 4:5)
265 *Hanc amavi et exquisivi in iuventute mea* (Wisdom 8:2)
266 Cf. Song 2:5; 5:8
267 Cf. Wisdom 8:3
268 *Non sumus sufficientes* (2 Corinthians 3:5)
269 *Vota mea Domino reddam in atriis domus Domini, in medio tui, Ierusalem* (Psalm 116:18-19)
270 St. Camilla Battista uses the word "pessimo", which is the superlative form of bad; i.e. "worst"; I translated it as "lowest" to emphasize that she is speaking of humility.
271 *Pone me, Domine, iuxta te at cuiusvis manus pugnet contra me* (Job 17:3)
272 *Tu es, Domine, patientia mea* (Psalm 70:5)
273 *orietur in diebus eius iustitia et abundantia pacis* (Psalm 71:7)
274 *Pax illa [quae] exsuperat omnem sensum* (Philippians 4.7)
275 Cf. Psalm 121:1
276 *Tota pulchra es, amica mea, formosa mea* (Song 4:7; 2:10)
277 *Quam pulchri sunt gressus tui* (Song 7:1)
278 *O filia principis* (Ibid.)
279 Cf. Song 2:14
280 *Petra autem erat Christus* (1 Cor 10:4)
281 *In caverna* (Song 2:14)
282 *Factum est cor meum tamquam cera liquescens* (Psalm 22:15)
283 Cf. Matthew 11:30
284 *Oleum effusum nomen tuum, ideo dilexerunt te nimis adulescentulae* (Song 1:2)
285 *curremus in odorem unguentorum tuorum* (Song 1:3)
286 *in terra sitiente* (Psalm 63:2)
287 *Venerunt mihi omnia bona pariter cum illa* (Wisdom 7:11)
288 *Qui vult venire post me, abneget semetipsum* (Matthew 16:24)
289 Cf. Wisdom 7:26
290 *speciosus prae filiis hominum* (Psalm 45:3)
291 Cf. 2 Corinthians 5:21
292 *in gaudium Domini sui* (Matthew 25:21)

293 *Quaesivi eum et non inveni* (Song 3:1)
294 *Adiuro vos, filiae Ierusalem* (Cf *Song* 2:7; 3:5; 5:8; 8:4)
295 *Qualis est dilectus tuus, O pulcherrima mulierum* (Ibid.)
296 *O vos omnes, qui transitis per viam* (cf. Lamentations 1: 12; St. Camilla Battista repeats this often in "Spiritual Life.")
297 *Pater meus et mater mea fuit amor meus.* N.B. There is no biblical reference to this phrase.
298 Cf Ezekiel 16:8.
299 *Leva eius sub capite meo* (Song 2:6)
300 That is, live a worldly life outside the monastery.
301 *unxit me oleo laetitiae* (Psalm 45:8)
302 *Calceavit me auro amoris, et argento puritatis honoravit me* (Ezekiel 16:13)
303 *Insuper lac et mel ex ore eius suscepi* (Song 5:1)
304 She is describing her entrance into the monastery.
305 But now she describes feeling the absence of God's presence.
306 *Audite, coeli, quae loquor, et tu, terra, auribus percipe* (Deuteronomy 32:1)
307 Isaiah 1:2
308 *Ad vos, O filiae Ierusalem, patet os meum* (Cf. Song 5:16; 2 Corinthians 6:11)
309 Songs 5:10
310 *caput eius aurum optimum, oculi eius divini, genae eius sicut aureolae aromatum, labia eius stillantia mirram, guttur eius suavissimum, manus eius plenae hyacinthis, verba eius verba vitae aeternae* (Song 5:11, 13, 6, 14)
311 John 6: 68
312 Cf. Song 5:10
313 Cf. Songs 5:6
314 *quia magna est velut mare contritio mea* (Lamentation 2:13)
315 *Repulit Dominus altare suum* (Lamentation 2:7)
316 *et ego oblitus sum bonorum* (Lamentation 3:17)
317 *qui biberit ex hac aqua* (John 4:13)
318 John 8:12
319 Mark 11:24
320 *Versa est ad alienos haereditas tua* (Lamentation 5:2)
321 *Intellectum da mihi et vivam* (Psalm 119:144)
322 *Parce, Domine; parce et deprecabilis esto super servos tuos.* N.B. This was not found in Scripture.
323 Cfr. Mark 10: 38: "Can you drink the cup that I drink?"
324 *Pereat dies in qua natus sum ... quare posuisti me contrarium tibi et factus sum mihimet ipsi gravis?* (Job 3:3; 7:20)
325 Cf. Job 2: 11
326 *Rugiebam a gemitu cordis mei* (Psalm 38: 9)
327 *Taedet animam meam vitae mae* (Job 10:1)
328 *Infixus sum in limo profundi et non est substantia spiritualis* (Psalm 69:3)
329 *misit Dominus manum suam ad omnia delectabilia animae meae* (Lamentations 1:10)
330 *Abstulit omnes magnificos meo[s]; de medio, effusum est in terra iecur meum et ideo spreverunt me omnes qui glorificabant me* (Lamentation 1:15, 2:11, 1:8)
331 She is saying that when souls turn their hearts away from God and turn to earthly things because of "dryness and weakness of spirit," God does them a favor by taking these things away; human consolations, therefore, are useless and are even against God.

332 *dies calamitatis et miseriae, dies magna et amara valde*. N.B. This is a citation from *Dies irae* by Thomas of Celano.
333 Cf. Job 2:6
334 Cf. Song 8:6
335 *Quaerentem me dilectum meum invenerunt custodes civitatis ci percusserunt me, insuper tulerunt a me pallium meum custodes murorum* (Song 5:7)
336 Cf. Ezekiel, chapter 34
337 *Gladius contritionis et compassionis intret in corda eorum et arcus eorum confringatur* (Psalm 37:15)
338 *Ego autem induam me cilicio et oratio mea pro salute eorum in sinu meo convertatur* (Psalm 35:13)
339 While not totally clear, this appears to be a reference to the ordeal suffered by St. Camilla when her father was excommunicated by Pope Alexander VI for political motives and later murdered with his three sons under the order of Cesare Borgia (the pope's son). If so, it is the only reference to this brutal episode in any of her writings.
340 *Faciam, inquit Dominus, te columnam in templo Dei tui et foras non egredieris amplius, et dabo tibi stellam matutinam* (Revelation 3:12; 2:28)
341 *O sponsa pulchra nimis et decora, labia tua distillaverunt favum mellis* (Song 6:3; 4:11)
342 *Hortus conclusus est anima tua, O sponsa nobilis et inclita, fons signatus* (Song 4:12)
343 This expression in Latin *Libera nos, Domine* is a liturgical invocation that recalls *Libera nos a malo* from the Lord's Prayer in Matthew 6:13.
344 *Tu eras Domina gentium et plena populo* (Cf. Lamentation 1:1)
345 *Paraverunt laqueum pedibus meis, foderunt ante faciem foveam* (Psalm 57:7)
346 *faciem Dei Iacob* (Psalms 24:6)
347 Song 5:3
348 2 Cor 12:2,7
349 Psalm 22:2; Matthew 27:46
350 Cf. John 19:30
351 *Moriatur animo mea hac morte* (Numbers 23:10)
352 *pretiosa in conspectu Domini mors sanctorum eius* (Psalm 116:15)
353 *En dilectus meus stat post parietem prospiciens per cancellos* (Song 2:9)
354 *Qui vicerit non laedetur a morte [secundo]; et dabo illi manna absconditum* (Revelation 2:11,17)
355 *Obliviscere ergo opprobrii viduitatis tuae, quia dominabitur tui qui fecit te* (Isaiah 54:4-5)
356 *In modico dereliqui te, sed miseratìonibus magnis congregabo te; in momento indignationis absondi faciem meam a te et in misericordia sempiterna misertus sum tui* (Isaiah 54:6-7)
357 *Ecce ego per ordinem sternam lapides* (Cf. Isaiah 28:16)
358 *fundabo te in sapphiris et ponam in lapides sculptos; fundaberis in iustitia et multitudine pacis; quia assimilavi te equitatui meo dum eras in curribus Pharaonis* (Isaiah 54:11-14; Song 1:8)
359 *Iam hiems transiit; imber abiit et recessit. Surge, amica mea, et veni* (Song 2:11,13)
360 Cf. Romans 8:28
361 *lauda, Ierusalem, Dominum* (Psalm 147:1)
362 *induere vestimentis gloriae tuae* (Isaiah 52:1)
363 *et in aeternum requiscet in tabernaculo tuo* (Hosea 12:10)
364 *vidi caelum novum et terram novam* (Revelation 21:1)
365 *Surrexit Dominus vere, alleluia* (Easter Sunday declaration)
366 Cf. Genesis 28:18

367 Psalm 45:8
368 Genesis 28:16
369 Genesis 9:21
370 Cf. Proverb 2:4
371 *fons indeficiens aquarum viventium* (Song 4:15)
372 Cf. Revelation 21:27
373 Cf. Galatians 6:17
374 Cf. Romans 8:35
375 Cf. 2 Timothy 4:8
376 *Recogitabo tibi omnes annos meos, in amaritudine animae meae* (Isaiah 38:15)
377 Psalm 52:10
378 cf. Psalm 91:7,5
379 Cf. Phil 2:6-9
380 *merces mea magna nimis* (Genesis 15.1)
381 *vulnerasti cor meum soror mea sponsa* (Song 4:9)
382 *Nardus mea dedit odorem suavitatis* (Song 1:11)
383 *emitte lucem tuam et veritatem tuam* (Psalm 43:3)
384 *ubi charitas et amor, ibi Deus est* (N.B. This is a liturgical hymn from Holy Thursday.)
385 Psalm 94:12
386 *plenitudo ergo legis est dilectio* (Romans 13:10)
387 *Quid est homo, quia magnificas eum, aut quid apponis erga eum cor tuum?* (Job 7:17)
388 Cf. Luke 15:4
389 Cf. Isaiah 64:5
390 *qui inter angelos repervisti pravitatem* (Job 4:18)
391 *Abyssus abyssum invocat* (Psalm 42:8)
392 Luke 5:8
393 *Fuge, fuge dilecte mi, assimilare capraee hinnuloque cervorum super montes Bethel* (Song 8:14)
394 Cf. Gen 35:1
395 *O sol, qui nescis occasum* (This is taken from the Easter Vigil liturgy.)
396 Cf. Leviticus 2:9
397 Cf. Rev 21:23
398 Cf. 1 John 4:8
399 *O quam pulchra es, amica mea, in deliciis tuis* (Song 7:6; 4:1)
400 *Statura tua assimilata est palmae, comae capitis tui sicut purpura regis* (Cf. Song 7:5)
401 *Fuge, fuge, dilecte mi, super montes Bethel* (Song 8:14)
402 *Vidi namque lumen in lumine tuo* (Psalm 36:10)
403 *Elegi et sanctificavi te* (2 Chronicles 7:16)
404 *viae Sion lugent* (Lamentations 1:4)
405 Cf. 1 Kings 18:38
406 Cf. 2 Kings 4:34
407 bridegroom, *comedite, amici, et inebriamini carissimi* (Song 5:1)
408 i.e. those new to the spiritual life
409 i.e. those experienced in contemplation
410 *O filiae Sion* (Song 3:11)
411 Ibid.
412 *Surge Aquilo et Auster perfla hortum meum et fluant aromata illius, osculetur me osculo oris sui, quia meliora sunt ubera tua vino fragrantia unguentis optimis* (Song 4:16; 1:1)

413 Cf. 1 Corinthians 15.54
414 *Unum velle et unum nolle* is a classical expression meaning to be of one mind, desiring and not desiring the same thing.
415 *Veni dilecte mi, egrediamur in agrum salutis: veni mecum ad excolendas vineas: veni et commoremur in villis, ibi dabo tibi ubera mea* (Song 7:11,12)
416 Cf. John 15.5
417 2 Corinthians 11:29
418 *zelus domus tuae comedit me* (Psalm 69:10)
419 John 19:28
420 Cf. Revelation 12:1
421 John 12.25
422 Cf. Psalm 117:22
423 Cf. John 17:21
424 Cf. John 1:14,18
425 *Trahe me post te* (Song 1:3)
426 Luke 18:19
427 Cf. James 1:4
428 2 Chronicles 7:1